10

PENGUIN BOOKS

ARTIFICIAL PARADISE_

Mike Jay has also edited, with Michael Neve, *1900* (Penguin 1999)
and is the author of *Blue Tide: The Search for Soma* (1999).

ARTIFICIAL PARADISES

A Drugs Reader

Edited by
MIKE JAY

PENGUIN BOOKS

PENGUIN BOOKS

Published by the Penguin Group
Penguin Books Ltd, 27 Wrights Lane, London W8 5TZ, England
Penguin Putnam Inc., 375 Hudson Street, New York, New York 10014, USA
Penguin Books Australia Ltd, Ringwood, Victoria, Australia
Penguin Books Canada Ltd, 10 Alcorn Avenue, Toronto, Ontario, Canada M4V 3B2
Penguin Books (NZ) Ltd, Private Bag 102902, NSMC, Auckland, New Zealand

Penguin Books Ltd, Registered Offices: Harmondsworth, Middlesex, England

First published in Penguin Books 1999
10 9 8 7 6 5 4 3 2 1

Permissions on p. 379 constitute an extension of this copyright page

Set in 9.5/12.5 pt PostScript Adobe New Caledonia
Typeset by Rowland Phototypesetting Ltd, Bury St Edmunds, Suffolk
Printed in England by Clays Ltd, St Ives plc

Contents

Illustrations

Acknowledgements

Many thanks to the following for their generous help:

The Fitz High Ludlow Memorial Library, Schuyler Henderson, Anthony Henman, Institute for the Study of Drug Dependency, Dorothy Kamen-Kaye, Paul Keegan, Gary Lachman, Nigel Larcombe, Betty Leese, Toni Melechi, Michele Minto and Wellcome Reprographics, Michael Neve, Mark Pilkington, Nancy Robinson and NASA, Richard Rudgley, Andrew Sclanders, Anna South and Adisakdi Tantimedh.

Introduction

Philosophers describing the way we construct reality, neurologists decoding the processes of the human brain, artists striving to express the inexpressible, anthropologists searching for keys to unlock unfamiliar civilizations, party people relaxing at home with a smorgasbord of illegal chemicals, doctors and police battling addiction-led crimewaves – all of the above may be, in their different ways, seeking to advance our grasp of mind-altering drugs and the way we use them. Yet none of them would agree that they are all engaged in the same project, and most of them would be less than interested in the activities of the others. 'The truth about drugs' is a strap-line which is frequently offered but never delivered: indeed, it's impossible even to imagine what such a truth might resemble.

For this reason, mind-altering drugs and their uses are a subject which has always been particularly well suited to the anthology. The earliest 'drug texts', such as the Egyptian magico-medical papyri or the classical Greek *Materia Medica* of Dioscorides and others, were miscellanies of plant wisdom drawn from priestly learning, folk tradition and anecdote, a format which persisted more or less unchanged into the Middle Ages. The eighteenth- and nineteenth-century classics of drug scholarship, such as Linnaeus' *Inebriantia* (*see* p. 8) or Mordecai Cooke's popular *Seven Sisters of Sleep* (*see* p. 166), similarly combined botanical taxonomy and medical understanding with folkloric reports and first-person anecdotes of drug intoxication. True to form, the recent resurgence of a 'drug culture' has produced a steady stream of anthologies and selections of disparate texts, further recycled and recombined through the underground press and the Internet.

This compendium approach to drug writings is a response to the nature of the subject. Scientists, artists and amateurs, ancient and modern, have instinctively recognized that 'the truth about drugs' is most closely approximated by a juxtaposition of various, often contradictory, voices: expert medico-scientific opinion, accreted bodies of folklore and tradition, and the personal, subjective experiences of drug users.

The reason why the subject has so consistently been approached in this multivalent way is that the understanding of drugs requires an investigation of many large, separate and only tangentially related questions. What are drugs? What do they do? How do they do it? Why do people take them? What are the effects on those who do – and on the wider society around them?

All these questions can be asked and answered on various levels, and to map them on to our modern framework of academic disciplines is an interesting and instructive process. The fields which they touch on make the catch-all term 'multidisciplinary' seem inadequate indeed: neurology, social history, botany, psychology, cultural theory, metaphysics, anthropology, philosophy of mind, chemistry, aesthetics and the history of science are merely a few of the disciplines which shed light on the nature and effects of drugs. By the same token, none of these fields alone can construct clear and definitive answers to these inquiries – nor, indeed, in most cases, can they adequately frame the basic questions.

The texts included in this volume not only represent all of the above disciplines, but also show the many ways of thinking about drugs which either ignore these disciplines altogether, or leap between them in capricious ways. To classify the texts here requires some other criterion than the partitions of contemporary academia – a distinction, perhaps, where the intention of the writer is given more weight than his or her field of expertise.

Some of the texts here, for example, might broadly be classed as 'metaphysical' attempts to confront the implications of drug-induced alternative realities head-on: what are the effects that drugs have on our mental realities, and what do these insights tell us about the nature of the world in which we live? While science has increasingly relevant answers particularly to the first half of this question, there have always been voices which claim that the scientific account of such experiences is necessarily limited by its scope and language, and that drugs offer a radical understanding of the extent to which our states of mind construct reality – both our internal reality and that of the social consensus which we inhabit – which will never be entirely contained within the scientific *sine qua non* of objective measurement. While these 'ascientific' answers present a chaotic and varied range, most are underpinned by the contention that, in the words of the psychologist William James (*see* p. 122), 'no account of the universe in its totality can be final, which leaves these other forms of consciousness quite disregarded' – although some, like R. C. Zaehner (*see* p. 132) would profoundly disagree even with this basic contention.

Another strand of the texts included here is the attempt to explore the social and cultural manifestations of drug use. Drug-related cultures and subcultures, from prehistory to the present, have generated their own stories and symbolisms, even their own cosmologies and language. Drug use often presents a unique lens through which to view social organization: almost every culture has its intoxicants of choice, and its 'scapegoat substances' which must be repressed at all costs, driven into the wilderness for the benefit of society at large. There is, of course, no consensus on what exactly these substances are: in the Arab world, for example, they include alcohol, while in the West they include almost everything (including, increasingly, tobacco) but *not* alcohol. Although, as Thomas Szasz (*see* p. 278) has demonstrated, these choices and prohibitions are better understood as 'ceremonial' than scientific, they are not without their practical reasons – reasons which, when unpacked, reveal central and often unspoken rules at the core of the society in question.

Within the academic framework, the exploration of drugs in societies typically falls within the scope of anthropology; indeed, some of this century's greatest anthropological discoveries – like those of Richard Schultes (*see* p. 28) – have involved those traditional societies which remain structured around the ritual use of intoxicants. But the same tools can be applied across a far broader range. The illicit drug cultures of the modern West, for example – also represented here – are often most remarkable not for their overt content, but for the extent to which they, too, represent a traditional initiatory path within the framework of modern pluralist society – the transmission of a set of beliefs and behaviours through the classic initiatic routes of oral transmission, song and dance, and covertly circulated texts. And cultural patterns also reveal themselves through the use of the 'softest', most pervasive and familiar drugs. Tobacco, for example: the difference between Amazonian snuff rituals, communal Arabic hookah-smoking and the factory-rolled (and nicotine-sprayed) filter cigarette is something which speaks subtly but clearly of a spectrum of desires, social rituals and ultimately views of the world.

A third strand of the following texts deals with the effect of drugs on the imagination, and the processes by which this effect finds creative and artistic expression. It is often these expressions, more than scientific descriptions, which give form to the effects which drugs produce. Few clinical accounts of the drug experiences have had as much popular impact as the metaphors of artists and writers: Baudelaire's 'thirst for the infinite', Huxley's 'doors of perception' or Leary's 'turn on, tune in, drop out'. And yet words themselves have always seemed to many an inappropriate vehicle for the protean, 'ineffable' experiences which drugs produce: their more natural vehicles have traditionally been the symbolic and visual arts and, particularly, music. A recurring theme of many of the selections here is the experience which reveals language itself as too crude a tool to describe the alien shores of consciousness on which drug users can find themselves beached.

A fourth strand of the literature on drugs, and one which is only sparsely represented here, is the generalized advocacy either 'for' or 'against' drugs, and the crime-and-punishment debate around their use. The reasons for excluding this are partly that this debate already makes up the vast bulk of the popular discourse on drugs, and partly that much of it is less about drugs themselves than the ideological presumptions of the protagonists. While this volume includes some selections which praise the effects of drugs and, in reasonably equal measure, others which are sceptical about their use and value, it should be clear from the overall selection that both pro-drug evangelists and anti-drug crusaders are attempting to reduce a huge complex of ideas to a single question – 'Are drugs in themselves beneficent or evil?' – a question to which any simple answer is bound to be meaningless.

The title *Artificial Paradises* is one which begs many questions – not least our definitions of the terms. In what sense are the effects of drugs 'artificial'? Psychoactive drugs work because of their affinities with naturally occurring substances, and the existence within the brain of receptors designed for them: all of us have several illegal drugs inside our bodies at this moment. Opiates, for example, are analogues of the substances produced naturally by exercise, sex or simply 'non-artificial' good moods and relaxation responses. And what, within our modern framework, constitutes a 'paradise', either metaphorically or literally?

Artificial Paradises was the title coined by the French poet Charles Baudelaire for the collection of writings on wine, hashish and opium which he produced in the 1850s (*see* p. 15), and it has become an enduring slogan for the effects of drugs – *see*, for example, Havelock

Ellis's *Mescal: A New Artificial Paradise* (p. 77) or Ronald K. Siegel's *Intoxication: Life in Pursuit of Artificial Paradise* (p. 69). In contrast to the flamboyant poetics of his contemporaries like Théophile Gautier (*see* p. 362), Baudelaire produced elegantly measured descriptions of his intoxications on all these substances, and they remain among the finest such accounts ever written.

But his title was as ambiguous to his contemporaries as it remains to us, though in a different sense. In the nineteenth century, 'artificial' had not accreted the pejorative sense of 'ersatz' or 'fake' with which we use it today. Quite the opposite: in the decadent and modernist traditions, from Huysmans to the Italian Futurists, it was specifically intended as the ultimate 'modern' compliment. 'Artificiality' was a state to be striven for, a state of refinement and self-definition which was seen as an improvement on nature rather than a cheapening of it. Does an 'artificial paradise', then, represent an elevation of the human state, a conscious shaping of reality which transforms it into nothing less than heaven on earth?

There are many who might have argued this, but Baudelaire was not among them. His 'Artificial Ideal' required a quenching of the 'thirst for the infinite', an effect which, it seemed, could be achieved by alcohol, ether or – most satisfactorily in his view – by hashish and opium. But although he is frequently clear-minded about the extent to which drugs can reasonably be expected to achieve this effect, their use remained for him a 'forbidden game', fraught with danger and almost axiomatically self-defeating. 'Alas! The vices in man, however frightful they seem, contain the proof . . . of his taste for the infinite; and yet it is a taste that quite frequently goes astray.' For Baudelaire, the urge to experience the infinite partakes of a 'natural depravity', and its pursuit delivers us into the clutches of 'the Spirit of Evil'. Artificial, in Baudelaire's sense, is as tainted as it is in ours, though for a different reason: in attempting to explore our divine selves, we only succeed in manifesting the bestial.

When Gustave Flaubert, who had recently been tried on charges of obscenity over *Madame Bovary*, received a copy of *Artificial Paradises* from Baudelaire, his broadly enthusiastic response contained a pertinent objection to this cosmic fatalism. Was not Baudelaire, while attempting to observe and report on the effects of the drugs in question, in fact projecting upon them an ominous quality which in truth emerged not from the drug but from the author? 'You have insisted too much', Flaubert wrote, '. . . on the spirit of evil. One can sense a leavening of

Catholicism here and there. I would have preferred that you not *blame* hashish, opium and excess. Do you know what will come of them later?'

Baudelaire, with a humility which would not always be his hallmark, deferred to the great man. 'I realise that I had been continually obsessed', he replied, 'by an inability to accept certain of man's deeds or actions without the hypothesis that malevolent powers, external to himself, of themselves intervene.' So what, then, of Artificial Paradises? If it is no longer fated that the Spirit of Evil must defeat all efforts to quench our thirst for the infinite – if, as Baudelaire clearly states elsewhere in the essays, the use of drugs will always reflect no more and no less than the consciousness which we bring to them – does the pursuit of an Artificial Paradise not escape the status of a doomed quest, and become both a strategy and a tool for illumination?

Baudelaire's reply signs off with an indication that such a fundamental rethink is, in fact, unlikely: 'I reserve the right to change my mind, however, or to contradict myself at any time.'

The following selection of texts reserves a similar right.

Finally, a brief note on terminology. *Narcotic*, increasingly used to refer to all illicit drugs, is here used in its clinically correct sense of sleep-inducing or sedative, a category which includes opium, heroin and barbiturates. *Stimulant*, its opposite, is a category which includes amphetamines, cocaine and caffeine. For powerful mind-altering drugs such as LSD, mescaline and psilocybin, *psychedelic* is preferred both to the less accurate 'hallucinogenic' and to recent coinages such as 'entheogen'. *Psychoactive* refers to any drug which has a perceptible effect on consciousness, and includes all of the above.

1
Inebriantia: The Discovery of Drugs

The modern understanding of drugs and their effects is indebted to many diverse forms of knowledge. These include our recent understanding of the mind's chemical mechanisms and the ways in which they construct our consciousness; the social histories of our development from the Stone Age to the present; and the diversity of contemporary cultures and the ways in which drugs are used within them.

In order to unpick this complex mesh of disciplines, the introductory section of this volume presents a few texts, in broad historical sequence, which point the route to some of these discoveries and the ways in which they have combined to assemble the modern notions of psychoactive drugs and their effects on us.

The knowledge of drugs has been with us since the most distant days of prehistory: the earliest use of opium, for example, has now been pushed back far into the Stone Age. Accounts of the use of drugs form the subject matter of many of mankind's earliest texts. But, of course, these accounts lack any modern notions of chemical cause and effect. Here, for example, is the late Classical narrative The Golden Ass, *where the protagonist Lucius is transformed into an ass by a witch's potion.*

LUCIUS APULEIUS
The Golden Ass

(*fl.* second century AD)

We spent the next few nights in the same amorous way, and then one morning Fotis ran into my room, trembling with excitement, and told me that her mistress, having made no headway by ordinary means in her affair with the Boeotian, intended that night to become a bird and fly in to the object of her desire, and that I must make careful preparations if I wished to watch the performance.

At twilight, she led me on tip-toe, very quietly up to the loft, where she signed to me to peep through a chink in the door. I obeyed, and watched Pamphile first undress completely and then open a small cabinet containing several little boxes, one of which she opened. It contained an ointment which she worked about with her fingers and then smeared all over her body from the soles of her feet to the crown of her head. After this she muttered a long charm to her lamp, and shook herself; her limbs vibrated gently and became gradually fledged with feathers, her arms changed into sturdy wings, her nose grew crooked and horny, her nails turned into talons, and Pamphile had become an owl. She gave a querulous hoot and made a few little hopping flights until she was sure enough of her wings to glide off, away over the roof-tops.

Not having been put under any spell myself, I was utterly astonished and stood frozen to the spot. I rubbed my eyes to make sure that I was really Lucius and that this was no waking dream. Was I perhaps going mad? I recovered my senses after a time, took hold of Fotis' hand and laid it across my eyes. 'I beg you,' I said, 'to grant me a tremendous favour – one which I can never hope to repay – in proof of your perfect love for me. If you do this, honey, I promise, by these sweet breasts of yours, to be your slave for evermore. I want to be able to fly. I want to hover around you like a winged Cupid in attendance on my Venus.'

. . .

I quickly pulled off my clothes, greedily stuck my fingers into the box and took out a large lump of ointment which I rubbed all over my body.

I stood flapping my arms, one after the other, as I had seen Pamphile do, but no little feathers appeared on them and they showed no sign of turning into wings. All that happened was that the hair on them grew coarser and coarser and the skin toughened into hide. Next, my fingers bunched together into a hard lump so that the five fingers of my hands became single hooves, the same change came over my feet and a long tail sprouted from the base of my spine. Then my face swelled, my mouth widened, my nostrils dilated, my lips hung down and my ears bristled long and hairy. The only consoling part of this miserable transformation was the enormous increase in the size of my member; because I was by this time finding it increasingly difficult to meet all Fotis' demands upon it. At last, hopelessly surveying myself all over, I realized that I had been transformed not into a bird but into an ass.

Although this may seem like pure fantasy, the fact that Fotis' potion is rubbed on the skin suggests a knowledge of the pharmacology of the solanaceous plants such as belladonna and henbane which can be absorbed in this way. These were undoubtedly used during the medieval witch craze and passages such as The Golden Ass *suggest that they were a genuine inheritance from antiquity.*

In the mid-sixteenth century, the Spanish physician of Emperor Charles V, Andres Fernandez de Laguna, made one of the first 'clinical' trials' of these witches' potions in order to establish that much of the supposed power of witches is caused by their chemical action.

ANDRÉS FERNANDEZ DE LAGUNA
'Commentaries on Dioscorides' *Materia medica*'

(1555)

Among the materials found in the hermitage of . . . [a] wizard and witch [executed by the authorities] was a pot full of a certain green ointment like poplar ointment [salve], whose smell was so heavy and pungent that it proved to be composed of extremely cold (ultimate grade) and soporific herbs such as hemlock, nightshade, henbane, and mandrake. Through the constable, who was a friend of mine, I obtained a good supply of the ointment and later in the city of Metz I had the wife of the public executioner anointed with it from head to foot. She through jealousy of her husband had completely lost power of sleep and had become half insane in consequence. This seemed to me to be an excellent opportunity to undertake a test of the witch's ointment. And so it turned out, for no sooner did I anoint her than she opened her eyes wide like a rabbit, and soon they looked like those of a cooked hare when she fell into such a profound sleep that I thought I should never be able to awake her. However, by means of tight ligatures and rubbing her extremities and applications of castor oil as well as euphorbia and frequent inhalations, and finally with cuppings, I was so insistent that after a lapse of thirty-six hours, I restored her to her senses and sanity. Her first words were 'Why did you awaken me, badcess to you, at such an inauspicious moment? Why I was surrounded by all the delights in the world.' Then, turning her eyes toward her husband (he was beside her, she stinking like a corpse) and smiling at him, she said, 'Skinflint! I want you to know that I have put the horns on you, and with a younger and lustier lover than you.' Many other strange things she said, and she wore herself out beseeching us to allow her to return to her pleasant dreams. Little by little we distracted her from her illusions, but forever after she stuck to many of her crazy notions.

From all this we may infer that all that those wretched witches do and say is caused by potions and ointments which so corrupt their memory and their imagination that they create their own woes, for they firmly believe when awake all that they had dreamed when asleep.

An additional important argument is that all those women who carried out these infamous practices confessed with one voice that they had on many occasions copulated with the Devil. And when they were asked whether they had experienced special pleasure in such connections they invariably replied that they had felt no pleasure at all because of the unbearable coldness of the Devil's private parts from which a freezing humour seemed to course through their entrails like hailstones. This sensation can only have been caused by the excessive coldness of the ointment which penetrated the marrow of their bones . . .

Witches' flying ointment: a classic image from the 'witch craze'. In this woodcut from 1514, a witch flies to the Sabbat while, in the foreground, her companions prepare a plant brew. (Wellcome Trust)

*The first classification of plants by their psychoactive effect was made
by Linnaeus, the father of modern botany, in the eighteenth century.*

LINNAEUS
Inebriantia

(1762)

I

Intoxicants are commonly said to be those stimulants which
affect the nervous system in such a way that there is a change not only
in its motor but its sensory functions. These agents are extremely subtle
and light particles like those which rise from plants, as if by exhalation,
or by means of chemical fermentation, are highly subtilized and are
called spirituous. As to how these stimulants arouse and excite the
nerves daily experience shows in the case of those people who, overcome
by some fainting spell, lie still like dead men; but when the spirit of sal
ammoniac or vinegar or wine or even fragrant plants are put to their
noses, they are called back, as it were, from the gates of death, while
their bare nerves in the sinus of the forehead are brought to life and
stimulated by the spirituous essences. Similarly when some part of the
body is swollen, bruised, or inflamed, surgeons apply resolvents, which
are spirituous or volatile fragrances, which enter the body by their own
breath, and breathe life into the half-dead nerves; by this means it
happens that the activity of life restores health in that part of the
body; contrariwise, if the patient labors under severe pain or constant
wakefulness, physicians give them something malodorous to drink, like
opiates, or they even apply externally such plants as Anethum, Crocus,
Myristica, in order to produce sleep.

II

But too broad a field opens up here, so that I would be unequal to the
task of traversing it, if, following up all the examples which can be
imagined, I should wish to examine all its nooks and corners. For the

present let it suffice for me to consider briefly the marvellous effect which intoxicants, properly so called, produce. Almost no nations are without intoxicants, by means of which the weary, the exhausted, the dispirited, the fainthearted often console their minds and refresh their bodies. These intoxicants restore now physical, now mental power, quickly – something which foods do more slowly and not without delay, and not even then sufficiently. For as soon as some intoxicant is taken, the strength increases on the spot, the heart beats excitedly, weariness vanishes, the body grows warm, the mind becomes more expansive and eager to carry on its activities.

III

We Europeans use fermented intoxicants such as Beer, Wine, and distilled Spirits, primarily as an accompaniment in our daily food, when by a drug of that sort we desire to assure a pleasing taste. Other nations however, especially the Orientals who are much enslaved to intoxicants, care less about the accompanying food.

Assuredly, very many *natural* intoxicants are known, but many, which are found in some malodorous plants, are still unknown.

a   O P I U M is a milky juice, thickened by the sun, made from bruised immature capsules of *Papaver somniferum*; with which the fields in the kingdom of Turkey and in neighbouring lands are planted for the sake of the opium. Time was when the Turks abused opium more than they do today; now they take it from a grain to a dram, according as by extensive use it turns into a natural habit. Opium dispels cares, sadness and fear of dangers; it induces gaiety, laughter, forgetfulness, stupidity, frenzy; because of this quality their Emperors often issue each soldier a dram of opium when they are going to lead them into battle, so that they might approach the enemy unafraid. If, however, a larger dose than is proper is taken, it causes a dilation of the pupil, redness in the face, stuttering, hiccoughing, loosening of the jaw, and other such ill effects. Those who use this heroic drug for a long time become as a result dull, sluggish, stupid, speechless, thin, melancholic, tremulous with premature old age; but taken properly in reasonable doses, it is a heroic medicine, and is a more powerful dietetic restorative than any-thing else hitherto known; and Jones in his book on opium never found a more perfect peace with any other drug.

b PEGANUM *Harmala*, whose seeds the Turks have for sale in their markets, is an inebriant, according to Belon in his travel account, who relates (with Giovio as his witness) that the emperor Solimann used to eat this seed not knowing its nature, because it brought pleasure and took away the memory of troublesome affairs. Perhaps from this seed was that 'Bolus' of which Kaempfer ate at a banquet when staying among the Persians. As a result he was filled with unending joy, like something he had never experienced before; then followed embraces, laughter, joking, etc. But after dinner when he had mounted his horse, the power of the drug planted another idea in his brain, just as if he were sitting on Pegasus and had flown through the clouds and the most colorful rainbows of Iris, and as if he had eaten with the gods; on the morrow he had forgotten all these events.

c *Turkish* MASLAC or *Persian Bangue* is made from the pollen of the male *Cannabis sativa* passed through a sieve and shaped with spittle into pills, or in the following manner: Take two bundles of crushed leaves of cannabis, pour cold water into a closed vessel, press [the leaves] out a bit [to remove the too strongly charged water], let new water be that senility and its misfortunes must be sought in the nervous system rather than in the solid parts of the body.

Therefore just as these Dietetic Remedies rekindle the body and mind, so have various nations often sought comfort in them. But just as their nature is volatile, so is their effect volatile and short-lived; if any mortal should have the power to hold down such a winged Mercury, he would deservedly think that he had discovered the true Philosopher's stone and the true Panacea; but even up to our time men have searched for this in vain, and perhaps will always search in vain.

*The beginning of the next century saw a rapid evolution in the under-
standing of the effects of drugs on the mind. In his popular and ground-
breaking* Confessions of an English Opium Eater, *the journalist and
essayist Thomas De Quincey overturned the traditional descriptions of
opium use with his careful introspective observations.*

THOMAS DE QUINCEY
Confessions of an English Opium Eater

(1822)

First, one word with respect to its bodily effects: for upon all
that has been hitherto written on the subject of opium, whether by
travellers in Turkey (who may plead their privilege of lying as an old
immemorial right), or by professors of medicine, writing *ex cathedra* –
I have but one emphatic criticism to pronounce: Lies! lies! lies! I
remember once, in passing a bookstall, to have caught these words from
a page of some satiric author: 'By this time I became convinced that
the London newspapers spoke truth at least twice a week, viz., on
Tuesday and Saturday, and might safely be depended upon for – the
list of bankrupts.' In like manner, I do by no means deny that some
truths have been delivered to the world in regard to opium: thus it has
been repeatedly affirmed by the learned that opium is a dusky brown
in colour; and this, take notice, I grant: secondly, that it is rather dear;
which also I grant: for in my time, East India opium has been three
guineas a pound, and Turkey eight: and, thirdly, that if you eat a good
deal of it, most probably you must do – what is particularly disagreeable
to any man of regular habits, viz. die. These weighty propositions are,
all and singular, true: I cannot gainsay them: and truth ever was, and
will be, commendable. But in these three theorems, I believe we have
exhausted the stock of knowledge as yet accumulated by man on the
subject of opium. And therefore, worthy doctors, as there seems to be
room for further discoveries, stand aside, and allow me to come forward
and lecture on this matter.

First, then, it is not so much affirmed as taken for granted, by all who
ever mention opium, formally or incidentally, that it does, or can,
produce intoxication. Now, reader, assure yourself, *meo periculo*, that

no quantity of opium ever did, or could, intoxicate. As to the tincture of opium (commonly called laudanum), *that* might certainly intoxicate if a man could bear to take enough of it; but why? Because it contains so much proof spirit, and not because it contains so much opium. But crude opium, I affirm peremptorily, is incapable of producing any state of body at all resembling that which is produced by alcohol: and not in *degree* only incapable, but even in *kind*: it is not in the quantity of its effects merely, but in the quality, that it differs altogether. The pleasure given by wine is always mounting, and tending to a crisis, after which it declines: that from opium, when once generated, is stationary for eight or ten hours: the first, to borrow a technical distinction from medicine, is a case of acute – the second, of chronic pleasure: the one is a flame, the other a steady and equable glow. But the main distinction lies in this, that whereas wine disorders the mental faculties, opium, on the contrary (if taken in a proper manner), introduces amongst them the most exquisite order, legislation, and harmony. Wine robs a man of his self-possession: opium greatly invigorates it. Wine unsettles and clouds the judgment, and gives a preternatural brightness, and a vivid exaltation to the contempts and the admirations, the loves and the hatreds, of the drinker: opium, on the contrary, communicates serenity and equipoise to all the faculties, active or passive: and with respect to the temper and moral feelings in general, it gives simply that sort of vital warmth which is approved by the judgment, and which would probably always accompany a bodily constitution of primeval or antediluvian health

. . .

Wine constantly leads a man to the brink of absurdity and extravagance; and, beyond a certain point, it is sure to volatilize and to disperse the intellectual energies: whereas opium always seems to compose what had been agitated, and to concentrate what had been distracted. In short, to sum up all in one word, a man who is inebriated, or tending to inebriation, is, and feels that he is, in a condition which calls up into supremacy the merely human, too often the brutal, part of his nature: but the opium-eater (I speak of him who is not suffering from any disease, or other remote effects of opium,) feels that the diviner part of his nature is paramount; that is, the moral affections are in a state of cloudless serenity; and over all is the great light of the majestic intellect.

This is the doctrine of the true church on the subject of opium: of which church I acknowledge myself to be the only member – the alpha and the omega: but then it is to be recollected, that I speak from the ground of a large and profound personal experience: whereas most of the unscientific authors who have at all treated of opium, and even of those who have written expressly on the materia medica, make it evident, from the horror they express of it, that their experimental knowledge of its action is none at all.

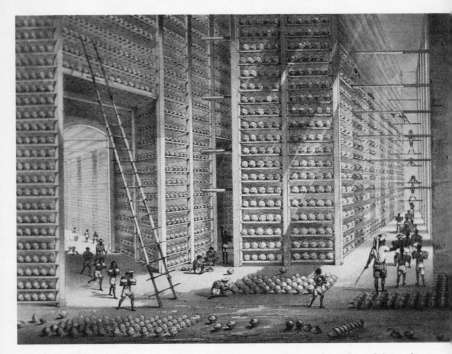

The prevalence of opium in De Quincey's day can be inferred from this vast stacking room in the British opium factory at Patna, India, *c*. 1850. (Wellcome Trust)

The poet Charles Baudelaire was a great admirer of De Quincey, translating his work into French. In his own writings on hashish, he also stresses that such drugs are not magical in their effects, but dependent on the expectations and constitution of the user.

CHARLES BAUDELAIRE
Artificial Paradises

(1860)

What will I feel? What will I see? Astounding marvels and extraordinary spectacles? Is it very beautiful, very terrible, or very dangerous? Those are the questions ordinarily asked, in tones of mingled curiosity and fear, by those who have no experimental knowledge of hashish. One might say that they show a childish impatience to know, like that of people who, having never ventured away from their hearth, find themselves face to face with a stranger who has come from remote, unknown lands. Hashish intoxication is a sort of fantastic landscape to them, a vast theatre of conjuring and illusion where all is miraculous and unforeseen. This is a preconception, an unfounded assumption. And since, for the majority of readers and inquisitive souls, the word *hashish* summons images of strangely altered worlds and the promise of prodigious dreams (or rather *hallucinations* which, however, occur less frequently than one might suppose), I will now comment on the most important difference separating the effects of hashish from the phenomena of sleep. In sleep, the adventurous voyage that fills our nights, there is something of the positively miraculous, a miracle whose mystery is dulled by repetitive punctuality. Man's dreams are of two types. The first is filled with his ordinary life, his preoccupations, desires, and vices, which combine in a more or less bizarre manner with objects encountered during the day to randomly fix upon the vast canvas of his memory. This is the natural dream; it is the man himself. But that other type of dream! the absurd and unpredictable dream, which has no bearing on, or connection to, the character, life, and passions of the dreamer! This dream, which I shall term hieroglyphic, evidently represents the supernatural side of life, and it is precisely because of its absurdity that the ancients thought it of divine origin. As this dream cannot be explained by any known cause, they attributed it to a cause external to man; and today, without mentioning oneiromancers, there is still a philosophic school which sees some sort of criticism or counsel in dreams of this nature, a symbolic and moral representation engendered in the very mind of the sleeping man. Such a dream is a dictionary to be studied, a language to which only the wise hold the key.

In hashish intoxication, we find nothing of the kind. Here we never leave the natural dream. Throughout its duration, the intoxication will be nothing but a fantastic dream, thanks to the intensity of colours and the rapidity of the conceptions, but it will always retain the particular quality of the individual. Man wished to dream and now the dream will govern man; but this dream will surely be as the son is to the father. The idler has contrived to artificially introduce an element of the supernatural into his life and thoughts: but he is, after all, and in spite of the heightened intensity of his sensations, only the same man augmented, the same number elevated to a much higher power. He is subjugated, but much to his displeasure, only by himself – that is to say, by the part of himself that is already dominant; *he wished to be an angel and he has become a beast*, temporarily very powerful, if one might call power an extreme sensitivity that is lacking the will to moderate or exploit it.

Thus let the sophisticates and novices who are curious to taste these exceptional delights take heed; they will find nothing miraculous in hashish, nothing but the excessively natural. The brain and body governed by hashish will yield nothing but their ordinary, individual phenomena, augmented, it is true, in number and energy, but always faithful to their origins. Man will not escape the destiny of his physical and moral temperament: for man's impressions and intimate thoughts, hashish will act as a magnifying mirror, but a pure mirror none the less.

Here is the drug we have before us: a morsel of green paste, the size of a nut, the smell of which is so potent that it gives rise to a certain repulsion and bouts of nausea, as will, for that matter, any fine and even appealing scent when carried to its maximum concentration and density, as it were. I might mention in passing that this proposition can be reversed, so that the vilest, most repugnant odour might perhaps become pleasurable were it reduced to its minimum of quantity and expansion. Here, then, is happiness! – it can be contained within an ordinary teaspoon! – happiness with all of its rapture, childishness, and folly! Swallow it without fear; you will not die of it. Your inner organs will suffer no harm. Later, perhaps, a too frequent invocation of the spell will diminish your power of resolve, perhaps you will be less a man than you are today, but the punishment is yet so distant and the future disaster of a nature so difficult to define! Where is the risk? Tomorrow, a slight touch of nervous exhaustion perhaps. Do you not each day risk greater chastisements for less recompense? So the matter is settled: to allow the drug its full range of expansion, you have dissolved your quantity of rich extract in a cup of strong coffee. You have arranged to take it on an empty stomach, postponing your dinner until at least nine or ten o'clock, to allow the poison free reign of action. In an hour a light soup alone will be tolerable. You are now sufficiently bolstered for a long, remarkable voyage. The steam whistle blows, the sails are set, and you, among all the other travellers, are a privileged exception, for you alone are unaware of your destination. You wished it to be so; long live destiny!

Baudelaire, self-portrait under hashish, 1844.

It's probable that Baudelaire was introduced to hashish by Dr Jacques-Joseph Moreau de Tours, the first psychologist to experiment with mind-altering drugs and to apply their effects to the phenomena of mental illness.

JACQUES-JOSEPH MOREAU DE TOURS
Hashish and Mental Illness

(1845)

At first, curiosity led me to experiment upon myself with hashish. Later, I readily admit, it was difficult to repress the nagging memory of some of the sensations it revealed to me. But from the very outset I was motivated by another reason.

I saw in hashish, or rather in its effect upon the mental faculties, a significant means of exploring the genesis of mental illness. I was convinced that it could solve the enigma of mental illness and lead to the hidden source of the mysterious disorder that we call '*madness*'.

I may be accused of being bold and presumptuous for expressing myself with so much assurance on a subject that so-called scientists avoid by relegating to the ill-defined area of metaphysics. This boldness, to which I admit, is justified by the conscientious research that characterizes this project. It will become apparent that it is based not upon arguments or inductions that can be questioned but upon simple, concrete facts derived from self-observation. As one can judge by what follows, I had only to transfer the main characteristics of delirium to those of hashish intoxication and to apply to my study the insights gathered from self-observation.

In this manner and guided solely by the kind of observation that enhances consciousness and self-awareness, I believe I was able to go back to the origin of the phenomenon of delirium. One fact seemed to be basic, seminal, and preliminary to all the others: I have called it the *primary fact*. Secondly, I had to postulate, for delirium in general, a psychological nature not only analogous but *absolutely identical* to a dream state.

This identity, which eludes casual observation since it cannot be seen in others, is definitely confirmed, and even *perceived*, by introspection

. . .

In the way in which it affects the mental faculties, hashish gives to whoever submits to its influence the power to study in himself the mental disorders that characterize insanity, or at least the intellectual modifications that are the beginning of all forms of mental illness.

By the end of the nineteenth century, the recreational use of drugs outside the world of science had become more widespread. James S. Lee, a mining foreman who worked in the British colonies of Africa and Asia around the turn of the century, represents the beginning of this century's 'underground drug culture'.

JAMES S. LEE
'The Underworld of the East'

(1935)

During the thirty years in which I was a constant user of drugs of many kinds, various people, including some doctors, and chemists, have asked me how it was that I was able to continue in the habit for so long a time, and use such large quantities of drugs, and still remain in good health.

This true story of my experiences will explain the reason, and also may show the drug habit in an entirely new aspect.

It is now many years since I gave up using all drugs, but during the thirty years with which this story deals, I have used morphia, cocaine, hashish, opium, and a good many other drugs, both singly and in combination.

The doses which I became able to take, after so many years of the habit, may seem almost impossible, yet it is a fact that I have increased my dose gradually, until I could inject eighty grains of pure cocaine a day; sufficient to kill many persons, if divided amongst them.

At other times when I favored morphia, I have injected as much as ten grains per day, although the medical dose is a quarter of a grain.

My arms, shoulders and chest, are a faint blue color, which, if magnified, reveals the marks of thousands of tiny punctures; hypodermic syringe marks.

Many years I have searched the jungles of the Far East for new drugs; testing strange plants, bulbs, and roots, making extracts, and then testing them first on animals, and in some cases on myself, and I will describe later some of the strange effects produced; particularly in the case of one drug, which I will call 'The Elixir of Life'.

If some of the things I describe are horrible, they are nevertheless true. What strange sights may a man not see during seven years in a country like China, if he goes to look for them below the surface? It is a country of camouflage and hidden ways. Innocent-looking junks, quietly floating down the rivers and canals, may be really sumptuously furnished gambling dens and drug haunts, where orgies of many kinds are carried on. No European, unless he is introduced by a trusted Chinese, will ever have the entry to these places.

The life of a drug taker can be a happy one, far surpassing that of any other; or it can be one of suffering and misery; it depends on the user's knowledge. The most interesting period will only be reached after many years, and then only if perfect health has been retained; using several kinds of drugs (for one drug alone spells disaster), and increasing the doses in a carefully thought-out system; a system which was first made known to me by the Indian doctor who initiated me into the drug habit.

Waking visions will then begin to appear when under the influence of very large doses, and it is these visions which are so interesting.

I have sat up through the night taking drugs until the room has been peopled with spirits. They may be horrible, grotesque, or beautiful, according to the nature of the drugs producing them. Strange scenes have been enacted before my eyes; scenes which were very real and lifelike, and which I will describe later.

When the Dangerous Drug Act came into force I gave up using all drugs, because the danger and risk of obtaining them was too great. The paltry quantities, about which the authorities make such a fuss, were of no use to me, and I was able to give them up without any trouble or suffering, owing to my experiments and discoveries.

The growing interest in psychedelic drugs was brought to popular attention by writers like Aldous Huxley. In his account of his first mescaline experiment, Huxley proposed an enduring metaphor for the effects of such drugs.

ALDOUS HUXLEY
The Doors of Perception

(1954)

From the books the investigator directed my attention to the furniture. A small typing-table stood in the centre of the room; beyond it, from my point of view, was a wicker chair and beyond that a desk The three pieces formed an intricate pattern of horizontals, uprights, and diagonals – a pattern all the more interesting for not being interpreted in terms of spatial relationships. Table, chair, and desk came together in a composition that was like something by Braque or Juan Gris, a still life recognizably related to the objective world, but rendered without depth, without any attempt at photographic realism. I was looking at my furniture, not as the utilitarian who has to sit on chairs, to write at desks and tables, and not as the cameraman or scientific recorder, but as the pure aesthete whose concern is only with forms and their relationships within the field of vision or the picture space. But as I looked, this purely aesthetic Cubist's-eye view gave place to what I can only describe as the sacramental vision of reality. I was back where I had been when I was looking at the flowers – back in a world where everything shone with the Inner Light, and was infinite in its significance. The legs, for example, of that chair – how miraculous their tubularity, how supernatural their polished smoothness! I spent several minutes – or was it several centuries? – not merely gazing at those bamboo legs, but actually *being* them – or rather being myself in them; or, to be still more accurate (for 'I' was not involved in the case, nor in a certain sense were 'they') being my Not-self in the Not-self which was the chair.

Reflecting on my experience, I find myself agreeing with the eminent Cambridge philosopher, Dr C. D. Broad, 'that we should do well to consider much more seriously than we have hitherto been inclined to do the type of theory which Bergson put forward in connection with memory and sense perception. The suggestion is that the function of the brain and nervous system and sense organs is in the main *eliminative* and not productive. Each person is at each moment capable of remembering all that has ever happened to him and of perceiving everything that is happening everywhere in the universe. The function of the brain and nervous system is to protect us from being overwhelmed and confused by this mass of largely useless and irrelevant knowledge, by shutting out most of what we should otherwise perceive or remember at any moment, and leaving only that very small and special selection which is likely to be practically useful.' According to such a theory, each one of us is potentially Mind at Large. But in so far as we are animals, our business is at all costs to survive. To make biological survival possible, Mind at Large has to be funnelled through the reducing valve of the brain and nervous system. What comes out at the other end is a measly trickle of the kind of consciousness which will help us to stay alive on the surface of this particular planet. To formulate and express the contents of this reduced awareness, man has invented and endlessly elaborated those symboli systems and implicit philosophies which we call languages. Every individual is at once the beneficiary and the victim of the linguistic tradition into which he or she has been born – the beneficiary inasmuch as language gives access to the accumulated records of other people's experience, the victim in so far as it confirms him in the belief that reduced awareness is the only awareness and as it bedevils his sense of reality, so that he is all too apt to take his concepts for data, his words for actual things. That which, in the language of religion, is called 'this world' is the universe of reduced awareness, expressed and, as it were, petrified by language. The various 'other worlds', with which human beings erratically make contact are so many elements in the totality of the awareness belonging to Mind at Large. Most people, most of the time, know only what comes through the reducing valve and is consecrated as genuinely real by the local language. Certain persons, however, seem to be born with a kind of bypass that circumvents the reducing valve. In others temporary bypasses may be acquired either spontaneously, or as the result of deliberate 'spiritual exercises', or through hypnosis, or by means of drugs. Through these permanent or temporary bypasses there flows, not indeed the perception 'of everything that is happening everywhere in the universe' (for the bypass does not abolish the reducing valve, which still excludes the total content of Mind at Large), but something more than, and above all something different from, the carefully selected utilitarian material which our narrowed, individual minds regard as a complete, or at least sufficient, picture of reality.

By the 1950s, the scientific community had realized that understanding the action of psychoactive drugs presented huge challenges and possibilities.

ROBERT S. DE ROPP
Drugs and the Mind
(1957)

Drugs that exert these effects have long been endowed with a halo of divinity by the people who used them. The *peyotl* was sacred to the Aztecs, the *coca* to the Incas. The gods in the Vedas drank *soma*, those of the Greeks *ambrosia*. *Nepenthe* was praised by Homer as the 'potent destroyer of grief' and the hemp plant with its potent resin *charas* was described by the sages of India as the 'delight giver'.

The properties of these plants were discovered accidentally, in many cases so long ago that we have no idea when their virtues first became known. Our hairy ancestors gained their knowledge of drugs the hard way. Impelled by hunger, they ate what they could find, root or berry, leaf, flower, or fungus. Often they sat in their caves ruefully clutching their stomachs, wondering what they had eaten that had caused them to feel so desperately ill. They purged, they vomited, they convulsed, they collapsed, and the sum of their writhings and spewings, accumulated through the ages, provided the basis for the science of pharmacology. Knowledge of the poisonous properties of plants was cherished by individuals, more discerning than their fellows, who guarded their secrets jealously and employed their understanding of poisons to further their own interests. Gradually, as religions evolved, these discerning characters became priests or witch doctors and their familiarity with poisons became a part of their sacred lore. Most precious of all to these early priests and witch doctors was their knowledge of the plants which affect the workings of the mind, which soothe griefs and relieve sufferings and flood the imagination with delightful visions.

Today the modern chemist is the heir to all this painfully accumulated knowledge. He is the lineal descendant of a long line of witch doctors, shamans, sorcerers, and alchemists. Their carefully guarded secrets have become his stock in trade but he has improved and enormously enlarged his heritage. The crude and often nauseous decoctions which our forefathers swallowed to soothe their griefs or delight their imaginations have now been fractionated by the skill of the analysts. The crystalline essences on which their effects depend have been isolated and characterized. The very places of the component atoms within their molecules have been determined. Nor has the modern chemist been satisfied with these triumphs of analysis but, liberating himself from his dependence on roots and berries, he has embarked on a voyage into the realm of synthesis, creating compounds not found in nature, the properties of which frequently represent a vast improvement on any known natural substance.

All these drugs act by affecting the chemistry of the brain, for it is out of this chemistry that what we call 'mind' emerges. The mind of man does not exist in a vacuum. It is associated with the chemistry of the brain and this chemistry underlies all our manifestations. Neither thought nor emotion can occur without some chemical change. The cruelty of the tyrant, the compassion of the saint, the ardour of lovers, the hatred of foes all are based on chemical processes. However hard we may try, however earnestly we may wish to do so, we cannot separate mind from matter or isolate what we call man's soul from his body. Were this not so the action of drugs on the mind could never be understood. It is precisely because all mental and emotional processes have a chemical basis that these drugs exert an action. If mind existed in a vacuum apart from matter we would not be able to influence it by drugs.

. . . as, at around the same time, anthropologists and botanists, such as the pioneering Harvard ethnobotanist Richard Schultes, began to realize that the use of plant drugs in traditional societies was an essential element in understanding their cultures.

RICHARD EVANS SCHULTES
'Plants and Plant Constituents as Mind-altering Agents Throughout History'

(1979)

From his earliest gropings as a distinct animal, man undoubtedly experimented with his vegetal surroundings. He put into his stomach anything from the plant kingdom in his frantic search for nourishment. He early discovered that some plants served to assuage hunger and sustain him; others relieved symptoms of illness; still others were dangerous, making him ill or killing him outright; but a few, he found, transported him from this monotonous and not-too-pleasant mundane existence to realms of ethereal wonder and inexplicable separation from everyday existence. He had discovered the narcotics, especially the hallucinogenic plants, capable of much more than activity on the physical body but able, through their psychoactivity on the central nervous system, to alter in ways most extraordinary the psyche and its relationship to the natural affairs of man.

Much of the experimentation that led man to his hallucinogens was very early. One of man's earliest cultigens, *Cannabis*, dates from well nigh the beginnings of agriculture in the Old World – 10,000 years ago. Specimens of coca leaves have been found in mummy bundles in some of the very early graves of Peru, in sites too early even for maize. Peyote buttons have recently been recovered from dry caves in New Mexico, which have been dated at 4,000 years of age.

Material evidence of the use of plant products as hallucinogens is certainly not lacking in archaeological sites. Yet from the importance of hallucinogens in aboriginal mythology and religion we know that they have played roles so ancient that they are basic concepts even in the origin myths of peoples in primitive societies around the world. There has been the suggestion that one of the oldest hallucinogens – *Amanita muscaria* – may go back as a narcotic so far in man's prehistory that it engendered the notion of divinity and the supernatural.

It requires only a glance at beliefs surrounding some of the hallucino-gens to appreciate their basic nature and significance to aboriginal concepts concerning the origin of man and his cultures: hence their great age. The fact that hallucinogens in many aboriginal societies permeate all aspects of living is evidence of their antiquity fully as convincing as material remains.

They reach into prenatal life and influence life after death; they operate throughout earthly existence. They play roles not only in health and sickness but in the relationships between individuals, villages, and tribes, in peace and war, at home and in travel, in hunting and in agriculture – there is hardly any aspect of living or dying where hallucin-ogenic plants do not play a major role.

It is not at all difficult to understand why hallucinogens have pen-etrated so deeply into all aspects of primitive societies. Man in primitive societies had to explain why a few plants possessed unearthly powers that could transfer him temporarily from everyday existence to realms of ethereal wonder. His explanation maintained that these plants were the abode of a divinity or spiritual force, and they became sacred. This concept, actually, is not wholly confined to so-called primitive societies, since many of the religions of the more advanced cultures are based on similar beliefs: witness the widespread Christian thesis that a divinity could incarnate itself into the body of a man, Jesus. But in societies based on the belief that all of nature is controlled by the supernatural, that all of man's existence – even sickness and death – is ruled by powers in outer realms, what is more logical than to assume that these plants enable mortal man – or at least certain individuals in society – to communicate through hallucinogens of various kinds with the ruling forces? As La Barre (1970) maintains: 'Sacred knowledge is commonly traceable, even by natives themselves, to an origin in revelation given to the ancestors or to some similarly charismatic individual, such as a shaman, visionary prophet or other culture hero believed to have been able to "tap" the unseen world of the "supernatural".'

There are many characteristics of hallucinations that can and do deeply influence primitive religion and ideas of the cosmos. Certain hallucinogenic plants – peyote, for example – induce indescribably deep and rich colours that are so unlike those normally experienced that only a supernatural origin seems possible; others produce only reds, oranges, or yellows; still others tend to be responsible for duller tones of blues, purples, or greys. The intoxication caused by some of these plants, especially those containing tryptamines, is characterized by macropsia and undoubtedly has played a role in mythology in connection with giants; others, however, have an opposite effect, micropsia, and have influenced belief – such as with the *oprita* of the Kofans – in the 'little people'. Other hallucinogens enable man to fly through the air by inducing the sense of levitation: shanshi of the Ecuadorian highlands; vinho de jurema in Brazil, the fly agaric in Siberia, the solanaceous species of medieval witches' brews of Europe.

Similarly, auditory hallucinations may enable medicine men and often others to speak with the controlling spirit forces: sinicuichi, gi-i-wa and gi-i-sa-wa, and thle-pela-kano in Mexico fall into this category. The peyote intoxication may, at certain phases, induce auditory aberrations and, like other hallucinogens such as *Cannabis*, may evoke peculiar response to chanting, singing, music, drumming, or natural sounds like that of rippling waters – an effect clearly suggesting in aboriginal thinking supernatural connections between the causative drug and man.

The combination of these various fields of enquiry led psychologists to conceive that drug-taking needed to be understood not merely in the context of abnormal behaviour, but as an essential dynamic in human nature.

ANDREW WEIL
The Natural Mind

(1975)

It is my belief that the desire to alter consciousness periodically is an innate, normal drive analogous to hunger or the sexual drive. Note that I do not say 'desire to alter consciousness by means of chemical agents'. Drugs are merely one means of satisfying this drive; there are many others, and I will discuss them in due course. In postulating an inborn drive of this sort, I am not advancing a proposition to be proved or disproved but simply a model to be tried out for usefulness in simplifying our understanding of our observations. The model I propose is consistent with observable evidence. In particular, the omnipresence of the phenomenon argues that we are dealing not with something socially or culturally based but rather with a biological characteristic of the species. Furthermore, the need for periods of non-ordinary consciousness begins to be expressed at ages far too young for it to have much to do with social conditioning. Anyone who watches very young children without revealing his presence will find them regularly practising techniques that induce striking changes in mental states. Three- and four-year-olds, for example, commonly whirl themselves into vertiginous stupors. They hyperventilate and have other children squeeze them around the chest until they faint. They also choke each other to produce loss of consciousness.

To my knowledge these practices appear spontaneously among children of all societies, and I suspect they have done so throughout history as well. It is most interesting that children quickly learn to keep this sort of play out of sight of grownups, who instinctively try to stop them. The sight of a child being throttled into unconsciousness scares the parent, but the child seems to have a wonderful time; at least, he goes right off and does it again. Psychologists have paid remarkably little attention to these activities of all children. Some Freudians have noted them and called them 'sexual equivalents', suggesting that they are somehow related to the experience of orgasm. But merely labelling a phenomenon does not automatically increase our ability to describe, predict, or influence it; besides, our understanding of sexual experience is too primitive to help us much.

Growing children engage in extensive experimentation with mental states, usually in the direction of loss of waking consciousness. Many of them discover that the transition zone between waking and sleep offers many possibilities for unusual sensations, such as hallucinations and out-of-the-body experiences, and they look forward to this period each night

. . .

It is only a matter of time before children find out that similar experiences may be obtained chemically; many of them learn it before the age of five. The most common route to this knowledge is the discovery that inhalation of the fumes of volatile solvents in household products induces experiences similar to those caused by whirling or fainting. An alternate route is introduction to general anaesthesia in connection with a child-hood operation – an experience that invariably becomes one of the most vivid early memories.

By the time most American children enter school they have already explored a variety of altered states of consciousness and usually know that chemical substances are one doorway to this fascinating realm. They also know that it is a forbidden realm in that grownups will always attempt to stop them from going there if they catch them at it. But, as I have said, the desire to repeat these experiences is not mere whim; it looks like a real drive arising from the neurophysiological structure of the human brain. What, then, happens to it as the child becomes more and more involved in the process of socialization? In most cases, it goes underground. Children learn very quickly that they must pursue antisocial behaviour patterns if they wish to continue to alter conscious-ness regularly. Hence the secret meetings in cloakrooms, garages, and playground corners where they can continue to whirl, choke each other, and, perhaps, sniff cleaning fluids or gasoline

. . .

It is noteworthy that most of the world's highest religious and philosophic thought originated in altered states of consciousness in individuals (Gautama, Paul, Mohammed, etc.). It is also noteworthy that creative genius has long been observed to correlate with psychosis and that intuitive genius is often associated with daydreaming, meditation, dreaming, and other non-ordinary modes of consciousness.

What conclusions can we draw from all this information? At the least, it would seem, altered states of consciousness have great potential for strongly positive psychic development. They appear to be the ways to more effective and fuller use of the nervous system, to development of creative and intellectual faculties, and to attainment of certain kinds of thought that have been deemed exalted by all who have experienced them.

So there is much logic in our being born with a drive to experiment with other ways of experiencing our perceptions, in particular to get away periodically from ordinary, ego-centred consciousness. It may even be a key factor in the present evolution of the human nervous system. But our immediate concern is the anxiety certain expressions of this drive are provoking in our own land, and we are trying to decide what to make of altered states of consciousness. Clearly, they are potentially valuable to us, not inherently undesirable as in our first hypothesis. They are also not abnormal in that they grade into states all of us have experienced. Therefore, to attempt to thwart this drive would probably be impossible and might be dangerous. True, it exposes the organism to certain risks, but ultimately it can confer psychic superiority. To try to thwart its expression in individuals and in society might be psychologically crippling for people and evolutionarily suicidal for the species. I would not want to see us tamper with something so closely related to our curiosity, our creativity, our intuition, and our highest aspirations.

2
Researches Chemical and Philosophical: Drugs and Science

The role of science in the understanding of drugs and their effects is complex and ambiguous. On the one hand, science claims the fundamental level of description of drugs, in increasingly microscopic detail — in fact, much of our understanding of neurochemistry has been reached by investigating the mechanics of drug action. On the other hand, many of the subjective realms of experience which drugs open up remain resolutely irreducible to the language of science.

This ambiguity has led to a prolonged and largely intractable debate about whether the scientific investigation of drugs should include the observation of their subjective effects on the scientist. Some claim that no true scientific understanding can be reached on the basis of external observation alone; others that self-experimentation can only lead to meaninglessly 'subjective' accounts.

*In the early days of chemical discovery, when Sir Humphry Davy first
isolated nitrous oxide in his search for 'pneumatic medicines', his own
experience of its effects was an essential part of the process.*

HUMPHRY DAVY

Researches Chemical and Philosophical; chiefly concerning nitrous oxide, or dephlogisticated nitrous air, and its respiration

(1800)

Having previously closed my nostrils and exhausted my lungs,
I breathed four quarts of nitrous oxide from and into a silk bag. The
first feelings were similar to those produced in the last experiment;
but in less than half a minute, the respiration being continued, they
diminished gradually and were succeeded by a sensation analogous to
gentle pressure on all muscles, attended by a highly pleasurable thrilling
in the chest and extremities. The objects around me became dazzling
and my hearing more acute.

[. . .] I now had a great disposition to laugh, luminous points seemed
frequently to pass before my eyes, my hearing was certainly more acute
and I felt a pleasant lightness and power of exertion in my muscles.

[. . .] I felt a sense of tangible extension highly pleasurable in every
limb; my visible impressions were dazzling and apparently magnified,
I heard every distinct sound in the room and was perfectly aware of my
situation. By degrees as the pleasurable sensations increased, I lost all
connection with external things; trains of vivid visible images rapidly
passed through my mind and were connected with words in such a
manner, as to produce perceptions perfectly novel. I existed in a world
of newly connected and newly modified ideas. I theorized; I imagined
I made discoveries. When I was awakened from this semi-delirious
trance by Dr Kinglake, who took the bag from my mouth, indignation
and pride were the first feelings produced by the sight of persons about
me. My emotions were enthusiastic and sublime; and for a minute I

walked round the room perfectly regardless of what was said to me. As I recovered my former state of mind, I felt an inclination to communicate the discoveries I had made during the experiment. I endeavoured to recall the ideas, they were feeble and indistinct; one collection of terms, however, presented itself; and with the most intense belief and prophetic manner, I exclaimed to Dr Kinglake, 'Nothing exists but thoughts! The Universe is composed of impressions, ideas, pleasures and pains!'

[. . .] The next morning the recollections of the effects of the gas were indistinct, and had not remarks written immediately after the experiment recalled them to my mind, I should even have doubted their reality.

Self-experimenting scientists: German medical students get high on ether in an illustration from 1847. (Mary Evans Picture Library)

Moreau de Tours (see p. 19) was explicit about the need for self-experimentation.

JACQUES-JOSEPH MOREAU DE TOURS
Hashish and Mental Illness

(1845)

Knowledge about hashish in the medical world is limited, at most, to recognition of the word for it. Mr Aubert-Roche, in his book *De la Peste, ou Typhus d'Orient* (1840) (*Concerning the Plague, or Oriental Typhus*), had already called attention to hashish. In 1841 in my treatise on the treatment of hallucinations with *Datura stramonium* (Jimson weed), I applied myself to the task of revealing the psychological effects of this substance. I had become acquainted with the effects of hashish through my own experience, and not merely from the reports of others. Indeed, there is essentially only one valid approach to the study; observation, in such cases, when not focused on the observer himself, touches only on appearances and can lead to grossly fallacious conclusions.

At the outset I must make this point, the verity of which is unquestionable: personal experience is the criterion of truth here. I challenge the right of anyone to discuss the effects of hashish if he is not speaking for himself and if he has not been in a position to evaluate them in light of sufficient repeated use.

Hopefully no one will be astonished to hear me speak in this manner. Since my travels in the Orient, I have steadfastly pursued a serious study of the effects of hashish. As much as I have been able and by diverse means (a large number of my colleagues, whom I could name here, will bear me witness), I have striven to disseminate such knowledge within the medical profession. My words have frequently been met with disbelief, but this disbelief would end whenever an individual, overcoming certain fears, and natural ones at that, had the courage to follow my example and try for himself.

. . . while his younger contemporary, the Catholic psychiatrist Benedict Augustin Morel, regarded drugs such as hashish and opium as degenerative poisons which should on no account be taken. It should be pointed out that, especially in the English translation here, Moreau de Tours ('M. Moreau') is spectacularly misquoted.

B A MOREL
'On the Degeneracy of the Human Race'

(1857; summary translation by Forbes Winslow)

*O*n Degenerations resulting from various Vegetable and Mineral Poisons

1. HACHISCH   The Indian hemp (*Cannabis Indica*) forms the basis of most of the intoxicating preparations used in Egypt, Syria, and most Oriental countries. The leaves are smoked alone or mixed with tobacco. But the most celebrated preparation is the fatty extract known as hachisch, which seems to be butter charged with the active principle. It is too nauseous to take alone, but is made up into various forms of cakes and electuaries, sometimes mixed with aphrodisiacs, and sometimes with other narcotics, as opium, stramonium, etc. The effects on the system have been so often described, and are so analogous, in many respects, to those of opium, shortly to be mentioned, that it is not necessary to recapitulate them. They are all referrable to the nervous system. The final results are thus alluded to by M. Moreau:

Besides the habitual hallucinations which the extract of Indian hemp produces in some individuals, I think its prolonged usage induces incurable dementia. I have reason to believe that such is the case in many persons met with in the cities of Egypt, who are venerated as holy men (*santons*) by the people, but who are merely fallen into a state of dementia from the use of hachisch.

2. OPIUM   'At no period of time has humanity witnessed a fact like that we have now to consider,' says M. Morel. 'Three hundred millions of individuals, united under one absolute government, speaking the same language, and having identical religious notions present to us the sad spectacle of a people menaced, as to its dearest interests, by

the most fatal and degrading habit that it is possible to conceive – that of smoking opium.'

An idea may be formed of the frightful increase of the consumption of opium in China by the following figures. China is selected as a typical illustration of the effects of this practice on the race. In 1810, 2,500 cases of opium were sent to Canton; in 1820, 4,770 cases; in 1830, 18,760 cases; and in 1838, 48,000 cases! And this in spite of the laws enacted against it! laws which the lawgivers are the first to infringe and set at nought.

The effects of smoking it, immediate and remote, are thus described:

The first impression is a feeling of content and slight excitement, manifested by loquacity and involuntary laughter. Sometimes there are fits of anger. Soon the eyes become brilliant, and the respiration and circulation are quickened and excited. At this stage of the nervous exaltation the smoker feels a peculiar comfort (*un bien-être tout à fait particulier*), and the temperature is augmented. The impressions are lively, and the imagination wanders into strange illusions. Now we observe a phenomenon frequently remarked in mental alienation. Facts and ideas, long forgotten, present themselves to the mind in all their original freshness. The future appears all bright, and every happiness ever wished for appears realized by the smoker. If he continues smoking, exaltation gives place to depression and utter prostration. The action of the senses is suspended. He hears nothing; he becomes silent; his face becomes pale, his tongue hangs out; a cold sweat inundates the whole body; and insensibility supervenes, often lasting for several hours. The awakening is what might be expected after such a debauch.

Such are the immediate effects, but neither tobacco nor Indian hemp (nor *perhaps* alcohol) are to compare with opium either in the constitutional results, or in the difficulty of breaking the habit. Except some few smokers, who, thanks to an exceptional organization, can restrain themselves within the bounds of moderation, all the others attain rapidly a fatal termination, having passed in quick succession the stages of idleness, debauch, misery, the ruin of their physical strength, and the utter depravation of their moral and intellectual faculties. Nothing can cure an advanced smoker of opium.

But the action of opium is more pernicious than that of alcohol in another particular – viz., the *rapidity* with which the nervous lesions declare themselves. Given the period at which a person begins to smoke opium, it is easy to predict the time of his death; his days are numbered. The physiological effects are uniform, and succeed each other with an unvarying regularity.

According to Dr Ainsley, a considerable fattening first occurs; then failure of strength, and irregularity of walk; then the memory is lost, the intellectual faculties fail, and dementia results. The termination is similar to that of the victims of alcoholism in Europe . . . *No smoker of opium attains an advanced age* and their offspring are blanched, miserable, and struck with premature mental decay. For obvious reasons, we have not yet the same opportunity of tracing the ultimate degenerating effect of this practice on the race, as we have of that of alcoholism; but it cannot be doubted that the same law will hold good; and we cannot but be alarmed for the intellectual, physical, and moral future reserved for China, Sumatra, and the other countries where this practice obtains.

The most celebrated self-experimental blunder of nineteenth-century science was Sigmund Freud's assessment of cocaine. Failing to notice its potential for metabolic dependence, he addicted several of his patients to it and was forced to retract the optimistic claims below. Nevertheless, he continued to use the drug himself.

SIGMUND FREUD
'Über Coca' ('On Cocaine')

(1884)

The psychic effect of *cocaïnum muriaticum* in doses of 0.05–0.10 g consists of exhilaration and lasting euphoria, which does not differ in any way from the normal euphoria of a healthy person. The feeling of excitement which accompanies stimulus by alcohol is completely lacking; the characteristic urge for immediate activity which alcohol produces is also absent. One senses an increase of self-control and feels more vigorous and more capable of work; on the other hand, if one works, one misses that heightening of the mental powers which alcohol, tea, or coffee induce. One is simply normal, and soon finds it difficult to believe that one is under the influence of any drug at all. This gives the impression that the mood induced by coca in such doses is due not so much to direct stimulation as to the disappearance of elements in one's general state of well-being which cause depression. One may perhaps assume that the euphoria resulting from good health is also nothing more than the normal condition of a well-nourished cerebral cortex which 'is not conscious' of the organs of the body to which it belongs.

During this stage of the cocaine condition, which is not otherwise distinguished, appear those symptoms which have been described as the wonderful stimulating effect of coca. Long-lasting, intensive mental or physical work can be performed without fatigue; it is as though the need for food and sleep, which otherwise makes itself felt peremptorily at certain times of the day, were completely banished. While the effects of cocaine last one can, if urged to do so, eat copiously and without revulsion; but one has the clear feeling that the meal was superfluous. Similarly, as the effect of coca declines it is possible to sleep on going to bed, but sleep can just as easily be omitted with no unpleasant consequences. During the first hours of the coca effect one cannot sleep, but this sleeplessness is in no way distressing.

I have tested this effect of coca, which wards off hunger, sleep, and fatigue and steels one to intellectual effort, some dozen times on myself; I had no opportunity to engage in physical work.

A very busy colleague gave me an opportunity to observe a striking example of the manner in which cocaine dispels extreme fatigue and a well justified feeling of hunger; at 6.00 p.m. this colleague, who had not eaten since the early morning and who had worked exceedingly hard during the day, took 0.05 g of *cocaïnum muriaticum*. A few minutes later he declared that he felt as though he had just eaten an ample meal, that he had no desire for an evening meal, and that he felt strong enough to undertake a long walk.

. . .

It seems probable, in the light of reports which I shall refer to later, that coca, if used protractedly but in moderation, is not detrimental to the body. Von Anrep treated animals for thirty days with moderate doses of cocaine and detected no detrimental effects on their bodily functions. It seems to me noteworthy – and I discovered this in myself and in other observers who were capable of judging such things – that a first dose or even repeated doses of coca produce no compulsive desire to use the stimulant further; on the contrary, one feels a certain unmotivated aversion to the substance. This circumstance may be partly responsible for the fact that coca, despite some warm recommendations, has not established itself in Europe as a stimulant.

The fiction of Freud's time reveals a growing ambivalence about self-experimentation with drugs. The early Sherlock Holmes used cocaine in a manner which Freud would have approved, though Conan Doyle later glossed over this character trait as the public perception of the 'cocaine fiend' became less sympathetic.

SIR ARTHUR CONAN DOYLE
The Sign of Four

(1889)

Sherlock Holmes took his bottle from the corner of the mantel-piece, and his hypodermic syringe from its neat morocco case. With his long, white, nervous fingers he adjusted the delicate needle, and rolled back his left shirt-cuff. For some little time his eyes rested thoughtfully upon the sinewy forearm and wrist, all dotted and scarred with innumerable puncture-marks. Finally, he thrust the sharp point home, pressed down the tiny piston, and sank back into the velvet-lined armchair with a long sigh of satisfaction.

Three times a day for many months I had witnessed this performance, but custom had not reconciled my mind to it. On the contrary, from day to day I had become more irritable at the sight, and my conscience swelled nightly within me at the thought that I had lacked the courage to protest. Again and again I had registered a vow that I should deliver my soul upon the subject; but there was that in the cool, nonchalant air of my companion which made him the last man with whom one would care to take anything approaching to a liberty. His great powers, his masterly manner, and the experience which I had had of his many extraordinary qualities, all made me diffident and backward in crossing him.

Yet upon that afternoon, whether it was the Beaune which I had taken with my lunch, or the additional exasperation produced by the extreme deliberation of his manner, I suddenly felt that I could hold out no longer.

'Which is it to-day,' I asked, 'morphine or cocaine?'

He raised his eyes languidly from the old black-letter volume which he had opened.

'It is cocaine,' he said, 'a seven-per-cent solution. Would you care to try it?'

'No, indeed,' I answered, brusquely. 'My constitution has not got over the Afghan campaign yet. I cannot afford to throw any extra strain upon it.'

He smiled at my vehemence. 'Perhaps you are right, Watson,' he said. 'I suppose that its influence is physically a bad one. I find it, however, so transcendently stimulating and clarifying to the mind that its secondary action is a matter of small moment.'

'But consider!' I said, earnestly. 'Count the cost! Your brain may, as you say, be roused and excited, but it is a pathological and morbid process, which involves increased tissue-change, and may at last leave a permanent weakness. You know, too, what a black reaction comes upon you. Surely the game is hardly worth the candle. Why should you, for a mere passing pleasure, risk the loss of those great powers with which you have been endowed? Remember that I speak not only as one comrade to another, but as a medical man to one for whose constitution he is to some extent answerable.'

He did not seem offended. On the contrary, he put his finger-tips together, and leaned his elbows on the arms of his chair, like one who has a relish for conversation.

'My mind,' he said, 'rebels at stagnation. Give me problems, give me work, give me the most abstruse cryptogram, or the most intricate analysis, and I am in my own proper atmosphere. I can dispense then with artificial stimulants. But I abhor the dull routine of existence. I crave for mental exaltation. That is why I have chosen my own particular profession, or rather created it, for I am the only one in the world.'

. . . while Robert Louis Stevenson's The Strange Case of Dr Jekyll and
Mr Hyde *remains the classic cautionary tale of the self-experimenting
scientist – allegedly written in less than a week under the influence of
cocaine.*

ROBERT LOUIS STEVENSON
The Strange Case of Dr Jekyll and Mr Hyde

(1886)

With every day, and from both sides of my intelligence, the
moral and the intellectual, I thus drew steadily nearer to that truth by
whose partial discovery I have been doomed to such a dreadful ship-
wreck: that man is not truly one, but truly two. I say two, because the
state of my own knowledge does not pass beyond that point. Others
will follow, others will outstrip me on the same lines; and I hazard the
guess that man will be ultimately known for a mere polity of multifarious,
incongruous and independent denizens

. . .

I was so far in my reflections when, a side light began to shine upon
the subject from the laboratory table. I began to perceive more deeply
than it has ever yet been stated, the trembling immateriality, the mist-like
transience, of this seemingly so solid body in which we walk attired.
Certain agents I found to have the power to shake and to pluck back
that fleshly vestment, even as a wind might toss the curtains of a pavilion.
For two good reasons, I will not enter deeply into this scientific branch
of my confession. First, because I have been made to learn that the
doom and burthen of our life is bound for ever on man's shoulders; and
when the attempt is made to cast it off, it but returns upon us with
more unfamiliar and more awful pressure. Second, because, as my
narrative will make, alas! too evident, my discoveries were incomplete.
Enough, then, that I not only recognised my natural body for the mere
aura and effulgence of certain of the powers that made up my spirit,

but managed to compound a drug by which these powers should be dethroned from their supremacy, and a second form and countenance substituted, none the less natural to me because they were the expression, and bore the stamp, of lower elements in my soul.

I hesitated long before I put this theory to the test of practice. I knew well that I risked death; for any drug that so potently controlled and shook the very fortress of identity, might by the least scruple of an overdose or at the least inopportunity in the moment of exhibition, utterly blot out that immaterial tabernacle which I looked to it to change. But the temptation of a discovery so singular and profound at last overcame the suggestions of alarm. I had long since prepared my tincture; I purchased at once, from a firm of wholesale chemists, a large quantity of a particular salt, which I knew, from my experiments, to be the last ingredient required; and, late one accursed night, I compounded the elements, watched them boil and smoke together in the glass, and when the ebullition had subsided, with a strong glow of courage, drank off the potion.

The most racking pangs succeeded: a grinding in the bones, deadly nausea, and a horror of the spirit that cannot be exceeded at the hour of birth or death. Then these agonies began swiftly to subside, and I came to myself as if out of a great sickness. There was something strange in my sensations, something indescribably new and, from its very novelty, incredibly sweet. I felt younger, lighter, happier in body; within I was conscious of a heady recklessness, a current of disordered sensual images running like a mill race in my fancy, a solution of the bonds of obligation, an unknown but not an innocent freedom of the soul. I knew myself, at the first breath of this new life, to be more wicked, tenfold more wicked, sold a slave to my original evil; and the thought, in that moment, braced and delighted me like wine. I stretched out my hands, exulting in the freshness of these sensations; and in the act, I was suddenly aware that I had lost in stature.

There was no mirror, at that date, in my room; that which stands beside me as I write was brought there later on, and for the very purpose of those transformations. The night, however, was far gone into the morning – the morning, black as it was, was nearly ripe for the conception of the day – the inmates of my house were locked in the most rigorous hours of slumber; and I determined, flushed as I was with hope and triumph, to venture in my new shape as far as to my bedroom. I crossed the yard, wherein the constellations looked down upon me, I could have thought, with wonder, the first creature of that sort that their unsleeping vigilance had yet disclosed to them; I stole through the corridors, a stranger in my own house; and coming to my room, I saw for the first time the appearance of Edward Hyde

. . .

And yet when I looked upon that ugly idol in the glass, I was conscious of no repugnance, rather of a leap of welcome. This, too, was myself. It seemed natural and human. In my eyes it bore a livelier image of the spirit, it seemed more express and single, than the imperfect and divided countenance, I had been hitherto accustomed to call mine. And in so far I was doubtless right. I have observed that when I wore the semblance of Edward Hyde, none could come near to me at first without a visible misgiving of the flesh. This, as I take it, was because all human beings, as we meet them, are commingled out of good and evil: and Edward Hyde, alone, in the ranks of mankind, was pure evil.

As the recreational use of drugs spread, new drugs were less easily contained within the scientific community. The psychiatrist William Sargant, in experimenting with the newly developed stimulant benzedrine, was led to discover applications for it beyond the strictly medical.

WILLIAM SARGANT
The Unquiet Mind

(1967)

In 1936 we at the Maudsley discovered the psychiatric value of benzedrine, or what is known as the amphetamine or benzedrine group of drugs, which now include dexedrine and methedrine. Dr Eric Guttman, and an American visiting doctor, Dr Peebles, who was sent supplies of benzedrine from America as a blood pressure raiser and a relief for narcolepsy, were testing it on a couple of depressives. The depressions suddenly lifted and Dr Peebles soon realized that benzedrine possessed greater virtues than he had suspected. This was the first time that we had ever watched a drug's sometimes immediate temporary benefit on melancholia. However, the improvement in mood never lasted for more than a couple of days and we eventually found that benzedrine's real value lay in treating cases of mild rather than acute severe depression, and in giving normal people a prolonged burst of confidence and energy to tide them over some important or dangerous period.

Observations on benzedrine as a temporary relief for mental depression were independently made in Boston at much the same time by Dr Abraham Myerson's team. Reports from both groups appeared almost simultaneously, and hope quickly spread all over the world that similar drugs more lasting in their effects would be found sooner or later: as has now happened. When Dr Peebles returned to America, I helped Guttman to explore further the actual clinical uses of benzedrine, and we were soon able to publish one of the earliest clinical reports of its effects on two hundred and fifty people, both normal and mentally depressed, of various types. On re-reading this report, some thirty years later, I find with relief that it agrees substantially with the present consensus of medical opinion.

On first using benzedrine, we could only guess at its proper dosage.

I still preserve a few of the original tablets brought over from America; they proved to contain four times more than the modern clinical dose. Though I have rarely taken drugs for experimental purposes, lest they might bias my judgment, I did try one of these tablets one Saturday afternoon, then I walked energetically around the Zoological Gardens with a most delightful sense of confidence and not the least fatigued. Returning to the hospital, I worked hard all that evening, still happy and vigorous. It suddenly occurred to me that, unless this top-of-the-world feeling were due to some other cause, benzedrine should clearly help me to pass examinations. Soon afterwards I sat for the Diploma of Psychological Medicine, which gave me a perfect opportunity for testing my theory. Having obtained the Diploma, I naturally wanted to know whether perhaps the drug, like alcohol, had made me feel that I was doing very well, when in point of fact my efficiency showed a marked decrease. I approached one of the examiners, a senior person at the Maudsley, who was himself interested in benzedrine, and asked him, strictly as a matter of scientific interest, what my actual marks had been. They proved high enough, by comparison with my knowledge of the subject, to rule out every possibility of false confidence.

With the help of a Maudsley psychologist, Dr F. A. Blackburn, I then arranged a series of intelligence tests with and without the taking of benzedrine; and found that it noticeably improved the percentage of correct answers. This did not necessarily mean that the drug improved intelligence; only that it enabled examinees suffering from mild depressions to give more confident answers and thus score higher marks. We published these findings in the *Lancet*.

Thus the English firm which marketed benzedrine realized that they had a highly saleable product to offer.

We urgently begged that they should refrain from selling it to the general public, or even to doctors, until we had worked out all its side effects, especially its possible addictive qualities, and had clearly explained the dangers that might attend the use of even so beneficial a drug. But we soon found that not only were free samples of benzedrine being distributed to all general practitioners, but it could be freely bought at any chemist's shop without a doctor's prescription. Imprudent people began using benzedrine at random, often with disastrous results. One woman, for instance, threw herself from the window of a London hotel after mixing large doses of it with alcohol; and all the publicity helped to provoke a new fashion for benzedrine cocktails.

Our discovery that intelligence quotients could be improved by benzedrine unfortunately also made headlines in the Press. Hundreds of students took the drug before and during examinations, without first testing its effects on themselves. Although, as a rule, benzedrine inspires confidence and lessens fatigue or minor anxiety, yet if an examinee panics in the examination hall its action on his autonomic nervous system accentuates the emotion. Though I had myself tested its effects beforehand and found that it agreed with my particular constitution, many students who were now drugging themselves for the first time, failed examinations which they might otherwise have passed easily enough. The doping of race horses and of athletes with benzedrine – now called pep pills – were other later displeasing results of the publicity originally given to our clinical research articles and all those that inevitably followed them.

We continued these benzedrine researches at the Maudsley until 1938, by which time its benefits still seemed confined mainly to prolonging and sustaining effort in mildly depressed, tired or quite normal people; and a combination of benzedrine with short-acting barbiturates, such as sodium amytal, also started to be used at the Maudsley which often assisted the treatment of severer anxieties.

Warned by the disastrous results of our publications, this powerful combined preparation was kept out of the news, and so out of the hands of drug houses. It was not until after the publication of 'Physical Methods of Treatment in Psychiatry' by Slater and myself six years later, that drug manufacturers got wind of this combination. It was marketed and became so popular in the form of tablets such as 'Drinamyl' or 'Purple Hearts', which psychopaths, drug addicts and simple delinquents used as a source of cheap 'kicks', that an Act of Parliament had finally to be passed in England specially to control their distribution. Fantastic amounts of drinamyl were before this being made and sold everywhere, often quite illegally, just as happened legally when we first reported on the chemical value of benzedrine itself in psychiatry.

The final pay-off to our early work on benzedrine came very early in World War II. The Press reported that German parachutists were coming down behind the French line, heavily drugged, fearless and berserk. The German conquest of France was largely attributed to the success of these formidable parachutists who caused such havoc in their drugged state when they landed. When this wonder drug at last was found in the possession of a captured monster, it proved to be no more than a very small benzedrine tablet! The Germans had been prudent enough to sustain their men's capacity for occasional prolonged effort. Soon airmen, parachutists and special contingents on both sides were using these tablets for the very same effects that I had once observed in myself during my walk around the Zoo; but by the end of the war, though the sale of the drug was already well controlled, benzedrine addicts had started to be seen.

*The powerful psychedelic LSD is perhaps the best-known example of
a new drug whose use has 'leaked' from the medical profession into the
wider community. This use might never have been discovered without
its inventor's unwitting self-experimentation.*

ALBERT HOFMANN
LSD, My Problem Child

(1979)

Time and again I hear or read that LSD was discovered by
accident. This is only partly true. LSD came into being within a
systematic research programme, and the 'accident' did not occur until
much later: when LSD was already five years old, I happened to
experience its unforeseeable effects in my own body or, rather, in my
own mind.

. . .

[. . .] In the spring of 1929, on concluding my chemistry studies at
the University of Zurich, I joined the Sandoz Company's pharmaceutical–chemical research laboratory in Basel, as a co-worker with
Professor Arthur Stoll, founder and director of the pharmaceutical
department. I chose this position because it afforded me the opportunity to work on natural products, whereas two other job offers from
chemical firms in Basel had involved work in the field of synthetic
chemistry.

. . .

[. . .] My first years in the Sandoz laboratories were devoted almost
exclusively to studying the active principles of Mediterranean squill. Dr
Walter Kreis, one of Professor Stoll's earliest associates, launched me in
this field of research. The most important constituents of Mediterranean
squill already existed in pure form. Their active agents, as well as those
of woolly foxglove (*Digitalis lanata*), had been isolated and purified,
chiefly by Dr Kreis, with extraordinary skill.

. . .

[. . .] My main contribution to the [. . .] research, in which I participated with enthusiasm, was to elucidate the chemical structure of the common nucleus of *Scilla glycosides*, showing on the one hand their differences from the *Digitalis glycosides*, and on the other hand their close structural relationship with the toxic principles isolated from skin glands of toads. In 1935, these studies were temporarily concluded.

Looking for a new field of research, I asked Professor Stoll to let me continue the investigations on the alkaloids of ergot, which he had begun in 1917 and which had led directly to the isolation of ergotamine in 1918. Ergotamine, discovered by Stoll, was the first ergot alkaloid obtained in pure chemical form.

. . .

[. . .] The first mention of a medicinal use of ergot, namely as an ecbolic (a medicament to precipitate childbirth), is found in the herbal of the Frankfurt city physician Adam Lonitzer (Lonicerus) in the year 1582. Although ergot, as Lonitzer stated, had been used since olden times by midwives, it was not until 1808 that this drug gained entry into academic medicine, on the strength of a work by the American physician John Stearns entitled *Account of the* Putvis Parturiens, *a Remedy for Quickening Childbirth*. The use of ergot as an ecbolic did not, however, endure. Practitioners became aware quite early of the great danger to the child, owing primarily to the uncertainty of dosage, which when too high led to uterine spasms. From then on, the use of ergot in obstetrics was confined to stopping postpartum haemorrhage (bleeding after childbirth).

. . .

[. . .] The early 1930s brought a new era in ergot research, beginning with the determination of the chemical structure of ergot alkaloids, as mentioned, in English and American laboratories. By chemical cleavage, W. A. Jacobs and L. C. Craig of the Rockefeller Institute of New York succeeded in isolating and characterizing the nucleus common to all ergot alkaloids. They named it lysergic acid.

. . .

[. . .] I set as my first goal the problem of preparing this alkaloid synthetically, through chemical linking of the two components of ergobasine, lysergic acid and propanolamine.

. . .

[. . .] Lysergic acid proved to be a rather unstable substance, and its rebonding with basic radicals posed difficulties. In the technique known as Curtius' Synthesis, I ultimately found a process that proved useful for combining lysergic acid with amines. [. . .] With this synthesis, the other alkaloids existing abundantly in ergot could now be converted to ergobasine, which was valuable in obstetrics

. . .

[. . .] I further employed my synthetic procedure to produce new lysergic acid compounds for which uterotonic activity was not prominent, but from which, on the basis of their chemical structure, other types of interesting pharmacological properties could be expected. In 1938, I produced the twenty-fifth substance in this series of lysergic acid derivatives: lysergic acid diethylamide, abbreviated LSD-25 for laboratory usage.

. . .

[. . .] The new substance, however, aroused no special interest in our pharmacologists and physicians; testing was therefore discontinued.

. . .

For the next five years, nothing more was heard of the substance LSD-25. Meanwhile, my work in the ergot field advanced further in other areas.

. . .

[. . .] The solution of the ergotoxine problem had led to fruitful results, described here only briefly, and had opened up further avenues of research. And yet I could not forget the relatively uninteresting LSD-25. A peculiar presentiment – the feeling that this substance could possess properties other than those established in the first investigations – induced me, five years after the first synthesis, to produce LSD-25 once again so that a sample could be given to the pharmacological department for further tests. This was quite unusual; experimental substances, as a rule, were definitely stricken from the research programme if once found to be lacking in pharmacological interest.

. . .

Nevertheless, in the spring of 1943, I repeated the synthesis of LSD-25. As in the first synthesis, this involved the production of only a few centigrams of the compound. In the final step of the synthesis, during the purification and crystallization of lysergic acid diethylamide in the form of a tartrate (tartaric acid salt), I was interrupted in my work by unusual sensations. The following description of this incident comes from the report that I sent at the time to Professor Stoll:

Last Friday, April 16, 1943, I was forced to interrupt my work in the laboratory in the middle of the afternoon and proceed home, being affected by a remarkable restlessness, combined with a slight dizziness. At home I lay down and sank into a not unpleasant intoxicated-like condition, characterized by an extremely stimulated imagination. In a dreamlike state, with eyes closed (I found the daylight to be unpleasantly glaring), I perceived an uninterrupted stream of fantastic pictures, extraordinary shapes with intense, kaleidoscopic play of colours. After some two hours this condition faded away.

This was, altogether, a remarkable experience both in its sudden onset and its extraordinary course. It seemed to have resulted from some external toxic influence; I surmised a connection with the substance I had been working with at the time, lysergic acid diethylamide tartrate. But this led to another question: how had I managed to absorb this material? Because of the known toxicity of ergot substances, I always maintained meticulously neat work habits. Possibly a bit of the LSD solution had contacted my fingertips during crystallization, and a trace of the substance was absorbed through the skin. If LSD-25 had indeed been the cause of this bizarre experience, then it must be a substance of extraordinary potency. There seemed to be only one way of getting to the bottom of this. I decided on a self-experiment.

Exercising extreme caution, I began the planned series of experiments with the smallest quantity that could be expected to produce some effect, considering the activity of the ergot alkaloids known at the time: namely, 0.25 mg (mg = milligram = one thousandth of a gram) of lysergic acid diethylamide tartrate. Quoted below is the entry for this experiment in my laboratory journal of 19 April 1943.

> 4/19/43 16.20: 0.5 cc of ½ promil aqueous solution of diethylamide tartrate orally = 0.25 mg tartrate. Taken diluted with about 10 cc water. Tasteless.

> 17.00: Beginning dizziness, feeling of anxiety, visual distortions, symptoms of paralysis, desire to laugh.

> Supplement of 4/21: Home by bicycle. From 18.00 – ca. 20.00 most severe crisis. (See special report.)

Here the notes in my laboratory journal cease. I was able to write the last words only with great effort. By now it was already clear to me that LSD had been the cause of the remarkable experience of the previous Friday, for the altered perceptions were of the same type as before, only much more intense. I had to struggle to speak intelligibly. I asked my laboratory assistant, who was informed of the self-experiment, to escort me home. We went by bicycle, no automobile being available because of wartime restrictions on their use. On the way home, my condition began to assume threatening forms. Everything in my field of vision wavered and was distorted as if seen in a curved mirror. I also had the sensation of being unable to move from the spot. Nevertheless, my assistant later told me that we had travelled very rapidly. Finally, we arrived at home safe and sound, and I was just barely capable of asking my companion to summon our family doctor and request milk from the neighbours. In spite of my delirious, bewildered condition, I had brief periods of clear and effective thinking and chose milk as a nonspecific antidote for poisoning.

The dizziness and sensation of fainting became so strong at times that I could no longer hold myself erect, and had to lie down on a sofa. My surroundings had now transformed themselves in more terrifying ways. Everything in the room spun around, and the familiar objects and pieces of furniture assumed grotesque, threatening forms. They were in continuous motion, animated, as if driven by an inner restlessness. The lady next door, whom I scarcely recognized, brought me milk. In the course of the evening I drank more than two litres. She was no longer Mrs R., but rather a malevolent, insidious witch with a coloured mask.

. . .

[. . .] By the time the doctor arrived, the climax of my despondent condition had already passed. My laboratory assistant informed him about my self-experiment, as I myself was not yet able to formulate a coherent sentence. He shook his head in perplexity, after my attempts to describe the mortal danger that threatened my body. He could detect no abnormal symptoms other than extremely dilated pupils. Pulse, blood pressure, breathing were all normal. He saw no reason to prescribe any medication. Instead he conveyed me to my bed and stood watch over me. Slowly I came back from a weird, unfamiliar world to reassuring everyday reality. The horror softened and gave way to a feeling of good fortune and gratitude, the more normal perceptions and thoughts returned, and I became more confident that the danger of insanity was conclusively past.

Now, little by little I could begin to enjoy the unprecedented colours and plays of shapes that persisted behind my closed eyes. Kaleidoscopic, fantastic images surged in on me, alternating, variegated, opening and then closing themselves in circles and spirals, exploding in coloured fountains, rearranging and hybridizing themselves in constant flux. It was particularly remarkable now every acoustic perception, such as the sound of a door handle or a passing automobile, became transformed into optical perceptions. Every sound generated a vividly changing image, with its own consistent form and colour.

Late in the evening my wife returned from Lucerne. Someone had informed her by telephone that I was suffering a mysterious breakdown. She had returned home at once, leaving the children behind with her parents. By now, I had recovered myself sufficiently to tell her what had happened.

Exhausted, I then slept, to awake next morning refreshed, with a clear head, though still somewhat tired physically. A sensation of well-being and renewed life flowed through me. Breakfast tasted delicious and gave me extraordinary pleasure. When I later walked out into the garden, in which the sun shone now after a spring rain, everything glistened and sparkled in a fresh light. The world was as if newly created. All my senses vibrated in a condition of highest sensitivity, which persisted for the entire day.

The discoverer of LSD: Albert Hofmann on his eightieth birthday, performing Tai Chi while holding a ling chi mushroom. (Christian Rätsch)

The case for self-experimentation is still put by scientists, but only those who are prepared to battle with the professional establishment. The neuroscientist John Lilly's principled stand made him a cause célèbre, *and an eventual casualty of his own ideology (see p. 292).*

JOHN C. LILLY
The Centre of the Cyclone: An Autobiography of Inner Space

(1973)

If you are a scientific investigator interested in using human subjects, it is necessary that you follow J. B. S. Haldane's dictum: 'You will not understand what is necessary in the way of scientific control unless you are the first subject in your experiments.' Professor Bazett taught me this unequivocally.

When he wanted to find out what the end organs (the sensitive endings within the skin) were, he performed psycho-physiological experiments with a cold bath alternating with a hot bath to determine the temperature-sensitive endings in the foreskin on his penis. He marked these with ink, had himself circumcised and found through microscopic sectioning and staining techniques the end organs responsible for the sensations that he had recorded.

Later, when it was important for him to know the temperature within the human brain, he had thermocouples inserted in his own brain through his jugular vein from the neck region. He measured the temperature within the brain and blood flow through his own brain. He never asked anyone else to do what he had not already done on himself.

This was the scientific policy that I was following when I did the isolation tank work at the National Institute of Mental Health and in the Virgin Islands. I followed the same policy when I did the isolation work with the LSD. I did not ask any other subjects to do it until after I had done it myself. Sometimes, one does not use another subject after one has done it oneself, because one realizes either that it is not necessary on a second subject or that it is too dangerous to do on a second subject. One then waits for another mature scientific investigator to do it on himself. This point of view was used by Walter Reed in his experiments to find the cause of yellow fever. This has been a medical and scientific research tradition among the older mature investigators for many years.

In recent years there has been much talk and much regulation both within the National Institutes of Health themselves and in their grants to medical schools. They prohibit the use of human subjects until a jury of one's peers judges whether or not the experiments should be done. This was the restriction placed upon the psychotherapy experiments using LSD at the Spring Grove State Hospital. The protocol of the experiments was exposed to several committees for a decision as to whether or not the group that proposed the experiments would be authorized to do them. I went over the protocols of the proposal from the Spring Grove State Hospital. In no case was it proposed that investigators be exposed to the experimental procedure first.

This lack of involvement of the investigators in their own scientific research as first subjects comes from another line of tradition than the one that I have been brought up and trained in. The justification of the opposing school, if you wish, is as follows: the patient has a disease, say, cancer. The investigator does not have this disease, therefore if you are trying some new therapeutic procedure to try to cure the disease you can't use yourself because you don't have the disease to cure.

I do not agree with this argument at all. You should not do to a patient what you are not willing to do to yourself. You do not know whether or not you are willing to do it on yourself until you try it on yourself. Even if you don't have the disease, whatever the procedure is that you propose using, it should not be damaging enough to prevent you from doing it on yourself. If it is, it should not be done on others. Therefore, until you've proved to your own satisfaction that it is not damaging on animals and then proved to your own satisfaction that it is not damaging on yourself, it is better not to use it.

Back in the fifties, this was the argument that I used against putting brain electrodes into humans. I knew from my animal studies that no matter how you put brain electrodes in a brain some damage to the brain took place during the insertion procedure. Unless one was willing to undergo this amount of damage by inserting electrodes into one's own brain, I didn't feel there was any justification for inserting electrodes into anybody else's brain. This turned out to be a very cogent argument in suppressing the use of brain electrodes.

I began to apply the same argument to the LSD work. I found that, in reality, at Spring Grove no one was doing psychotherapeutic work with LSD until they had been through the LSD session themselves as a training procedure. Therefore, when I arrived at Spring Grove, it was obvious that they were following the ethic that I was already following myself despite the official protocol.

Even though I'd had extensive experience with LSD in the isolation tank under the particular conditions that I had set up for myself in the Virgin Islands, I had not taken LSD under the circumstances prevailing at Spring Grove. By that time I had a very high respect for what LSD could do and for what it did do or what happens under the influence of LSD, which varies considerably with what is going on inside one's self and with what is going on in the surroundings at the same time. Therefore, until I had taken LSD, that is, in the 'psychotherapeutic' setting used with the patients, I would not know what was really happening inside these patients.

Lilly's work with sensory deprivation and psychedelic drugs became the basis for Paddy Chayevsky's novel Altered States, *which replays the Jekyll and Hyde story against the backdrop of me-generation California.*

PADDY CHAYEFSKY
Altered States

(1978)

He met Arthur Rosenberg in Bethesda. Rosenberg was working right across the street in the NIMH, studying the effects of LSD on schizophrenics. This was back in 1964, when LSD was still considered an interesting therapeutic drug and available for responsible research. Jessup was struck by the similarity between the tank experience and the psychotomimetic experience of LSD and other psychedelic drugs. He looked around for literature on the subject. There wasn't much work being done in isolation and sense deprivation, most of it brain-washing studies which the Army funded in the wake of the Korean War, but there was a voluminous, even chaotic, literature on LSD, some fifteen hundred papers. The experiences of LSD subjects are anar-chically variable, he told Emily. Some subjects see things brilliantly illuminated, some subjects see everything shrouded in gloomy shadows. Some people are exhilarated, some feel paranoid. Some people recall things lost in their consciousness, some people see projections of the future. Some people don't feel anything at all. It was clear that the big problem with research in interior experience and altered states of consciousness was its total subjectivity and the fact that the com-munication between subject and observer frequently deteriorated. A subject is induced into altering his normal consciousness in an iso-lation tank or by a pharmacological agent or by hypnosis or self-induced trance, and his experiences are entirely personal, in fact, suprapersonal. The visions, hallucinations, distortions and deformities of cognition are his entirely, and he frequently cannot communicate them at all; and when he does communicate them, they frequently cannot be understood by the experimenter-observer he is communicating them to. Nor is there any way of knowing whether the information being communi-cated by a subject on an inner high is true or valid or accurately reported. The experimenter has no way of repeating them to check them out.

It seemed to Jessup that the whole world of inner and other conscious-ness was being improperly explored. The work being done in it was all radical stuff, an outgrowth of the contentious sixties, polemical in nature, a reaction against the establishment psychology of the times, tinged by Timothy Leary messianism. There were some good people working in the field, Tart, Ornstein, Deikman, but most of the literature was political rather than scientific, more interested in attacking Jensen and the behaviourists and Western science, exalting the irrational and intuitive over the rational and quantifiable. What had to be done, it seemed to Jessup, was to work out some kind of methodology for studying our other consciousnesses under controlled conditions

. . .

Rosenberg was ranging around the dinner table trying to get everyone to sign a petition demanding that the NIH guidelines on recombinant DNA research be reviewed and made stricter. 'For Pete's sake,' Emily paused in her own chattering to comment. 'You haven't been in Boston four days, Arthur, and you're already a member of the Committee of Concerned Scientists.' She signed nevertheless

. . .

And Jessup, who had had more wine than was his wont, was loudly explaining the Buddhist concept of self to Sylvia Rosenberg and to anybody else whose attention he could grab.

'As a matter of fact,' he announced to Sylvia, 'the whole yogic experi-ence was a little disappointing. No matter how you slice it, it's still a state-specific technology operating in the service of an *a priori* belief system, not much different from other trance-inducing techniques. The breathing exercises are effective as hell. The breathing becomes an entity in itself, an actual state of consciousness in its own right, so that your body breathing becomes the embodiment of your breath. But it's still a renunciatory technique to achieve a predetermined trance-like state, what the Zen people call an isness, a very pure narcissism, Freud's oceanic feeling. What dignifies the yogic practices is that the belief system itself is not truly religious. There is no Buddhist god *per se*. It is the Self, the individual Mind, that contains immortality and ultimate truth – '

'What the hell's not metaphysical about that?' shouted Emily from her end of the table, interrupting her own colloquy. 'You've simply replaced God with the Original Self.'

'Yes, but we've localized it, haven't we!' Jessup shouted back. 'At least we know where the Self is! It's in our own minds, somewhere in those hundred-odd billion neural and glial cells in our own minds! It's a form of human energy! If there is an Original Consciousness or a Jungian consciousness or whatever the hell you want to call it, it took in a lot of sensory input, and that input is stored away somewhere in our minds in the quantifiable form of memory! Memory is energy! It doesn't disappear! It's still in there!' He was on his feet now, staggering a little, not really able to hold four flagons of red wine. He wheeled to Rosenberg. 'I'm telling you there's a physiological pathway to our earlier conscious-nesses! And I'm telling you it's somewhere in the goddamned limbic system! If I could stick a couple of microelectrodes into your skull, I'll bet my last shirt we would revive long-term memory and even prenatal recall, and if that isn't a prior consciousness, I'll eat my hat!'

'Jessup, you are a whacko!' roared Parrish happily.

Jessup, who had wandered some steps away from his seat, found his way back, sat down, poured himself another glass of wine. One of those inexplicable hushes had descended on the gathering, out of which Jessup's abruptly quiet, contemplative voice could be clearly heard. 'What's whacko about it, Mason?' he asked agreeably. 'I'm a man in search of his true self. How archetypically American can you get? Everybody's looking for his true self. We're all trying to fulfil ourselves, understand ourselves, get in touch with ourselves, get a hold of ourselves, face the reality of ourselves, explore ourselves, expand ourselves. Ever since we dispensed with God, we've got nothing but our selves to explain this meaningless horror of life. We're all weekending at est or meditating for forty minutes a day or squatting on floors in a communal O M or locking arms in quasi-Sufi dances or stripping off the deceptions of civilized life and jumping naked into a swimming pool filled with other naked searchers for self. Well, I think that true self, that original self, that first self, is a real, mensurate, quantifiable thing, tangible and incarnate. And I'm going to find the fucker.'

Science has, meanwhile, developed an increasingly sophisticated range of methodologies for analysing the subjective effects of drugs by external observation. Some of the most elegant experiments have been devised by the behavioural psychologist Ronald Siegel.

RONALD K. SIEGEL
Intoxication: Life in Pursuit of Artificial Paradise

(1989)

I gave a group of rhesus monkeys in the laboratory an opportunity to tell us something about the nature of these perceptions. The monkeys would sit in a special chair at a desk. On the desk would be two M & M chocolate candies. At least that is what it looked like from the monkey's perspective. Actually, only one M & M was real, the other was a three-dimensional projection arranged by parabolic mirrors hidden inside the desk. The illusion was remarkably convincing. The two candies looked much the same in terms of colour, size, and shape. When the desk was pushed up to the chair, the monkey could easily reach out and grab the real M & M; if it reached for the illusory M & M, its hand would only go through the projection. Initially, monkeys, like the children and adults who have played with this illusion device in toy stores and museums, make the mistake of grasping at the projected object as if it were real.

. . .

Our monkeys had a confusing time differentiating between the real and illusory candies. Yet, after several months, they mastered the discrimination and learned to reach quickly for the real treats, which they either ate right away or stuffed into their cheek pouches for a later snack. The test proved to be extremely sensitive to injections of THC.° Low doses impaired the ability of the monkeys to pick the real M & M. When their

° tetrahydrocannabinol, the active ingredient in cannabis.

grasp literally went through the projection of the illusory M & M, they would display facial expressions of surprise. It also frustrated the animals; Groucho, a six-month-old male rhesus, would give an alarm bark and kick the desk whenever he missed. As the dose of THC increased, the monkeys took longer and longer to decide which M & M to go for and, increasingly, it would be the wrong choice. At high doses, they seemed to lose interest in the test. They performed only at chance levels and appeared just as interested in the mirage as in the real candy, often playing with the projected image by poking and probing it with their fingers. The frustration also disappeared. Groucho would emit a short series of grunting sounds between 0.5 and 1.5 kilocycles. The sounds are called *girning*, noises associated with pleasure and contentment. Groucho's girning was laughter to my ears.

The laughter vanished when I experimented with more extreme dosages. While most other behaviour was also suppressed and I could not use these dosages in the formal tests with the illusion device, I noticed the monkeys adopting a familiar stance. The extreme doses of THC caused the monkeys to assume a typical crouched posture in the chair: they leaned forward and supported their head with one hand, a posture reminiscent of Rodin's *Thinker*. If left undisturbed they would remain in this *Thinker* position for sixty to ninety minutes; their gaze was fixed and they appeared lost in thought. I, too, wondered what they were seeing and thinking.

. . .

Years before I had asked this same question about Mr Nodell's pigeons when, in the midst of their intoxication from the *Cannabis* extract, they would sit on the bottom of the loft and peck at 'things' in the air. Pigeons can fly through these gates of perception, so to speak, and report information on what they see. Because a pigeon's visual system is similar to those of monkeys and people, psychopharmacologists have used this animal to study the effects of drugs on vision. To find out what pigeons might be seeing during a *Cannabis* session, I arranged a series of elaborate experiments with Mr Nodell's birds. In one of the early preliminary studies, the pigeons were trained to watch a screen on which visual stimuli were rear-projected by a special slide projector. The stimuli might be geometric forms, colours, or even complex patterns. Several response keys were located near the screen and each key displayed a different visual stimulus. One of the keys would always display the same pattern that was shown on the screen, and the pigeon was trained to peck at that key, thus matching its response to the sample projected on the screen. When the pigeon pecked the key that correctly matched the screen's pattern, it was rewarded with some grain.

After learning this 'matching-to-sample' procedure, the birds were injected with various drugs and then periodically shown blank screens. They had been trained not to peck a key when the screen was blank. Under the influence of THC or a *Cannabis* extract they pecked certain keys when the screen was blank. In effect, their key pecks were indicating that they saw something on the screen and it looked like the pattern on the particular response key they were pecking. When provided with a vast array of different patterns on the response keys to match to whatever they were seeing on the blank screen, the pigeons pecked out a particular message over and over again: *blue geometric patterns*.

Now I arranged a similar experiment for Groucho. Instead of pecking the response keys, Groucho could simply tap them with his fingers and earn his reward of fruit juice. During the test with THC, he tapped out his vision: *blue geometric patterns*!

I conducted similar experiments with human volunteers. Instead of pecking or tapping, they were trained in a very precise psychophysical language to describe the colours, forms, and movements they saw in their mind's eye while lying down in a completely dark room. Here they were given capsules of THC or marijuana cigarettes. They laughed and called out their measurements of the images: 'lattice-tunnels overlaying repeating lines pulsating at 470 millimicrons' – *blue geometric patterns*! And they were moving!

(a)

(c)

What do psychoactive drugs do to spiders? In these tests run by NASA scientists in Alabama, marijuana (a) caused them to produce webs which progressively lacked detail; the stimulant benzedrine (b) produced webs which were woven quickly but with descreasing attention to the overall design. The most deranged-looking webs, which seemed to have no structure at all, were produced on caffeine (c); and narcotic sedatives like chloral hydrate (d) led to sketchy, impoverished designs. (NASA, Marshall Space Flight Centre, Alabama)

But for some scientists self-experimentation remains an essential part of the process. For the pioneering chemist Alexander Shulgin, who has synthesized dozens of new psychoactive drugs, the process retains Sir Humphry Davy's ambivalent description – 'researches chemical and philosophical'.

ALEXANDER SHULGIN
Tihkal

(1997)

The world of chemistry is, to me at least, without any question the most exciting of all the disciplines of science. It is developing with extraordinary rapidity, it is continuously providing discoveries that are unexpected, and there seems to be no logical limit as to where it might go. Astronomy, mathematics, archaeology, all continuously reward us with the discovery of the unknown. The things discovered have always been there. It is just that we did not know them.

Chemical syntheses also provide discovery of the unknown, but all the unknowns are without any earlier history, at least here on earth. Each new compound produced by a chemist is a glimpse into a universe of the unprecedented, without any history and without any agenda. As far as we know, at the moment before its creation, no hint of it existed anywhere in the cosmos. At the moment of its creation, it exists in full beauty. This is why I am totally captivated by the art of chemistry, and why I say it is the most exciting of all the scientific disciplines. Everything that is newly created in my laboratory is also new in the known universe, as far as I am aware, and therefore there can be no one who can advise me as to what its properties will be. There is a thrill in creating new things. Let me share this excitement with you.

. . .

What are the motives for designing new chemicals? There are three that are obvious to me: the circumvention of drug law, the circumvention of patent claims, and the development of research tools

. . .

This is the work that I choose to do, in this third area of the designing of drugs; one which I have found to be unbelievably exciting. I want to describe to you a little bit of this particular world of tools. I will use the vocabulary of a tool-maker. When you design a new tool, a new compound, a potential drug, you are playing very much the role of an artist. You have a blank canvas in front of you. You have a pallet of oil paints, which is your collection of chemicals, and solvents, and catalysts, and reagents. You have the skill and talent in your hands of creating. With the artist, this is painting; with the chemist, this is synthesizing. And you have an inspired image of what the final picture might be. You have a target. You may be quite surprised as to where you eventually get to, but you indeed have a goal. Let me give one example of this form of artistry. I would like to walk you through the act of creation, from the initial design, to the actual birth of the new drug, to the introduction and getting-to-know this new individual, and up to the final definition and understanding of the completed product.

The example I have chosen is a research drug called N,N-diisopropyl tryptamine, or DIPT for short. As to the initial design consideration, I had a pretty good vision of what I wanted to create. I have produced my most satisfying creations using one of two types of canvases, the nucleus of phenethylamine or the nucleus of tryptamine. Here I knew that a tryptamine was needed, but how was I to embroider it? My past work had assured me that if I were to put lots of bulky stuff on the basic nitrogen, I might get a compound with oral activity. Should I place a group on the aromatic ring? Nah. Keep it simple. Go for a simple product, and maybe it just might be a clean and instructive product. Forgive me the mixing of the metaphors of artist and chemist but many of the concepts of designing a painting or a compound are identical.

Let me continue the mental picture. What kind of chemical shrubbery should I put on the right hand side of the canvas, on that basic nitrogen? How about a couple of isopropyl groups? They have never been used in this particular situation and they have an appealing, interlocking three-dimensional nature. A nice kind of bulkiness. Once the concept, the design, is pretty much complete, it's time to put oil to canvas. This stage of the process can be difficult, or it can be straightforward. But it always gives promise of being instructive. It can be especially informative when everything goes wrong. It is then that new and unexpected things can be learned about chemistry. In this particular case, however, there were no surprises. In the tight jargon of the world of chemistry, let me sum up the 'how' part by simply stating that the indole was converted – via oxalyl chloride and diisopropylamine – to the glyoxamide – which was reduced with LAH to give me DIPT. The hydrochloride salt was a fine white solid.

So, having designed a potential drug and given it birth, so to speak, I now must meet it and get to know it. Looking at these fine white crystals is, in one way, like looking at a newborn baby. Either one, the compound or the baby, is a total unknown. True, I know the structure of the compound, and its obvious physical properties, but in no way do I really 'know' the chemical. The structure it possesses is only one of the many brushes that I have used in this creation process. I must begin to interact with my creation by employing a mixture of caution, curiosity, and excitement. I will learn from this creation, and it will learn from me. It is a truly mutual development. With time I will gradually discover the inherent properties, the unique nature of this compound. But as I learn, I always become aware that some of these very properties that I am observing have been instilled into it by me. It is by this give-and-take interaction that we become familiar with one another. The first clue of the nature of this friendship between DIPT and me was when I became aware of the fact that I was listening to a recording of 'The Young Person's Guide to the Orchestra' on the radio in my study. It sounded absolutely terrible. I had accepted some 18 milligrams of DIPT into my body a short time earlier, and I now had my first hint as to just how it might become a useful tool some day. Its value might be in learning how we interpret sounds.

I knew that there was no way possible that any symphonic group could be so awful and still be tolerated in the recording of this little gem of Benjamin Britten. I began to pay attention to what was inside me, not outside me. Somehow, a certain number of cycles were being removed from the perceived sound, so that a lowering of the apparent pitch was being experienced. Different notes were distorted to different extents. It was not like putting your finger on the edge of a record player turntable, and slowing it down. There was no distortion of the sense of time. But there was a complex distortion of chords, and that which would otherwise have been an acceptable harmonic relationship sounded terrible. This type of highly specific distortion gives promise of a tool for looking at the interface between an actual physical sound and how we hear it. These two realities, what actually goes into the ear, and what we think went into the ear, can be very, very different. A recent study has established that DIPT is primarily associated with the auditory process and that this property can be demonstrated in others. Two subjects with absolute pitch were able to state what the exact pitch was of any one of several single musical notes that were generated for them by an independent observer. They provided their opinions before, during, and after exposure to DIPT. Their assignments were very accurate before the drug was given and quite inaccurate while the drug was present inside them, then accurate again after the effects of the drug had dissipated. This allowed an objective time-curve of effects to be constructed, and satisfactorily confirmed this unique property of the drug.

Here is a potentially superb tool to explore and begin to understand one of the complex functions of the human mind. Perhaps it can be defined pharmacologically by the neurotransmitters it replaces or interferes with. Perhaps it can be labeled with carbon-11 and its dynamics observed with a PET camera in a human subject. What would be the scan of its distribution in a tone-deaf subject? What would be its effect on a schizophrenic subject who is hearing the voice of God?

And the most exciting part of any discovery such as this, is that perhaps this tool might be a prototype for another. You must ask yourself a sequence of questions. What do you want from a new drug or a new tool? How would you design it? How can you learn what you have? And having learned this, now what new tool do you want to create? This cycle can be repeated as often as you wish. Nothing might come out of this series of questions, the next time around. But just maybe, out of it might come some totally different and unexpected tool; one that might some day be used to explore a little further into the miracle of the human mind.

If the 'objective' approach to the science of drugs is limiting and problem-
atic, it doesn't necessarily follow that the 'subjective' approach is any
less so. Individual responses to drugs can be so varied that it's often
impossible to find any meaningful common ground. To illustrate this,
consider five different subjective accounts of the effects of the psychedelic
drug mescaline.

The first is among the earliest Western self-experiments with the drug,
conducted by the writer and serologist Havelock Ellis in his rooms in
London's Inner Temple in 1898.

HAVELOCK ELLIS
'Mescal: A New Artificial Paradise'

(Annual Report of the Smithsonian Institute, 1898)

On Good Friday I found myself entirely alone in the quiet
rooms in the Temple which I occupy when in London, and judged the
occasion a fitting one for a personal experiment. I made a decoction (a
different method from that adopted in America) of three buttons, the
full physiological dose, and drank this at intervals between 2.30 and
4.30 p.m. The first symptom observed during the afternoon was a certain
consciousness of energy and intellectual power. This passed off, and
about an hour after the final dose I felt faint and unsteady; the pulse
was low, and I found it pleasanter to lie down. I was still able to read,
and I noticed that a pale violet shadow floated over the page around
the point at which my eyes were fixed. I had already noticed that objects
not in the direct line of vision, such as my hands holding the book,
shows a tendency to look obtrusive, heightened in colour, almost monstrous, while, on closing my eyes, afterimages were vivid and prolonged.
The appearance of vision with closed eyes was very gradual. At first
there was merely a vague play of light and shade which suggested
pictures, but never made them. Then the pictures became more definite,
but too confused and crowded to be described, beyond saying that
they were of the same character as the images of the kaleidoscope,
symmetrical groupings of spiked objects. Then, in the course of the
evening, they became distinct, but still indescribable – mostly a vast
field of golden jewels, studded with red and green stones, ever changing.

This moment was, perhaps, the most delightful of the experience, for at the same time the air around me seemed to be flushed with vague perfume – producing with the visions a delicious effect – and all discomfort had vanished, except a slight faintness and tremor of the hands, which, later on, made it almost impossible to guide a pen as I made notes of the experiment; it was, however, with an effort, always possible to write with a pencil. The visions never resembled familiar objects; they were extremely definite, but yet always novel; they were constantly approaching, and yet constantly eluding, the semblance of known things. I would see thick, glorious fields of jewels, solitary or clustered, sometimes brilliant and sparkling, sometimes with a dull rich glow. Then they would spring up into flower-like shapes beneath my gaze, and then seem to turn into gorgeous butterfly forms or endless folds of glistening, iridescent, fibrous wings of wonderful insects; while sometimes I seemed to be gazing into a vast hollow revolving vessel, on whose polished concave mother-of-pearl surface the hues were swiftly changing. I was surprised, not only by the enormous profusion of the imagery presented to my gaze, but still more by its variety. Perpetually some totally new kind of effect would appear in the field of vision; sometimes there was swift movement, sometimes dull, somber richness of colour, sometimes glitter and sparkle, once a startling rain of gold, which seemed to approach me. Most usually there was a combination of rich, sober colour, with jewel-like points of brilliant hue. Every colour and tone conceivable to me appeared at some time or another

. . .

Thus, once the objects presented to me seemed to be made of exquisite porcelain, again they were like elaborate sweetmeats, again of a somewhat Maori style of architecture; and the background of the pictures frequently recalled, both in form and tone, the delicate architectural effects as of lace carved in wood, which we associated with the mouchrabieh work of Cairo. But always the visions grew and changed without any reference to the characteristics of those real objects of which they vaguely reminded me, and when I tried to influence their course it was with very little success. On the whole, I should say that the images were most usually what might be called living arabesques

. . .

It would be out of place here to discuss the obscure question as to the underlying mechanism by which mescal exerts its magic powers. It is clear from the foregoing descriptions that mescal intoxication may be described as chiefly a saturnalia of the specific senses, and, above all, an orgy of vision. It reveals an optical fairyland, where all the senses now and again join the play, but the mind itself remains a self-possessed spectator. Mescal intoxication thus differs from the other artificial paradises which drugs procure. Under the influence of alcohol, for instance, as in normal dreaming, the intellect is impaired, although there may be a consciousness of unusual brilliance; hasheesh, again, produces an uncontrollable tendency to movement and bathes its victim in a sea of emotion. The mescal drinker remains calm and collected amid the sensory turmoil around him; his judgment is as clear as in the normal state; he falls into no oriental condition of vague and voluptuous reverie. The reason why mescal is of all this class of drugs the most purely intellectual in its appeal is evidently because it affects mainly the most intellectual of the senses. On this ground it is not probable that its use will easily develop into a habit. Moreover, unlike most other intoxicants, it seems to have no special affinity for a disordered and unbalanced nervous system; on the contrary, it demands organic soundness and good health for the complete manifestation of its virtues. Further, unlike the other chief substances to which it may be compared, mescal does not wholly carry us away from the actual world, or plunge us into oblivion; a large part of its charm lies in the halo of beauty which it casts around the simplest and commonest things. It is the most democratic of the plants which lead men to an artificial paradise. If it should ever chance that the consumption of mescal becomes a habit, the favorite poet of the mescal drinker will certainly be Wordsworth. Not only the general attitude of Wordsworth, but many of his most memorable poems and phrases can not – one is almost tempted to say – be appreciated in their full significance by one who has never been under the influence of mescal. On all these grounds it may be claimed that the artificial paradise of mescal, though less seductive, is safe and dignified beyond its peers.

For the French writer and painter Henri Michaux the visual effects which consumed Ellis were 'tawdry' and the overall experience was profoundly unsatisfying.

HENRI MICHAUX
Miserable Miracle (Mescaline)

(1956)

In the huge light-churn, with lights splashing over me, drunk, I was swept headlong without ever turning back.

How to describe it! It would require a picturesque style which I do not possess, made up of surprises, of nonsense, of sudden flashes, of bounds and rebounds, an unstable style, tobogganing and prankish

. . .

I was not neutral either, for which I do not apologize. Mescaline and I were more often at odds with each other than together. I was shaken, broken, but I refused to be taken in by it.

Tawdry, its spectacle. Moreover it was enough to uncover one's eyes not to see any more of the stupid phantasmagoria. Inharmonious mescaline, an alcaloid derived from the Peyotl which contains six, was really like a robot. It knew only how to do certain things.

Yet I had come prepared to admire. I was confident. But that day my cells were brayed, buffeted, sabotaged, sent into convulsions. I felt them being caressed, being subjected to constant wrenchings. Mescaline wanted my full consent. To enjoy a drug one must enjoy being a subject. To me it was too much like being on 'fatigue duty'.

It was with *my* terrible buffetings that *It* put on its show. I was the fireworks that despises the pyrotechnist, even when it can be proved that it is itself the pyrotechnist. I was being shoved about, I was being crumpled. In a daze, I stared at this Brownian movement – disturbance of perception.

I was distraught and tired of being distraught, with my eye at this microscope. What was there supernatural about all this? You scarcely got away from the human state at all. You felt more as if you were caught and held prisoner in some workshop of the brain.

Should I speak of pleasure? It was unpleasant.

Once the agony of the first hour is over (effect of the encounter with the poison), an agony so great that you wonder if you are not going to faint (as some people do, though rarely) you can let yourself be carried along by a certain current which may seem like happiness. Is that what I thought? I am not sure of the contrary. Yet, in my journal, during all those incredible hours, I find these words written more than fifty times, clumsily, and with difficulty: *Intolerable, Unbearable.*

Such is the price of this paradise(!)

. . .

I used to have a kind of respect for people who saw apparitions. No longer! I have no doubt they really see them, but in what a state! (Certainly not a normal one, for then they would really be extraordinary.)

To the eye and the mind of someone who is, or has been, in another state, everything moves, everything is vibrant and teeming with reality.

In bed one evening about three weeks after my last dose of mescaline, I decided to read Quercy on Hallucination. Later, I tossed the book toward the couch and missed my aim. It fell to the floor and opening, revealed a wonderful colored reproduction inserted in the volume. I immediately picked up the book again, eager to examine those marvellous colors and to find out who had painted the original of the reproduction which I had barely glimpsed, but which I should recognize among all others. I turn the pages: Nothing. I shake the volume trying to make the loose page fall out. Impossible. I go over the book once more, page by page, and again the next morning, even getting a friend to examine it too: Nothing.

At the word 'Hallucination' I had had one.

Seeing the word on the cover I had functioned. Quick as thought it appeared. And, failing to understand I had kept on searching in vain for the admirable colored reproduction, more real than a real one, among the colorless pages of the book whose title had provoked it.

When the Polish avant-gardist Stanislaw Witkiewicz took mescaline (in the form of peyote), his wife recorded the experience as he reported it.

STANISLAW I. WITKIEWICZ
Report about the Effects of Peyote on Stanislaw Ignacy Witkiewicz

(1933)

At 5:40 W. took 2 ground-up pills of pan-peyote. After a few minutes he began to feel lightness and cold throughout his body and became afraid of being sick to his stomach. 6 o'clock – yawning and chills, pulse 88. 6:15 feels wonderful, nerves completely soothed. W. takes another dose (2 pills) and eats 2 eggs with tomatoes and drinks a small cup of coffee with just a drop of milk. 6:25 feels a little bit abnormal, like after a small dose of cocaine, pulse 80. The tired feeling after three portrait sittings disappeared totally. W. walks around the room with a steady step and closed the blinds on the windows tightly. 6:40 pulse 72 – feels slight, agreeable stupor and light-headedness. The inactivity bothers him, he's bored and would like to smoke a cigarette. 6:50 W. takes a third dose – stares with tremendous interest at an airplane in flight – then lowers the blinds again and lies down on the bed. Pupils normal, pulse 84. Strange feeling, waits for visions without any results, finally out of boredom smoked a cigarette but didn't finish it. 7:20 got up, took the last pill and lay down again. Starts to feel apathetic and disheartened. After lying down for half an hour, W. got up and felt sick, pulse a little weak, pupils somewhat enlarged, voice changed. Asked for coffee and stays lying down, as soon as he tries to get up, feels sick. 8:30 sees swirls of filaments, bright against a dark background. Next there start to appear animal phantoms, sea monsters, little faces, a man with a beard, but he still does not consider this to be visions, only the kind of heightened images that occur before falling asleep. Someone in a black velvet hat leans from an Italian balcony and speaks to the crowd. Definitely feels a heightening of the imagination, but still nothing extraordinary. Feels better, but when he gets up has dizzy spells and feels 'odd', in an unpleasant way, at the same time a strange feeling in his muscles. 9 o'clock begins to see rainbow colors, but still does not consider this to be visions. 9:30 – various sculpture in sharp relief, tiny faces, feels 'weird', but good. Sees rainbow stripes, but incomplete – the following colors predominate: dirty-red and lemon-yellow. Desire to forget reality. Huge building, the bricks turn into gargoyle faces, like on the cathedral of Nôtre-Dame in Paris. Monsters similar to plesiosauruses made out of luminous filaments. The trees turned into ostriches. A corpse's brain, abscesses, sheaves of sparks bursting out of them. On the whole unpleasant apparitions. On the ceiling, against a red background horned beasts. A gigantic abdomen with a wound – the insides turn into coral at the bottom of the sea. A battle among sea monsters. Dr Sokolowski turns into a cephalopod. Spatial 'distortion'. Cross-section of the earth. Fantastic luxuriousness of plant life. 10 o'clock languor continues. Stupor. Battle among senseless things. A series of chambers which change into an underground circus, some strange beasts appear, interesting class of people in the boxes, the boxes turn into (?). Impressions of two visible layers – the images are only black and white, and the rainbow colors are as it were separately. Land and sea monsters and frightful human mugs predominate in the visions. Snakes and giraffes, a sheep with a flamingo's nose, cobras crawled out of this sheep, a double-crested grebe with a seal's tail – bursting jaws, volcanoes change into fish. African vision. 11 o'clock terrific appetite, but at the same time total laziness so that eating a few tomatoes took over half an hour. With the monsters in the background a yellow pilot's cap appeared, then a uniform, then the face of Col. Beaurain in a yellow light. Out of the wild, chaotic coils a splendid beach came to the fore, across it along by the sea a Negro boy rides a bicycle and changes into a man with a small beard, and the toys which the Negro boy was apparently carrying turned into Mexican sculpture which, while looking at W., climbed up ladders. A series of female sex organs, out of which spill out guts and live worms as well as a green embryo turning somersaults.

The existentialist writer Jean-Paul Sartre's experiment with mescaline in 1935, described here by Simone de Beauvoir, coincided with the onset of an extended period of depression and psychosis.

SIMONE DE BEAUVOIR
The Prime of Life

(1960)

He took a marked interest in dreams, dream-induced imagery, and anomalies of perception. In February one of his former fellow students, Dr Lagache (who had passed his state examinations the year Sartre failed, qualified as a medical practitioner, and specialized in psychiatry) suggested that he should come to Sainte-Anne's Hospital and undergo a mescaline injection. This drug induced hallucinations, and Sartre would be able to observe the phenomenon in himself. Lagache warned him that it would be a mildly disagreeable experience, although not in the least dangerous. The worst that could happen was that Sartre might 'behave rather oddly' for a few hours afterwards.

I spent the appointed day with Madame Lemaire and Pagniez at their place on the Boulevard Raspail. Late that afternoon, as we had arranged, I telephoned Sainte-Anne's, to hear Sartre telling me, in a thick, blurred voice, that my phone call had rescued him from a battle with several devil-fish, which he would almost certainly have lost. Half an hour later he arrived. He had been made to lie down on a bed in a dimly lit room, he said. He had not exactly had hallucinations, but the objects he looked at changed their appearance in the most horrifying manner: umbrellas had become vultures, shoes turned into skeletons, and faces acquired monstrous characteristics, while behind him, just past the corner of his eye, swarmed crabs and polyps and grimacing Things. One of the housemen was amazed at these reactions; on him, as he told Sartre when the session was over, mescaline had produced wholly different effects. *He* had gone romping through flowery meadows, full of exotic houris. Sartre reflected, a little regretfully, that if he had waited till his nightmares turned into something more pleasant, he too might have gravitated towards such paradisaic visions. But he had been influenced by Lagache's predictions. He spoke listlessly, staring all the time in a distrustful way at the telephone cord that ran across the carpet. In the train he said very little. I was wearing a pair of crocodile-skin shoes, the laces of which ended in two acornlike objects; he expected to see them turn into gigantic dung beetles at any moment. There was also an orang-utan, doubtless hanging on to the roof of the carriage by its feet, which kept its leering face glued to the window. The next day Sartre was quite himself again, and talked about Sainte-Anne's with cheerful detachment.

A Sunday or two later Colette Audry came with me to Le Havre. Normally with people he liked, Sartre put himself out to be pleasant, and I was amazed at his surliness on this occasion. We walked along the beach collecting starfish, and hardly a word was exchanged between us. Sartre looked as though he had no idea what Colette and I – or indeed he himself – were doing there. I was somewhat irritated when I left him.

The next time we met, he explained what had happened. For several days he had been in a state of deep depression, and the moods that came upon him recalled those that had been induced by mescaline. This frightened him. His visual faculties became distorted: houses had leering faces, all eyes and jaws, and he couldn't help looking at every clockface he passed, expecting it to display the features of an owl – which it always did. He knew perfectly well that such objects were in fact houses and clocks, and no one could say that he *believed* in their eyes and gaping maws – but a time might well come when he *would* believe in them; one day he could really be convinced that there was a lobster trotting along behind him. Already he had a black spot persistently dancing about in his line of vision, at eye level. One afternoon, as we were walking along the left bank of the Seine at Rouen through a wilderness of railway tracks, sidings, goods trucks, and patches of leprous grass, he said abruptly: 'I know what the matter with me is: I'm on the edge of a chronic hallucinatory psychosis.' As defined at the time, this was an illness which in ten years would inevitably produce total insanity. I disagreed violently – not, for once, because of my natural optimism, but through plain common sense. Sartre's symptoms were not in the least like those produced by the onset of psychotic hallucinations. Neither the black spot nor his obsession with houses that gnashed their jaws suggested the inception of an incurable psychosis. Besides, I knew how readily Sartre's imagination tended towards disaster. 'Your only madness,' I told him, 'is believing that you're mad.'

'You'll see,' he replied gloomily.

I saw nothing, apart from this depression of his, which he had the greatest difficulty in shaking off. Sometimes, though, he managed to do so. At Easter we went down to the Italian Lakes; we took a canoe out on Lake Como, and one night we saw a torchlight procession in the narrow streets of Bellagio, and all the time Sartre seemed in very high spirits. But after our return to Paris he could not even pretend to be in a normal state. Fernando had an exhibition of paintings at the Galerie Bonjean; and all through the day of the *vernissage* Sartre sat huddled in a corner, his face expressionless, not saying a word. Whereas a short time ago he missed nothing, now he simply did not bother to look. Sometimes we would sit side by side in a café or walk down the street together without a word passing between us. Madame Lemaire, who thought he had been overworking, sent him to see one of her friends who was a doctor. The doctor, however, refused to grant him a certificate of leave; in his opinion what Sartre needed was as little solitude and leisure as possible. He did, however, prescribe a small dose of belladonna morning and evening. Sartre therefore went on with his teaching and writing; and it is true that he was less liable to fall a prey to his fears when there was someone with him. He began to go out a lot with two of his former pupils, of whom he was very fond, Albert Palle and Jacques Bost, who was Pierre Bost's youngest brother: their presence protected him from crabs and similar monsters. When I was busy teaching in Rouen, Olga kept him company, and became very attached to her role of nurse-companion. Sartre told her endless stories, which amused her and distracted him from his own problems.

Doctors have told me that the mescaline could not possibly have provoked this attack. All that his session at Sainte-Anne's did for Sartre was to furnish him with certain hallucinatory patterns. It was, beyond any doubt, the fatigue and tension engendered by his philosophical research work that brought his fears to the surface again. We afterwards concluded that they were the physical expression of a deep emotional malaise: Sartre could not resign himself to going on to 'the age of reason', to full manhood.

When the British Member of Parliament Christopher Mayhew experi-
mented with mescaline in the presence of scientists and journalists, he
became almost entirely preoccupied with its effects on his perceptions
of time.

CHRISTOPHER MAYHEW
'An Excursion out of Time'

(*Observer*, 28 October 1956)

What happened to me between 12.30 and 4 o'clock on Friday, December 2, 1955? After brooding about it for several months, I still think my first, astonishing conviction was right – that on many occasions that afternoon I existed *outside time*.

I don't mean this metaphorically, but literally. I mean that the essential part of me (the part that thinks to itself 'This is me') had an existence, quite conscious of itself, enjoying itself, reflecting on its strange experience, in a timeless order of reality outside the world as we know it.

And I believe this in spite of the fact that the experience was induced by a drug, the much discussed mescaline.

People who are drugged, of course, often suffer from delusions; and the common-sense explanation of my experience is simply that I took an hallucinogen and had an hallucination. And if I dispute this now, when I am undrugged, there is, says common sense, nothing strange about that either. People who have hallucinations often cannot believe that they *are* hallucinations.

This common-sense attitude is persuasive, but I don't think it is wrong; and at the risk of making a complete fool of myself, I would like to put forward an alternative explanation. At least this may stir up some controversy, and perhaps even encourage some research along what seems an extremely promising line of scientific inquiry.

Let me first explain how I came to take the drug. I am an old school friend of Dr Humphry Osmond, who is the Medical Superintendent of a mental hospital in Saskatchewan. In his search for a cure for his schizophrenic patients, Dr Osmond has for some years past been experimenting with a particular range of drugs known as 'psychotomimetics', which produce in those who take them some of the symptoms of insanity.° It was Dr Osmond who administered one of these drugs – mescaline – to Mr Aldous Huxley in the fascinating experiment described in Huxley's *The Doors of Perception*.

For years I had been in desultory correspondence with Dr Osmond, and in the course of this he had told me about his research work and expounded the exciting theory that certain drugs can, by inhibiting parts of our brain which act as a 'filter', enable us to receive a wider, more representative range of signals from the outside world – i.e., to experience the outside world more nearly as it 'really' is, before our minds impose their pattern on it.

Last autumn, in anticipation of a visit to Britain, Dr Osmond asked me to approach the BBC about the possibility of his doing some broadcasts on his work. I replied by suggesting that we should make a television film together about mescaline, in the course of which he would give me the drug and I would describe my reactions.

Dr Osmond liked this idea, and so did the BBC. So on December 2, a BBC producer and film team – old colleagues of mine – arrived at our home in Surrey, converted our drawing-room into a studio, and at 12.05 p.m. filmed me drinking down 400 mg of mescaline hydrochloride.

For half an hour nothing happened. Then I began feeling sick; and various nerves and muscles started twitching unpleasantly. Then, as this wore off, my body became more or less anaesthetised, and I became 'de-personalised', i.e., I felt completely detached from my body and the world, and was aware of my eyes seeing, my ears hearing and my mouth speaking as though at some distance below me.

By 1.15 I was in the full flood of the extraordinary visual phenomena described in *The Doors of Perception*. I will not describe these fully, as Huxley has done it so well already. Perspectives and colours everywhere had an astonishing, mysterious beauty. The red curtains of our drawing-room took on a dozen ethereal shades of mauve and purple.

This experience alone would have fully justified the entire experiment for me (e.g., I think I shall always be more sensitive in future to certain kinds of painting), but at about 1.30 all interest in these visual phenomena was abruptly swept aside when I found that *time* was behaving even more strangely than colour. Though perfectly rational and wide awake

---

° 'Psychotomimetics', by Humphry Osmond, MRCS, DPM, New York Academy of Science Proceedings (special number), 1956.

(Dr Osmond gave me tests throughout the experiment which showed no significant falling-off in intelligence) I was not experiencing events in the normal sequence of time. I was experiencing the events of 3.30 before the events of 3.0; the events of 2.0 after the events of 2.45, and so on. Several events I experienced with an equal degree of reality more than once.

I am not suggesting, of course, that the events of 3.30 *happened* before the events of 3.0, or that any events *happened* more than once. All I am saying is that I experienced them, not in the familiar sequence of clock time, but in a different, apparently capricious sequence which was outside my control.

By 'I' in this context I mean, of course, my disembodied self, and by 'experienced' I mean learned by a special kind of awareness which seemed to comprehend yet be different from, seeing, hearing, etc.

In films, 'flash-backs' transpose us backwards and forwards in time. We find events of 1956 being suddenly interrupted by events of 1939. In the same way I found later events in our drawing-room – events in which I myself was participating at the bodily level – being interrupted by earlier events and vice versa.

I count this experience, which occurred when, as I say, I was wide awake and intelligent, sitting in my own armchair at home, as the most astounding and thought-provoking of my life.

The experience lasted about two and a half hours, when the drug began wearing off. An amusing by-product was that I never knew whether or when the experiment was ending. True – I could, and constantly did, consult my watch; and would be aware of my eyes registering, say, three o'clock; but this information would be of no value to me myself, in my strange detachment, since I knew I might soon be transported to some earlier part of the experiment, when I would be aware of my eyes registering, say, 2.30.

However, as the drug wore off, I managed to work out a way of telling that the experiment was ending. I noticed that I was experiencing events of a particular type with increasing frequency and regularity. These were events associated with our tea-trolley (which was brought in at the end of the experiment). Their increasing frequency of recurrence gave them a special importance and significance. After a time, they held the field, and were no longer interrupted by earlier events. The tea-trolley stayed there all the time, and I judged from this (it was my only clue) that I was back in the normal world of time.

Time perception under the influence of drugs is a good example of the
difficulties of describing the experience in scientific language. For the
Hungarian writer, doctor and opiate addict Géza Csáth, the manipu-
lation of time was the most salient effect of drugs, and one which science
could only dream of mastering.

GÉZA CSÁTH
'The Surgeon'

(1910, translated 1980)

I noticed the surgeon the first time I went to that seedy café on
the edge of the town. His one black coat was threadbare, though clean.
A scraggly, graying chestnut mustache and large, deepset eyes suited
his pale face. His watery eyes glittered with the light of café nights. He
spoke softly, almost whispering, as doctors consulting do. During the
most casual of conversations, over a piece in the newspaper with one
of the customers, say, he would gaze into the other's eyes. As though
taking a special interest in him. His opinion was always delivered in
periods too, like instructions to a patient. I was impressed by the
aristocratic demeanor of this shabby man, just as I have been by the
faded, fine velvets one sees in the antique chateaux of ancient nobility.
   —Who is that gentleman? I asked the garçon.
   —A doctor. Surgeon once. Been coming over a year now.
   He heard me calling for one of the medical papers one time, and
approached me. Lauded the profession, inquired about the university.
We chatted a bit, and he showed himself to be learned. I was particularly
struck by some psychosomatic views I'd never read before. I was fascinated by his insights and the imaginativeness which he invested even
trivial matters with in talking about them. It surprised me to see how
he'd adapted to circumstances, compromised with his life – he even
seemed at ease in it. We had our coffee and I left. (I was still in a hurry
in those days.)
   Once I stopped by late at night. He sat alone, drinking. Eyes shut,
he raised the absinthe to his lips with such desirous seeking, draining
the green syrup so slowly and pleasurably that I realized the surgeon
was alcoholic. More, that he was a confirmed, passionate drunk, lost

and drifting steadily towards the DTs. In that moment I was hit by the odd glint in his eyes, the disinterested gaiety and hairsplitting sharp intellect: the man must once have been very different. Alcohol's transmogrified him.

He started, seeing me. I saw he was mortified by my presence, a colleague's. He asked me over. I ordered an absinthe for myself, which relieved him. In a little while I felt the beginnings of a bit of soul-baring; in ten minutes he was deeply into it.

—After all, my friend, what's most important in life? Why do we suffer? Why do we eat? Why do we love? Why is a man joyful? Because of life. How ridiculous, when life comes suddenly to a halt, and that's it. But why? What prevents a scientist from completing his work, an artist from exploring his ideas, fathers from seeing their children to maturity? I know why. It's quite simple: why does time move on? That's the basic question.

Listen, and I'll tell you

. . .

I have found time in the brain. It doesn't differ externally from an ordinary brain cell. Yet it's the nucleus of misery, sickness, the senseless sorrow of passing on. It can be quantitatively greater in one man than another. It elaborates its appendages, its branches and forks like a polyp into the fresh and healthy brain – hence into every aspect of our thoughts.

Of course, this is a great task for the surgeon, but it's absolutely simple. All we have to know is what to cut. I know it. And I'll offer my discovery to the man who wishes above all to be rid of time, who is borne down by the idea of passing on. Him I shall help.

I'll rent a huge operating theatre. It will be jammed with observers. In its centre we set up the operating table. Three assistants make preparations. The aristocrats of finance and science crowd the hall, mingling with the poor. Finally, silence. I put on my gown; I'm helped into my rubber boots. Calmly I scrub up and give the order: Start the anaesthesia! I tie the apron around me and pull on my gloves. Is he out? Good! Blood pressure? Fine! I touch his head. Slowly I make my incision from the base of the skull to the parotid. The audience watches, holding its breath. Binoculars are trained on me. I stop the bleeding. I peel back scalp and muscles in an area about half a palm's size. Raspatory for the periostal! I have now reached bone. Auger, please! Trepanation.

I have made the hole . . . I am at the *dura mater*. I carefully cut the membrane, fold it aside. With my fingers I penetrate one of the folds, the one I alone know – and extract time.

And as easily as that I just spoon out this evil hornet's nest of human grief. In a few minutes the whole thing's finished. I hand the time cells round in a dish. Then I sew up the arachnoid, the *pia mater* and *dura mater*, and reset the pieces of skull-bone I've cut out . . . tying up the veins. Stitch the scalp, muscles and skin, and dress the wound. I am all done. I waken the fellow. (Here the surgeon rose from his chair and continued almost shouting.) This is the man of the future, the really new man who's able to solve today's secrets and tomorrow's truth with his fresh clean brain. He has total recall because facts don't pass away for him – they line themselves up as equal powers in his consciousness. The audience applauds wildly. I remove my surgical gown and take my bows in my dove-grey morning attire. The happiness of mankind addresses me, jubilant. In three days' time the wound's healed. Why three days precisely? My friend, have you any idea why? It's quite simple, too.

Because time has exhausted itself! All of the psychic energy stolen from us by the silent madness of mortality is left over for us in the form of tremendous life-energy.

And all the rulers of the world will come to me to be operated on. Sorry, ladies and gentlemen, but the poor come first and so I have to take care of them – besides, their condition's more critical. Emperors will have to wait their turn, of course.

My discovery's rather elementary, isn't it, my dear colleague? Definitely worth having been thought of.

But until the hour for surgical intervention arrives, we are provided with a drug to be taken orally, and which is useful against time, temporarily: absinthe. Merely a symptomatic treatment. We won't be needing it much longer, since the surgical method's both radical and excellent. Cheers, my dear colleague!

. . . and H. G. Wells, another scientist-turned-writer, postulated a fictional drug called 'The New Accelerator' which might enable its subjects to escape from 'the Garment of Time' at will.

H. G. WELLS
'The New Accelerator'

(1903)

So it was I had my first experience of the New Accelerator. Practically we had been running about and saying and doing all sorts of things in the space of a second or so of time. We had lived half an hour while the band had played, perhaps, two bars. But the effect it had upon us was that the whole world had stopped for our convenient inspection. Considering all things, and particularly considering our rashness in venturing out of the house, the experience might certainly have been much more disagreeable than it was. It showed, no doubt, that Gibberne has still much to learn before his preparation is a manageable convenience, but its practicability it certainly demonstrated beyond all cavil.

Since that adventure he has been steadily bringing its use under control, and I have several times, and without the slightest bad result, taken measured doses under his direction; though I must confess I have not yet ventured abroad again while under its influence. I may mention, for example, that this story has been written at one sitting and without interruption, except for the nibbling of some chocolate, by its means. I began at 6.25, and my watch is now very nearly at the minute past the half-hour. The convenience of securing a long, uninterrupted spell of work in the midst of a day full of engagements cannot be exaggerated. Gibberne is now working at the quantitative handling of his preparation, with especial reference to its distinctive effects upon different types of constitution. He then hopes to find a Retarder with which to dilute its present rather excessive potency. The Retarder will, of course, have the reverse effect to the Accelerator; used alone it should enable the patient to spread a few seconds over many hours of ordinary time, and so to maintain an apathetic inaction, a glacierlike absence of alacrity, amidst the most animated or irritating surroundings. The two things together must necessarily work an entire revolution in civilized existence. It is the beginning of our escape from that Time Garment of which Carlyle speaks. While this Accelerator will enable us to concentrate ourselves with tremendous impact upon any moment or occasion that demands our utmost sense and vigour, the Retarder will enable us to pass in passive tranquillity through infinite hardship and tedium. Perhaps I am a little optimistic about the Retarder, which has indeed still to be discovered, but about the Accelerator there is no possible sort of doubt whatever. Its appearance upon the market in a convenient, controllable, and assimilable form is a matter of the next few months. It will be obtainable of all chemists and druggists, in small green bottles, at a high but, considering its extraordinary qualities, by no means excessive price. Gibberne's Nervous Accelerator it will be called, and he hopes to be able to supply it in three strengths: one in 200, one in 900, and one in 2000, distinguished by yellow, pink, and white labels respectively.

No doubt its use renders a great number of very extraordinary things possible; for, of course, the most remarkable and, possibly, even criminal proceedings may be effected with impunity by thus dodging, as it were, into the interstices of time. Like all potent preparations it will be liable to abuse. We have, however, discussed this aspect of the question very thoroughly, and we have decided that this is purely a matter of medical jurisprudence and altogether outside our province. We shall manufacture and sell the Accelerator, and, as for the consequences – we shall see.

3
The Taste of God: Drugs and Religion

The role of drugs in religion, as in science, revolves around a central paradox. On the one hand, it is now established that the sacred and ritual use of drugs was central to most of the original religions in both the Old and the New Worlds, and that it retains this central position in many of the animist or traditional religions which survive today. On the other hand, the synoptic religions – Judaism, Islam, Christianity and others – generally regard the use of drugs as contrary to their teachings and the 'spiritual' role of drugs as, at best, delusional.

Perhaps the paradigmatic example of the 'drug sacrament' in ancient religions is the unknown plant or plants which constituted soma, *the sacrament of the Indo-European Vedic religion. The* Rig Veda, *among the earliest known texts, contains dozens of hymns describing its preparation and psychoactive properties.*

RIG VEDA

Hymn to Soma: 'We Have Drunk the Soma'

(*c.* 1000 BC)

1   I have tasted the sweet drink of life, knowing that it inspires good thoughts and joyous expansiveness to the extreme, that all the gods and mortals seek it together, calling it honey.

2   When you penetrate inside, you will know no limits, and you will avert the wrath of the gods. Enjoying Indra's friendship, O drop of Soma, bring riches as a docile cow brings the yoke.

3   We have drunk the Soma; we have become immortal; we have gone to the light; we have found the gods. What can hatred and the malice of a mortal do to us now, O immortal one?

4   When we have drunk you, O drop of Soma, be good to our heart, kind as a father to his son, thoughtful as a friend to a friend. Far-famed Soma, stretch out our lifespan so that we may live.

5   The glorious drops that I have drunk set me free in wide space. You have bound me together in my limbs as thongs bind a chariot. Let the drops protect me from the foot that stumbles and keep lameness away from me.

6   Inflame me like a fire kindled by friction; make us see far; make us richer, better. For when I am intoxicated with you, Soma, I think myself rich. Draw near and make us thrive.

7   We would enjoy you, pressed with a fervent heart, like riches from a father. King Soma, stretch out our lifespans as the sun stretches the spring days.

*Many parallel traditions survive today, such as the use of the psychedelic
plant* iboga *among the Bwiti people of West Africa. Iboga is used in the
initiatory rites of passage for young men, and some of the visions it
produces are recorded here.*

JAMES W. FERNANDEZ
Bwiti: An Ethnography of the Religious Imagination in Africa

(1982)

8.   The vision of Ndong Asseko (Onwan Misengue). Age 22, Clan
Essabam. Not married, he is an 'aide-chauffeur' but also plants coffee
in his father's village. District of Oyem, Bwiti Chapel at Kwakum. Taken
several weeks after initiation.

REASONS GIVEN: Nzambi Evanga Beyogo Ondo mwan Evon gave
me the *eboga*. I was a Christian but I found no truth in it. Christianity
is the religion of the whites. It is the whites who have brought us the
Cross and the Book. All the things in their religion one hears by the
ears. But we Fang do not learn that way. We learn by the eyes, and
eboga is the religion that enables us to actually see!

VISION: When I ate *eboga* I found myself taken by it up a long road
in a deep forest until I came to a barrier of black iron. At that barrier,
unable to pass, I saw a crowd of black persons also unable to pass. In
the distance beyond the barrier it was very bright. I could see many
colours in the air but the crowd of black people could not pass. Suddenly
my father descended from above in the form of a bird. He gave to me
then my *eboga* name. Onwan Misengue, and enabled me to fly up after
him over the barrier of iron. As we proceeded, the bird who was my
father changed from black to white – first his tail feathers, then all his
plumage. We came then to a river the colour of blood, in the midst of
which was a great snake of three colours – blue, black, and red. It closed
its gaping mouth so that we were able to pass over it. On the other side
there was a crowd of people all in white. We passed through them and
they shouted at us words of recognition until we arrived at another

river, all white. This we crossed by means of a giant chain of gold. On the other side there were no trees but only a grassy upland. On the top of the hill was a round house made entirely of glass and built upon one post only. Within I saw a man. The hair on his head piled up in the form of a bishop's hat! He had a star on his breast, but on coming closer I saw that it was his heart in his chest beating. We moved around him, and on the back of his neck there was a red cross tattooed. He had a long beard. Just then I looked up and saw a woman in the moon – a bayonet was piercing her heart, from which a bright white fire was pouring forth. Then I felt a pain in my shoulder. My father told me to return to earth. I had gone far enough. If I went farther I would not return.

9. The vision of Eman Ela (Misango ki Nanga). Aged 30, Clan Essameny-ang. One wife, who is a Banzie, and no children. He is the oldest of his brothers and a planter. District of Mitzik, Bwiti Chapel at Akuruzok.

REASONS GIVEN: A man of the Mvang Clan gave me the *eboga*. I ate the *eboga* for other black men. I am sorry for the other black men and their suffering. I also ate the *eboga* to be able to play the *ngombi* well. I also searched in it to have many children. Years ago my father, who was a Banzie for a time, gave me some *eboga*. But I saw nothing in it.

VISION: When I ate *eboga*, very quickly my father came to me. First he had black skin. Then he returned and he had white skin. My grandfather then appeared in the same way [i.e., in a white skin]. It was he that gave me my *eboga* name. Because my grandfather was dead before I was born, he asked me if I knew how I recognized him. It was through *eboga*. He then seized me by the hand and we found ourselves embarked on a grand route. I didn't have the sense of walking but just of floating along. We came to a table in that path. There we sat and my grandfather asked me all the reasons I had eaten *eboga*. A man there wrote all these down. He gave me others. Then my grandfather dis-appeared, and suddenly a white spirit appeared before me. He grasped me by the arm and we floated along. Then we came to a crossroads. The path on which we were travelling was red. The other two routes were black and white. We passed over. Finally we arrived at a large house on a hill. It was built on one post. Within, I found the wife of my mother's father. She gave me my *eboga* name a second time and also gave me the talent to play the *ngombi* harp. She told me to work it until eternity. We passed on and finally arrived, after passing over more crossroads, at a great desert. Nothing was there! There I saw descend from the sky – from the moon – a giant circle, which came down and encircled the earth, as a rainbow of three colours – blue, red, and white. There were two women in white at each side of that circle. I began playing the *ngombi* under the rainbow and I heard the applause of men. I returned. All the Banzie thought I had gone too far and was dead. Since then I have seen nothing in *eboga*. But each time I take it I hear the spirits who give the power to play the *ngombi*. I play what I hear from them. Only if I come into the chapel in a bad heart does *eboga* fail me.

*One of the most striking of such surviving rituals is the peyote hunt of
the Huichol Indians in Mexico, who undertake an annual pilgrimage to
gather the psychedelic cactus.*

PETER T. FURST
'Peyote among the Huichol Indians in Mexico'

(1972)

THE PRIMORDIAL PEYOTE QUEST

This comes to us from ancient, ancient times. The times of my great-
great-grandfathers, those who were the fathers of my great-grandfather, fathers
of my grandfather who was the *mara'akáme*,° fathers of my father. This is a
story from those very ancient times . . .

Those ancient ones of whom I speak, they began to say to one another, 'How
will it turn out well, so that there will be unity of all, this unity we have?' And
another said, 'Ah, that is a beautiful thing, that which is our life. It is the *hikuri*
[peyote].' And another said, 'It is like a beautiful flower, as one says. It is like
the Deer. It is our life. We must go so that it will enable us to see our life.'

So begins an account by my long-time Huichol friend Ramón Medina
Silva of the original journey to *Wirikúta* – the primordial quest of the
gods that provides the mythological model for the Huichol peyote
pilgrimage.

According to the myth, the ancient gods had come together in the
first *túki*, the prototypical Huichol sanctuary constructed by *Tatewarí*,
so that each might have his proper place. When they were met together
they discovered that all were ill – one suffered a pain in his chest,
another in his stomach, a third in his eyes, a fourth in his legs, and so
forth. Those responsible for rain were giving no rain; those who were

---

° This refers to the narrator's grandfather, who was a prestigious *mara'akáme*, or
shaman-priest and singer. Ramón's sister, Concha, is one of the few female shamans
in the Huichol Sierra today.

masters of animals were finding nothing to hunt. It was a time of general malaise in the Sierra, and none knew how to 'find his life'.

Into this assembly of the ailing gods entered the *Mara'akáme*, *Tatewarí*, tutelary deity of Huichol shamans. It was *Tatewarí* who had called them together, as the singing shaman of the temple to this day calls the supernaturals together 'to take their proper places'. 'What can be ailing us?' they asked, and each spoke of his infirmities. 'How shall we be cured? How shall we find our life?'

Tatewarí told them that they were ill because they had not gone to *Wirikúta* (Real de Catorce), the sacred land of the peyote, the place to the east where the Sun was born. If they wished to regain their health, they must prepare themselves ritually and follow him in their proper order on the long and difficult journey to the peyote. They must fast and touch neither salt nor *chile*. No matter how hungry or thirsty they became, they must nibble only dried tortillas and assuage their thirst with but a drop or two of water.

And so he placed them in their proper order, one after the other. No females were present – they would join the men later, at the sacred lakes or water holes called *Tatéi Matiniéri* (Where Our Mother Dwells), which lie within sight of the sacred mountains of *Wirikúta*

. . .

The Huichol are unique among contemporary Indians north of the tropical rain forests of South America in that not merely certain individuals or groups but, practically speaking, everyone is an active or a passive participant in a pre-European philosophical and ritual system. The primary focus of this system is the 'peyote hunt'. It is a 'hunt' in the literal sense, because to the Huichol, peyote and deer are synonymous. The first of the sacred plants to be seen by the leader of the hunting party contains the essence of Elder Brother *Wawatsári*, 'master' of the deer species, and manifests itself as deer, which in turn explains why it is first 'shot' with bow and arrow before being dug from the ground and ritually divided among the participants in the hunt. At the same time Deer-Peyote embodies the equally sacred and life-giving Maize, so that deer, peyote, and maize together form a symbol complex. On the peyote pilgrimage, or 'hunt', these three elements become fused, the mythic 'first times' that existed before the separation of man, plants, animals, and 'gods' are recreated, man reunites with his ancestors, and contradictions between what is and what is thought to be or desired, between life and death, and between the sexes are resolved, bringing about the state of unity and continuity between past, and present, 'between man, nature, society, and the supernatural', that epitomizes the Huichol view of 'the good' (Myerhoff, 1968). This is what the Huichol mean when they say that on the peyote hunt 'we go to find our life'

. . .

The Huichol regard their peyote experiences as private and do not, as a rule, discuss them with anyone, except in the most general terms ('there were many beautiful colours', 'I saw maize in brilliant colours, much maize', or simply, 'I saw my life'). Under certain conditions the *mara'akáme* might be called upon to assist in giving form and meaning to a vision, especially for a *matewáme*, or in a cure. This much is clear, however: beyond certain 'universal' visual and auditory sensations, which may be laid to the chemistry of the plant and its effect on the central nervous system, there are powerful cultural factors at work that influence, if they do not actually determine, both content and interpretation of the drug experience. This is true not only between cultures but even within the same culture. Huichol are convinced that the *mara'akáme*, or one preparing himself to become a *mara'akáme*, and the ordinary person have different kinds of peyote experiences. Certainly a *mara'akáme* embarks on the pilgrimage and the drug experience itself with a somewhat different set of expectations than the ordinary Huichol. He seeks to experience a catharsis that allows him to enter upon a personal encounter with *Tatewarí* and to travel to 'the fifth level' to meet the supreme spirits at the ends of the world. And so he does. Ordinary Huichol also 'experience' the supernaturals, but they do so essentially through the medium of their shaman. In any event, I have met no one who was not convinced of this essential difference or who laid claim to the same kinds of exalted and illuminating confrontations with the Otherworld as the *mara'akáme*. In an objective sense his visions might be similar, but subjectively they are differently perceived and interpreted.

This sixteenth-century Aztec statue of Xochipilli, the 'Prince of Flowers', shows a figure in the grip of a transcendental ecstasy and surrounded by the iconic representations of a range of psychoactive plants including *psilocybe* mushrooms, morning-glory flowers and tobacco. (Werner Forman Archive)

*In 1936 the theatrical innovator, opiate addict and eventual lunatic
Antonin Artaud went to Mexico to participate in a similar peyote ritual
with the Tarahumara Indians. For the rest of his life he insisted that
the few days of the ritual were the only time when he had been at peace
with the world.*

ANTONIN ARTAUD
The Peyote Dance

(1936, translated from the French by Helen Weaver)

On the side where the sun rises they drove into the ground ten
crosses of unequal height but arranged in a symmetrical pattern, and
to each cross they attached a mirror.

Twenty-eight days of this horrible waiting after the dangerous withdrawal were now culminating in a circle peopled with Beings, here
represented by ten crosses.

Ten, of the Number of ten, like the Invisible Masters of Peyote, in
the Sierra.

And among these ten: the Male Principle of Nature, which the Indians
call *San Ignacio*, and its female, *San Nicolás*!

Around this circle is a zone of moral abandonment in which no Indian
would venture: it is told that birds who stray into this circle fall, and
that pregnant women feel their embryos rot inside them.

There is a history of the world in the circle of this dance, compressed
between two suns, the one that sets and the one that rises. And it is
when the sun sets that the sorcerers enter the circle, and that the dancer
with the six hundred bells (three hundred of horn and three hundred
of silver) utters his coyote's howl in the forest.

The dancer enters and leaves, and yet he does not leave the circle.
He moves forward deliberately into evil. He immerses himself in it with
a kind of terrible courage, in a rhythm which above the Dance seems
to depict the Illness. And one seems to see him alternately emerging
and disappearing in a movement which evokes one knows not what
obscure tantalizations. He enters and leaves: *'leaves the daylight, in the
first chapter'*, as is said of Man's Double in the *Egyptian Book of the
Dead*. For this advance into the illness is a voyage, a *descent in order*

to RE-EMERGE INTO THE DAYLIGHT. He turns in a circle in the direction of the wings of the Swastika, always from right to left, and from the top.

He leaps with his army of bells, like an agglomeration of dazed bees caked together in a crackling and tempestuous disorder.

Ten crosses in the circle and *ten* mirrors. *One* beam with *three* sorcerers on it. *Four* priests (*two* Males and *two* Females). The epileptic dancer, and *myself*, for whom the rite was being performed

. . .

Of the three sorcerers who were there, two, the two smallest and shortest, had had the right to handle the rasping stick for three years (for the right to handle the rasp is acquired, and in fact this right determines the nobility of the caste of the Peyote sorcerers among the Tarahumara Indians); and the third had had the right for ten years. And I must admit that it was the one most experienced in the rite who pissed the best and who farted the loudest and most expressively.

And a few moments later the same man, with the pride of this manner of crude purgation, began to spit. He spat after drinking the Peyote, as we all did. For after the twelve phases of the dance had been performed, and since dawn was about to break, we were passed the ground-up Peyote, which was like a kind of muddy gruel; and in front of each of us a new hole was dug to receive the spit from our mouths, which contact with the Peyote had henceforth made sacred.

'Spit,' the dancer told me, 'but as deep in the ground as possible, for no particle of *Ciguri* must ever emerge again.'

And it was the sorcerer who had grown old in the harness who spat most abundantly and with the largest and most compact gobs. And the other sorcerers and the dancer, gathered in a circle around the hole, had come to admire him.

After I had spat, I fell to the ground, overcome with drowsiness. The dancer in front of me passed back and forth endlessly, turning and crying *unnecessarily*, because he had discovered that his cry pleased me.

'Get up, man, get up,' he shouted each time he passed me, with diminishing effect.

Aroused and staggering, I was led toward the crosses for the final cure, in which the sorcerers shake the rasp on the very head of the patient.

Thus I took part in the rite of water, the rite of the blows on the skull, the rite of that kind of mutual cure which the participants give each other, the rite of immoderate ablutions.

They uttered strange words over my head while sprinkling me with water; then they sprinkled each other nervously, for the mixture of corn liquor and Peyote was beginning to make them wild.

And it was with these final movements that the Peyote dance ended.

The conflict between the traditional and synoptic religions can be clearly seen in the European treatment of the Native American peyote rites. The Spanish conquistadores were horrified by the 'sacred intoxication' of peyote, as shown by this Inquisition edict from 1620.

OMER C. STEWART
Peyote Religion: A History

(1987)

We, the Inquisitors against heretical perversity and apostasy in the City of Mexico, states and provinces of New Spain, New Galicia, Guatemala, Nicaragua Yucatán, Verapaz, Honduras, Philippine Islands and their districts and jurisdictions, by virtue of apostolic authority . . .

Inasmuch as the use of the herb or root called peyote has been introduced into these Provinces for the purpose of detecting thefts, of divining other happenings, and of foretelling future events, it is an act of superstition condemned as opposed to the purity and integrity of our Holy Catholic Faith . . .

Said abuse has increased in strength and is indulged in with the frequency observed. As our duty imposes upon us the obligation to put a stop to this vice . . . We order that henceforth no person of whatever rank or social condition can or may make use of the said herb, peyote, nor any other kind under any name or appearance for the same or similar purposes, nor shall he make the Indians or any other person take them, with the further warning that disobedience to these decrees shall cause us . . . to take action against such disobedient and recalcitrant persons as we would against those suspected of heresy to our Holy Catholic Faith . . . Given in the Hall of our Court on the 29th day of June, 1620, Licenciado D. Pedro Nabarre de Isla (Rubric).

. . .

Similar sentiments led to the US state and federal laws prohibiting the use of peyote by Indians, such as this statute of 1899.

Section 2652 – That it shall be unlawful for any person to introduce on

any Indian reservation or Indian allotment situated within this Territory
or to have in possession, barter, sell, give, or otherwise dispose of, any
'Mescal Bean', or the product of any such drug, to any allotted Indian
in this Territory . . . Any person who shall violate the provisions of this
Act in this Territory, shall be deemed guilty of a misdemeanor, and,
upon conviction, thereof, shall be fined in a sum not less than twenty-five
dollars, nor more than two hundred dollars, or be confined in the county
jail for not more than six months, or be assessed both such fine and
imprisonment in the discretion of the court.

. . .

*The response of the Native American community was to form a 'peyote
church', thereby claiming constitutional freedom of worship. The Native
American activist Albert Hensley put their case in the following words
in 1908.*

Sir: Having read in some of the state newspapers that you are about to
investigate 'Mescal' and its use by Indians I wish to do everything that
lies in my power to assist you in this investigation. I am the leader of
the 'Mescal' Winnebagos, who number probably three hundred, and in
this letter I speak not only for myself but also for all of those who believe
as I believe.

As you are doubtless aware, the term 'Mescal' is a misnomer. The
correct name for the plant is Peyote, the same growing in New Mexico
and Arizona, but it may be that you are not aware of the veneration in
which we hold it. We do not call it mescal, neither do we call it peyote.
Our favorite term is 'Medicine', and to us it is a portion of the body of
Christ, even as the communion bread is believed to be a portion of
Christ's body by other Christian denominations.

We read in the Bible where Christ spoke of a Comforter who was to
come. Long ago this Comforter came to the Whites, but it never came
to the Indians until it was sent by God in the form of this Holy medicine.
We know whereof we speak. We have tasted of God and our eyes have
been opened.

It is utter folly for scientists to attempt to analyze this medicine. Can
science analyze God's body? No White man can understand it. It came
from God. It is a part of God's body. God's Holy Spirit enveloped in it.
It was given exclusively to Indians and God never intended that White

men should understand it, hence the folly of any such attempt. It cures us of our temporal ills, as well as those of the spiritual nature. It takes away the desire for strong drink. I, myself, have been cured of a loathsome disease, too horrible to mention. So have hundreds of others. Hundreds of confirmed drunkards have been dragged from their downward way.

Proof of any statement I have made, or will make, is not wanting. In the face of all this, is it any wonder that the use of this medicine is increasing? Is it any wonder that our ranks are constantly increasing in number?

You know better than I, although I know well enough, what has been the result when any man or body of men have endeavored to oppose God's will; and I know, whether you do or not, what will be the result if any man or body of men attempt to oppose the onward march of this movement. It will not cease nor falter 'till every Indian within the boundaries of our great country has learned the truth, and knows God as God intends they should know him.

I am forwarding this through our Superintendent, who is also sending you a sample of the medicine.

The discovery of the prevalence of sacred drug use in the ancient world has led many modern scholars to posit the use of drugs in Classical rites such as the Eleusinian Mysteries. The suggestion that the Eleusinian potion contained ergot, a rye mould which secretes a natural analogue of LSD, allows the unknown mysteries to be dramatically reimagined.

R. GORDON WASSON, ALBERT HOFMANN,
CARL A. P. RUCK

The Road to Eleusis: Unveiling the Secret of the Mysteries

(1978)

Clearly ergot of barley is the likely psychotropic ingredient in the Eleusinian potion. Its seeming symbiotic relationship to the barley signified an appropriate expropriation and transmutation of the Dionysian spirit to which the grain, Demeter's daughter, was lost in the nuptial embrace with earth. Grain and ergot together, moreover, were joined in a bisexual union as siblings, bearing at the time of the maiden's loss already the potential for her own return and for the birth of the phalloid son that would grow from her body. A similar hermaphroditism occurs in the mythical traditions about the grotesquely fertile woman whose obscene jests were said to have cheered Demeter from her grief just before she drank the potion

. . .

Thus we may now venture past the forbidden gates and reconstruct the scene within the great initiation hall at Eleusis. The preparation of the potion was the central event. With elaborate pageantry, the hierophant, the priest who traced his descent back to the first performance of the Mystery, removed the sclerotia of ergot from the free-standing room constructed inside the *telesterion* over the remains of the original temple that had stood there in Mycenaean times. As he performed the service, he intoned ancient chants in a falsetto voice, for his role in the Mystery was asexual, a male who had sacrificed his gender to the Great Goddess.

He conveyed the grain in chalices to the priestesses, who then danced throughout the hall, balancing the vessels and lamps upon their heads. The grain was next mixed with mint and water in urns, from which the sacred potion was then ladled into the special cups for the initiates to drink their share. Finally, in acknowledgment of their readiness, they all chanted that they had drunk the potion and had handled the secret objects that had come with them on the Sacred Road in sealed baskets. Then, seated on the tiers of steps that lined the walls of the cavernous hall, in darkness they waited. From the potion they gradually entered into ecstasy. You must remember that this potion – an hallucinogen – under the right set and setting, disturbs man's inner ear and trips astonishing ventriloquistic effects. We can rest assured that the hierophants, with generations of experience, knew all the secrets of set and setting. I am sure that there was music, probably both vocal and instrumental, not loud but with authority, coming from hither and yon, now from the depths of the earth, now from outside, now a mere whisper infiltrating the ear, flitting from place to place unaccountably. The hierophants may well have known the art of releasing into the air various perfumes in succession, and they must have contrived the music for a crescendo of expectation, until suddenly the inner chamber was flung open and spirits of light entered the room, subdued lights I think, not blinding, and among them the spirit of Persephone with her new-born son just returned from Hades. She would arrive just as the hierophant raised his voice in ancient measures reserved for the Mystery: 'The Terrible Queen has given birth to her son, the Terrible One.' This divine birth of the Lord of the Nether World was accompanied by the bellowing roar of a gong-like instrument that outdid, for the ecstatic audience, the mightiest thunderclap, coming from the bowels of the earth

. . .

Until yesterday we knew of Eleusis only what little a few of the initiates told us but the spell of their words had held generations of mankind enthralled. Now, thanks to Dr Hofmann and Gordon Wasson, those of us who have experienced the superior hallucinogens may join the fellowship of the ancient initiates in a lasting bond of friendship, a friendship born of a shared experience of a reality far deeper than we had known before.

The Dead Sea Scrolls scholar John Allegro provoked outrage and ridicule when he applied a similar argument to Christianity, suggesting that Christ was, in fact, the symbolic representation of a mushroom cult.

JOHN M. ALLEGRO

The Sacred Mushroom and the Cross: A study of the nature and origins of Christianity within the fertility cults of the ancient Near East

(1970)

The fungus recognized today as the *Amanita muscaria*, or Fly Agaric, had been known from the beginning of history. Beneath the skin of its characteristic red- and white-spotted cap, there is concealed a powerful hallucinatory poison. Its religious use among certain Siberian peoples and others has been the subject of study in recent years, and its exhilarating and depressive effects have been clinically examined. These include the stimulation of the perceptive faculties so that the subject sees objects much greater or much smaller than they really are, colours and sounds are much enhanced, and there is a general sense of power, both physical and mental, quite outside the normal range of human experience.

The mushroom has always been a thing of mystery. The ancients were puzzled by its manner of growth without seed, the speed with which it made its appearance after rain, and its equally rapid disappearance. Born from a volva or 'egg' it appears like a small penis, raising itself like the human organ sexually aroused, and when it spread wide its canopy the old botanists saw it as a phallus bearing the 'burden' of a woman's groin. Every aspect of the mushroom's existence was fraught with sexual allusions, and in its phallic form the ancient saw a replica of the fertility god himself. It was the 'son of God', its drug was a purer form of the god's own spermatozoa than that discoverable in any other form of living matter. It was, in fact, God himself, manifest on earth. To the mystic it was the divinely given means of entering heaven; God had come down in the flesh to show the way to himself, by himself.

To pluck such a precious herb was attended at every point with peril. The time – before sunrise, the words to be uttered – the name of the guardian angel, were vital to the operation, but more was needed. Some form of substitution was necessary, to make an atonement to the earth robbed of her offspring. Yet such was the divine nature of the Holy Plant, as it was called, only the god could make the necessary sacrifice. To redeem the Son, the Father had to supply even the 'price of redemption'. These are all phrases used of the sacred mushroom, as they are of the Jesus of Christian theology

. . .

Our study, then, begins at the beginning, with an appreciation of religion in terms of a stimulation of the god to procreation and the provision of life. Armed with our new understanding of the language relationships of the ancient Near East, we can tackle the major problems involved in botanical nomenclature and discover those features of the more god-endued plants which attracted the attention of the old medicine men and prophets. The isolation of the names and epithets of the sacred mushroom opens the door into the secret chambers of the mystery cults which depended for their mystic hallucinatory experiences on the drugs found in the fungus. At long last identification of the main characters of many of the old classical and biblical mythologies is possible, since we can now decipher their names. Above all, those mushroom epithets and holy invocations that the Christian cryptographers wove into their stories of the man Jesus and his companions can now be recognized, and the main features of the Christian cult laid bare.

But it can be more credibly asserted that drugs such as opium and hashish have long played a sacred role in the margins of Islam.

PETER LAMBORN WILSON
Scandal: Essays in Islamic Heresy

(1900)

The Shariah forbids all intoxicants. A Moslem who drinks wine or uses hashish acts against the Shariah, but someone who uses an intoxicant for spiritual purposes can rightly be called not just a sinner but a heretic

. . .

The medieval arch-bigot Ibn Taymiyya lumped hashish-eaters in the same damnable category with boy-lovers and sufis. The three tastes appear linked in much Islamic literature. The great Abu Nowas is supposed to have written this Khayyamian quatrain:

A pound of roast meat, a few loaves of bread
A jug of wine, at least one willing boy,
A pipe of hashish. Now the picnic's spread
My garden beggars paradise's joy.

The following verses are variously attributed to the thirteenth-century Spaniard Ibn Khamis or the twelfth-century Syro-Egyptian Ibn al-A'ma:

Swear off wine and drink from the cup of Haydar,
    amber-scented, smarigdite green.
Look: it is offered to you by a slender Turkish gazelle
    who sways delicate as a willow bough.
As he prepares it, you might compare it
    to the traces of fine down on a blushing cheek
since even the slightest breeze makes it move
    as if in the coolness of a drunken morning
when silvery pigeons might whisper in branches

> filling its vegetal soul with their mutual emotions.
> How many meanings it has, significances unknown to wine!
> So close your ears to the Old Censor's slander!

('Haydar', a legendary Khorassanian sufi ascetic, was supposed to have discovered the spiritual uses of hashish.)

One of the companions of Ibn Arabi, an 'elegant young poet' from North Africa named Afif Tilimsani, compared the tresses of the Beloved to hashish and the mouth to wine. Once however at a party he was offered hashish by a friend named Juban al-Qawwas, who said,

> When opportunity arises, seize it,
>   since the time for savoring it is brief.
> Take pleasure from something amber-scented,
>   touched with green as myrtle-leaf.

Tilimsani refused the drug and answered:

> They say it expands the consciousness, this grass.
> Why then, the greatest intellect must be the ass!

Other sufis however were prepared to defend hashish in the highest terms. The Turkish sufi poet Fuzuli (author of a *Layla and Majnun* which has been translated into English) wrote a treatise on 'Bhang and Wine' in which he claimed that wine is merely 'an eager disciple setting the world afire', but hashish is the sufi master himself. Wine shows the way to the hermitage of the Shaykh of Love – but hashish is the refuge itself. Once a certain sufi of Basra began to consume hashish regularly; his shaykh realized this meant he had reached the ultimate degree of perfection, and no longer stood in need of guidance. This (says Fuzuli) 'proves that hashish is the perfect being, sought after by mankind with great eagerness. It may not be the perfect being for everybody, but it most certainly is for the seeker of mystical experience.'

. . .

Humankind in its 'ordinary' state lacks the attentiveness and will to recognize the Real. We need help. And since the Real itself is 'generous', constantly revealing itself to 'those with eyes to see', such help can come from many sources.

Intoxication provides one major source of aid in breaking out of the shell of our stale illusions. Sufis have argued *ad nauseum* whether Sobriety is better than Intoxication. Among those who supported spiritual drunkenness perhaps the most famous was Mansur al-Hallaj, who was executed for heresy.

But God himself approves of intoxication, since he promises it to the inhabitants of paradise in innumerable Koranic passages. However, 'he who tastes the wine of this world will not taste that of Paradise' (hadith). Material wine is forbidden, only spiritual wine permitted. Many sufi poets never drank a drop, for all their mystic wine-songs. To paraphrase Rumi, if grape wine could make one into a mystic, then every sot in the gutter would be a saint. The mystic lends his intoxication to wine, not the wine to the mystic. This is the orthodox mystical view.

'Do not approach prayer while intoxicated.' This hadith is given a radical exegesis by some sufis. They take it to mean that intoxication is better than prayer and that the esotericist is absolved from ritual duty by his spiritual state. As the Ismailis would say, those who have tasted the kernel can discard the shell. Those who adopt this attitude may still consider themselves Moslems, but have decidedly stepped outside the Shariah.

For such a heretic the sources of intoxication lose all moral stigma. A vagrant breeze, a beautiful face, a watered garden, a pitcher of wine or a pipe of hashish – these all become prayer in themselves, or better than prayer. For supplication need be made only by those who have not entered. For those who see here-and-now with the eyes of paradise, nothing which sharpens that vision can be considered forbidden.

. . . and the role of cannabis in some sacred traditions of Hinduism, such as the worship of Shiva, is both ancient and still prevalent. It's described here by J. M. Campbell, a British civil servant in nineteenth-century India, in his submission to the government-sponsored Indian Hemp Commission.

JAMES M. CAMPBELL
'On the Religion of Hemp'

(1893–4)

To the Hindu the hemp plant is holy. A guardian lives in the bhang leaf. As the wife of Vishnu, the preserver, lives in the hysteria-curing *tulsi*, or Holy Basil, and as Shiva dwells in the dysentery-scaring *bel*, *Aegle marmelos*, so the properties of the bhang plant, its power to suppress the appetites, its virtue as a febrifuge, and its thought-bracing qualities show that the bhang leaf is the home of the great Yogi or brooding ascetic Mahadev

. . .

Bhang the cooler is a febrifuge. Bhang acts on the fever not directly or physically as an ordinary medicine, but indirectly or spiritually by soothing the angry influences to whom the heats of fever are due. According to one account in the Ayurveda, fever is possession by the hot angry breath of the great gods Brahma, Vishnu, and Shiva. According to another passage in the Ayurveda, Shankar or Shiva, enraged by a slight from his father-in-law Daksha, breathed from his nostrils the eight fevers that wither mankind. If the fever-stricken performs the Vijayā abhishek, or bhang-pouring on the Ling of Shankar, the god is pleased, his breath cools, and the portion of his breath in the body of the fever-stricken ceases to inflame. The Kashikhanda Purana tells how at Benares, a Brahman, sore-smitten with fever, dreamed that he had poured bhang over the self-sprung Ling and was well. On waking he went to the Ling, worshipped, poured bhang and recovered . . . In . . . praise of the hemp the Makhazan or great Greek–Arab work on drugs joins. Ganja in excess causes abscess, even madness. In moderation bhang is the best of gifts. Bhang is a cordial, a bile absorber, an appetiser, a prolonger of life. Bhang quickens fancy, deepens thought, and braces judgment

. . .

oaths are taken on the bhang leaf. Even to a truthful witness an oath on the bhang leaf is dreaded. To one who foreswears himself the bhang oath is death

. . .

Even according to the straitest school of the objectors to stimulants, while to a high-caste Hindu the penalty for liquor-drinking is death, no penalty attaches to the use of bhang, and a single day's fast is enough to cleanse from the coarser spirit of *ganja*. Even among those who hold stimulants to be devil-possessed penalty and disfavour attach to the use of hemp drugs only when they are taken with no religious object and without observing the due religious rites.

At the other extreme of Hindu thought from the foes to stimulants, to the worshippers of the influences that, raising man out of himself and above mean individual worries, make him one with the divine force of nature, it is inevitable that temperaments should be found to whom the quickening spirit of bhang is the spirit of freedom and knowledge. In the ecstasy of bhang the spark of the Eternal in man turns into light the murkiness of matter or illusion and self is lost in the central soul-fire. The Hindu poet of Shiva, the Great Spirit that living in bhang passes into the drinker, sings of bhang as the clearer of ignorance, the giver of knowledge. No gem or jewel can touch in value bhang taken truly and reverently. He who drinks bhang drinks Shiva. The soul in whom the spirit of bhang finds a home glides into the ocean of being freed from the weary round of matter-blinded self. To the meaner man, still under the glamour of matter or *māyā*, bhang taken religiously is kindly thwarting the wiles of his foes and giving the drinker wealth and promptness of mind.

. . .

Much of the holiness of bhang is due to its virtue of clearing the head and stimulating the brain to thought. Among ascetics the sect known as Atits are specially devoted to hemp. No social or religious gathering of Atits is complete without the use of the hemp plant smoked in ganja or drunk in bhang. To its devotee bhang is no ordinary plant that became holy from its guardian and healing qualities. According to one account, when nectar was produced from the churning of the ocean, something was wanted to purify the nectar. The deity supplied the want of nectar-cleanser by creating bhang. This bhang Mahadev made from his own body, and so it is called *angaj* or body-born. According to another account some nectar dropped to the ground and from the ground the bhang plant sprang. It was because they used this child of nectar or of Mahadev in agreement with religious forms that the seers or Rishis became Siddha or one with the deity. He who, despite the example of the Rishis, uses no bhang shall lose his happiness in this life and in the life to come. In the end he shall be cast into hell. The mere sight of bhang cleanses from as much sin as a thousand horse-sacrifices or a thousand pilgrimages. He who scandalizes the user of bhang shall suffer the torments of hell so long as the sun endures. He who drinks bhang foolishly or for pleasure without religious rites is as guilty as the sinner of *lakhs* of sins. He who drinks wisely and according to rule, be he ever so low, even so his body is smeared with human ordure and urine, is Shiva. No god or man is as good as the religious drinker of bhang. The students of the scriptures at Benares are given bhang before they sit to study. At Benares, Ujjain, and other holy places yogis, beiragis and sanyasits take deep draughts of bhang that they may centre their thoughts on the Eternal. To bring back to reason an unhinged mind the best and cleanest bhang leaves should be boiled in milk and turned to clarified butter. Salamisri, saffron, and sugar should be added and the whole eaten. Besides over the demon of Madness bhang is Vijayā or victorious over the demons of hunger and thirst. By the help of bhang ascetics pass days without food or drink. The supporting power of bhang has brought many a Hindu family safe through the miseries of famine. To forbid or even seriously to restrict the use of so holy and gracious a herb as the hemp would cause widespread suffering and annoyance and to the large bands of worshipped ascetics deep-seated anger. It would rob the people of a solace in discomfort, of a cure in sickness, of a guardian whose gracious protection saves them from the attacks of evil influences, and whose mighty power makes the devotee of the Victorious, overcoming the demons of hunger and thirst, of panic, fear, of the glamour of Māyā or matter, and of madness, able in rest to brood on the Eternal, till the Eternal, possessing him body and soul, frees him from the haunting of self and receives him into the ocean of Being.

*Is it the case that drugs can produce a genuine transcendental experi-
ence? In his monumental survey* The Varieties of Religious Experience,
the psychologist William James suggested that they could.

WILLIAM JAMES

The Varieties of Religious Experience: A Study in Human Nature

(1902)

Nitrous oxide and ether, especially nitrous oxide, when sufficiently diluted with air, stimulate the mystical consciousness in an
extraordinary degree. Depth beyond depth of truth seems revealed to
the inhaler. This truth fades out, however, or escapes, at the moment
of coming to; and if any words remain over in which it seemed to clothe
itself, they prove to be the veriest nonsense. Nevertheless, the sense of
a profound meaning having been there persists; and I know more than
one person who is persuaded that in the nitrous oxide trance we have
a genuine metaphysical revelation.

Some years ago I myself made some observations on this aspect of
nitrous oxide intoxication, and reported them in print. One conclusion
was forced upon my mind at that time, and my impression of its
truth has ever since remained unshaken. It is that our normal waking
consciousness, rational consciousness as we call it, is but one special
type of consciousness, whilst all about it, parted from it by the filmiest
of screens, there lie potential forms of consciousness entirely different.
We may go through life without suspecting their existence; but apply the
requisite stimulus, and at a touch they are there in all their completeness,
definite types of mentality which probably somewhere have their field
of application and adaptation. No account of the universe in its totality
can be final which leaves these other forms of consciousness quite
disregarded

. . .

I just now spoke of friends who believe in the anaesthetic revelation. For them too it is a monistic insight, in which the *other* in its various forms appears absorbed into the One.

'Into this pervading genius,' writes one of them, 'we pass, forgetting and forgotten, and thenceforth each is all, in God. There is no higher, no deeper, no other, than the life in which we are founded. "The One remains, the many change and pass;" and each and every one of us *is* the One that remains   This is the ultimatum . . . As sure as being – whence is all our care – so sure is content, beyond duplexity, antithesis, or trouble, where I have triumphed in a solitude that God is not above.'

. . .

This has the genuine religious mystic ring! I just now quoted J. A. Symonds. He also records a mystical experience with chloroform, as follows:

After the choking and stifling had passed away, I seemed at first in a state of utter blankness; then came flashes of intense light, alternating with blackness, and with a keen vision of what was going on in the room around me, but no sensation of touch. I thought that I was near death; when, suddenly, my soul became aware of God, who was manifestly dealing with me, handling me, so to speak, in an intense personal present reality. I felt him streaming in like light upon me . . . I cannot describe the ecstasy I felt. Then, as I gradually awoke from the influence of the anaesthetics, the old sense of my relation to the world began to return, the new sense of my relation to God began to fade. I suddenly leapt to my feet on the chair where I was sitting, and shrieked out, 'It is too horrible, it is too horrible, it is too horrible,' meaning that I could not bear this disillusionment. Then I flung myself on the ground, and at last awoke covered with blood, calling to the two surgeons (who were frightened), 'Why did you not kill me? Why would you not let me die?' Only think of it. To have felt for that long dateless ecstasy of vision the very God, in all purity and tenderness and truth and absolute love, and then to find that I had after all had no revelation, but that I had been tricked by the abnormal excitement of my brain.

Yet, this question remains, Is it possible that the inner sense of reality which succeeded, when my flesh was dead to impressions from without, to the ordinary sense of physical relations, was not a delusion but an actual experience? Is it possible that I, in that moment, felt what some of the saints have said they always felt, the undemonstrable but irrefragable certainty of God?

With this we make connection with religious mysticism pure and simple. Symonds's question takes us back to those examples . . . of sudden realization of the immediate presence of God. The phenomenon in one shape or another is not uncommon.

The poet and visionary writer René Daumal had a similar experience to that of William James. It is interesting to note that both their accounts are based on experiments not with traditionally 'spiritual' plant psyche-delics such as peyote, but with industrial inhalants.

RENÉ DAUMAL
'A Fundamental Experience'

(1944, tr. Roger Shattuck © 1959/1987)

My memories of childhood and adolescence are deeply marked by a series of attempts to experience the beyond, and those random attempts brought me to the ultimate experiment, the fundamental experience of which I speak. At about the age of six, having been taught no kind of religious belief whatsoever, I struck up against the stark problem of death. I passed some atrocious nights, feeling my stomach clawed to shreds and my breathing half throttled by the anguish of nothingness, the 'no more of anything'. One night when I was about eleven, relaxing my entire body, I calmed the terror and revulsion of my organism before the unknown, and a new feeling came alive in me; hope, and a foretaste of the imperishable. But I wanted more, I wanted a certainty. At fifteen or sixteen I began my experiments, a search without direction or system.

Finding no way to experiment directly on death – on *my* death – I tried to study my sleep, assuming an analogy between the two. By various devices I attempted to enter sleep in a waking state. The undertaking is not so utterly absurd as it sounds, but in certain respects it is perilous. I could not go very far with it; my own organism gave me some serious warnings of the risks I was running. One day, however, I decided to tackle the problem of death itself. I would put my body into a state approaching as close as possible that of physiological death, and still concentrate all my attention on remaining conscious and registering everything that might take place. I had in my possession some carbon tetrachloride, which I used to kill beetles for my collection. Knowing this substance belongs to the same chemical family as chloroform (it is even more toxic), I thought I could regulate its action very simply and easily: the moment I began to lose consciousness, my hand would fall from my nostrils carrying with it the handkerchief moistened with the volatile fluid. Later on I repeated the experiment in the presence of friends, who could have given me help had I needed it. The result was always exactly the same; that is, it exceeded and even overwhelmed my expectations by bursting the limits of the possible and by projecting me brutally into another world.

First came the ordinary phenomena of asphyxiation: arterial palpitation, buzzings, sounds of heavy pumping in the temples, painful repercussions from the tiniest exterior noises, flickering lights. Then, the distinct feeling: 'This is getting serious. The game is up,' followed by a swift recapitulation of my life up to that moment. If I felt any slight anxiety, it remained indistinguishable from a bodily discomfort that did not affect my mind. And my mind kept repeating to itself: 'Careful, don't doze off. This is just the time to keep your eyes open.' The luminous spots that danced in front of my eyes soon filled the whole of space, which echoed with the beat of my blood – sound and light overflowing space and fusing in a single rhythm. By this time I was no longer capable of speech, even of interior speech; my mind travelled too rapidly to carry any words along with it. I realized, in a sudden illumination, that I still had control of the hand which held the handkerchief, that I still accurately perceived the position of my body, and that I could hear and understand words uttered nearby – but that objects, words, and meanings of words had lost any significance whatsoever. It was a little like having repeated a word over and over until it shrivels and dies in your mouth: you still know what the word 'table' means, for instance, you could use it correctly, but it no longer truly evokes its object. In the same way everything that made up 'the world' for me in my ordinary state was still there, but I felt as if it had been drained of its substance. It was nothing more than a phantasmagoria – empty, absurd, clearly outlined, and necessary all at once. This 'world' lost all reality because I had abruptly entered another world, infinitely more real, an instantaneous and intense world of eternity, a concentrated flame of reality and evidence into which I had cast myself like a butterfly drawn to a lighted candle. Then, at that moment, comes the *certainty*; speech must now be content to wheel in circles around the bare fact.

. . .

Little by little I discovered in my reading accounts of the same experience, for I now held the key to these narratives and descriptions whose relation to a single and unique reality I should not previously have suspected. William James speaks of it. O. V. de L. Milosz, in his *Letter to Storge*, gives an overwhelming account of it in terms I had been using myself. The famous circle referred to by a medieval monk, and which Pascal saw (but who first saw it and spoke of it?) ceased to be an empty allegory for me; I know it represented a devouring vision of what I had seen also. And, beyond all this varied and partial human testimony (there is scarcely a single true poet in whose work I did not find at least a fragment of it), the confessions of the great mystics and, still more advanced, the sacred texts of certain religions, brought me an affirmation of the same reality. Sometimes I found it in its most terrifying form, as perceived by an individual of limited vision who has not raised himself to the level of such perception, who, like myself, has tried to look into the infinite through the keyhole and finds himself staring into Bluebeard's cupboard. Sometimes I encountered it in the pleasing, plentifully satisfying and intensely luminous form that is the vision of beings truly transformed, who can behold that reality face to face without being destroyed by it. I have in mind the revelation of the Divine Being in the *Bhagavad-Gita*, the vision of Ezekiel and that of St John the Divine on Patmos, certain descriptions in the *Tibetan Book of the Dead* (*Bardo thôdol*), and a passage in the *Lankâvatâra-Sûtra*.

Not having lost my mind then and there, I began little by little to philosophize about the memory of this experience. And I would have buried myself in a philosophy of my own if someone had not come along just in time to tell me: 'Look, the door is open – narrow and hard to reach, but a door. It is the only one for you.'

The most celebrated 'clinical trial' of drugs and the religious experience was the Good Friday Experiment of 1962, where various theology students from Harvard Divinity School were given psilocybin in Boston University chapel. One of them described his experience as follows.

WALTER N. PAHNKE
'LSD and Religious Experience'
(1962)

I hesitate to attempt a summary of my drug experience as I am acutely aware of the inability of linguistic symbols to contain, or even accurately reflect, the dynamics of 'mystic' consciousness. In the words of the Russian poet Tyutchev, I feel as though 'A thought that's spoken is a lie'. To seek to condense any of my experiences into words is to distort them, rendering them finite and impure. In so acknowledging the profound ineffability of my experience, I am not trying to write poetry – although in the final analysis this may well be the only possible means of verbal expression – but intend only to convey the feelings of frustration and futility with which I begin this report.

Now, four days after the experience itself, I continue to feel a deep sense of awe and reverence, being simultaneously intoxicated with an ecstatic joy. This euphoric feeling . . . includes elements of profound peace and steadfastness, surging like a spring from a depth of my being which has rarely, if ever, been tapped prior to the drug experience. The spasmodic nature of my prayer life has ceased, and I have yielded to a need to spend time each day in meditation which, though essentially open and wordless, is impregnated by feelings of thanksgiving and trust. This increased need to be alone is balanced by what I believe to be a greater sensitivity to the authentic problems of others and a corresponding willingness to enter freely into genuine friendships. I possess a renewed and increased sense of personal integration and am more content simply to 'be myself' than previously.

. . .

Relatively soon after receiving the drug, I transcended my usual level of consciousness and became aware of fantastic dimensions of being, all of which possessed a profound sense of reality.

. . .

It would seem more accurate to say that I existed 'in' these dimensions of being as I had not only transcended my ego, but also the dichotomy between subject and object.

It is meaningful to say that I ceased to exist, becoming immersed in the ground of Being, in Brahman, in God, in 'Nothingness', in Ultimate Reality or in some similar religious symbol for Oneness . . .

The feelings I experienced could best be described as cosmic tenderness, infinite love, penetrating peace, eternal blessing and unconditional acceptance on one hand, and on the other, as unspeakable awe, overflowing joy, primeval humility, inexpressible gratitude and boundless devotion. Yet all of these words are hopelessly inadequate and can do little more than meekly point towards the genuine, inexpressible feelings actually experienced.

It is misleading even to use the words 'I experienced', since during the peak of the experience (which must have lasted at least an hour) there was no duality between myself and what I experienced. Rather, I *was* these feelings, or ceased to be in them and felt no loss at the cessation. This was especially evident when, after having reached the mystic peak, a recording of Bach's 'Fantasia and Fugue in G Minor' was played. At this time it seemed as though I was not M. R. listening to a recording, but paradoxically *was* the music itself. Especially at one climax in the Fantasia, the 'love' I was experiencing became so overwhelming as to become unbearable or even painful. The tears I shed at this moment were in no sense those of fear, but ones of uncontainable joy.

. . .

During the height of the experience, I had no consciousness of time or space in the ordinary sense. I felt as though I was beyond seconds, minutes, hours, and also beyond past, present, and future. In religious language, I was in 'eternity'.

. . .

Let me affirm that even with my acquaintance with mystic literature of both east and west, coupled with the profound appreciation of natural and artistic beauty I have always enjoyed, I know I could never have understood this experience, had I not lived it myself. The dimensions of being I entered surpassed the wildest fantasies of my imagination and, as I have said, leave me with a profound sense of awe . . . In no sense have I an urge to formulate philosophical or theological dogmas about my experience. Only my silence can retain its purity and genuineness.

TABLE I   SUMMARY OF PERCENTAGE SCORES AND SIGNIFICANCE
LEVELS REACHED BY THE EXPERIMENTAL VERSUS THE CONTROL
GROUP FOR CATEGORIES MEASURING THE TYPOLOGY OF MYSTI-
CAL EXPERIENCE

*% of Maximum Possible
Score for 10 Ss*

	Category	Exp.	Cont.	P°
1	Unity	62	7	.001
	A Internal	70	8	.001
	B External	38	2	.008
2	Transcendence of time and space	84	6	.001
3	Deeply felt positive mood	57	23	.020
	A Joy, blessedness and peace	51	19	.020
	B Love	57	33	.055
4	Sacredness	53	28	.020
5	Objectivity and reality	63	18	.011
6	Paradoxicality	61	13	.001
7	Alleged ineffability	66	18	.001
8	Transciency	79	8	.001
9	Persisting positive changes in attitude and behavior	51	8	.001
	A Toward self	57	3	.001
	B Toward others	40	20	.002
	C Toward life	54	6	.011
	D Toward the experience	57	31	.055

° Probability that the difference between experimental and control scores was
due to chance.

The psychologist Walter Pankhe's summary of the Good Friday experiment. Some of the experimental subjects were given psilocybin, others
a mild stimulant placebo: this table compares the reports of the genuine
experimental subjects with those of the control subjects, and demon-
strates the low probability that the disparity could be due to chance.
(Aaronson/Osmond: *Psychedelics* (Hogarth Press, 1971))

But the professor of ancient religions R. C. Zaehner made a similar experiment with very different results. His experience of taking mescaline in Oxford Cathedral was, in his words, 'anti-religious'.

R. C. ZAEHNER
'Mysticism, Sacred and Profane'

(1957)

On returning to my rooms I sat down, feeling rather tired. The time was now 2.45, and the investigators tried to elicit a more or less clear account of my experiences in the Cathedral.

'In the Cathedral,' I replied, 'I started looking at the rose window which at first seemed to be fairly clear and then it faded . . . I'm sorry, things are coming a bit odd . . . I don't seem to be able to remember, I can't express myself any more . . . I'm not feeling very . . . er . . . sensible at the moment.'

I was then asked about things around me and how they were behaving. I was feeling rather exhausted and had some difficulty in replying.

'They're going up and down rather,' I said, '. . . very misty . . . the bookcase pattern forms and reforms. I wish it'd stay where it was. Dr Allison is recognizable, I'm glad to say . . . (sigh). I'm sorry to look at you like this . . . (another sigh). Things are just *queer*. They don't stay in the same place very long, but they don't change very much.' In actual fact, though Dr Allison's face was much the same, his right ear had expanded quite considerably, but I somehow felt it would be impolite to draw attention to this.

I was then asked to look at the Gentile da Fabriano 'Adoration of the Magi'. At first it looked 'precisely as it was before', and for some time remained so

. . .

I was looking at the picture by daylight, and the investigators now shone a lamp on it. At this the picture appeared to come to life. It was the second Magus again who started it. He again moved his outstretched hand slightly forward and seemed to be trying hard to take his crown off

. . .

the poor Magus' predicament seemed to me wildly amusing. In any case I now broke into uncontrollable laughter which was to last, on and off, for over an hour. The occasion for this excessive hilarity was, I suppose, the Magus; but this did not seem wholly clear to me at the time.

'What do you find so funny,' Professor Zaehner?' an investigator asked.

R.C.Z. (ecstatically). 'Nothing.' This was true: everything had suddenly become so totally funny that to single out one thing rather than another would not at all have conveyed this experience of total funniness. I could only continue to laugh till I cried. The situation was not made one bit better by the behaviour of the Magi. The eldest, who is represented as kneeling and about to kiss the Infant Jesus' feet, seemed to advance while the Child attempted to push him back. And now it became clear that the Magus was not going to kiss the Child's feet: he was trying to bite them and the Child would not let him. Perhaps because, as I explained to the investigators before the experiment began, I had always admired this picture for the beauty and richness of its colouring, not for its religious content, I was not shocked by the thought of the Magus biting the feet of the Infant Jesus. I simply did not connect this grotesque scene with the actual subject of the picture. Even in my manic state I made a clear distinction between the world of 'funniness' and objects or pictures which seemed to me genuinely sacred.

. . .

I would not presume to draw any conclusions from so trivial an experience. It was interesting and it certainly seemed hilariously funny. All along, however, I felt that the experience was in a sense 'anti-religious', I mean, not conformable with religious experience or in the same category. In Huxley's terminology 'self-transcendence' of a sort did take place, but transcendence into a world of farcical meaninglessness. All things were one in the sense that they were all, at the height of my manic state, equally funny: the quality of 'funniness' and incongruity had swallowed up all others. I was never frightened, and as, under the influence of Berlioz, I slowly returned to sanity, my normal religious consciousness, which was never completely swamped, returned in full vigour. There was no longer any reason why I should be afraid.

I would not wish to take the drug again, but purely on moral grounds. I should be most interested to know whether the drug taken elsewhere and in a different and less friendly environment would produce different effects; but the more the experience fades into the past, the clearer does it seem to me that, in principle, artificial interference with consciousness is, except for valid medical reasons, wrong.

As far as I am concerned, mescalin was quite unable to reproduce the 'natural mystical experience' I have described elsewhere. I half hoped it would. However, once the drug started working and I was plunged into a universe of farce, I realized that this was not to be.

4

High Culture: Drugs and Art

The heightened perception and intensity of experience which drugs produce have been related to art throughout history and across cultures, but the equation of drugs and art remains vague and complex. In what sense, if any, do drugs 'produce' art? How exactly is an artist's use of drugs reflected in their work? Can we, with any accuracy, talk about 'drug literature' or 'drug music'? Is 'psychedelic' or 'visionary' painting produced more or less effectively by artists who have used drugs?

FRIEDRICH NIETZSCHE
Twilight of the Idols

(1889)

For art to exist, for any sort of aesthetic activity or perception to exist, a certain physiological precondition is indispensable: *intoxication*. Intoxication must first have heightened the excitability of the entire machine: no art results before that happens. All kinds of intoxication, however different their origin, have the power to do this . . .

It seems that the origins of art may have been closely connected with the use of drugs. Recent research suggests that, on a fundamental level, the signs and representations of the earliest Palaeolithic art may be drug-related. The basic building-blocks (or 'form-constants') of cave art correlate strongly with the optical patterning produced by psychedelic drugs.

J. D. LEWIS-WILLIAMS AND T. A. DOWSON
'The Signs of All Times: Entoptic Phenomena in Upper Palaeolithic Art'

(1988)

The so-called signs of European Upper Palaeolithic art have been a persistently intractable challenge to archaeologists. By and large, two approaches have been employed to elucidate their meaning. Some writers, especially those of earlier decades, invoked ethnographic analogies to argue that the signs were traps, huts, or shrines inhabited by spirits (e.g. Breuil 1952:24). More recently, writers have turned from ethnography to internal analysis, believing it possible to discover an inherent order and then, without recourse to analogues, to induce meaning from that order (e.g. Laming 1962; Leroi-Gourhan 1968*a*, *b*; Marshack 1972; Sauvet, Sauvet, and Wlodarczyk 1977; Sauvet and Sauvet 1979; Faris 1983). Various patterns have been suggested and supported, some more, some less convincingly, by quantitative work (Parkington 1969, Rosenfeld 1971, Stevens 1975), but the next step, induction of meaning, has run into snags, for it is logically impossible to induce meaning from numerical rock-art data, as it is from any data (Lewis-Williams 1983*b*:101; Lewis-Williams and Loubser 1986). Although much of this inductive work has proved valuable and provocative, no explanation for the signs has won general acceptance. Today there is a 'swing away from a fruitless search for meaning to a consolidation of all we know about the art' (Bahn 1986*b*:55; *see also* Conkey 1983).

. . .

The strong evidence that chimpanzees, baboons, monkeys, cats, dogs, and other animals hallucinate suggests that altered states of consciousness and hallucinations are a function of the mammalian, not just the human, nervous system (Siegel and Jarvik 1975:81–104) and that 'non-real' visual percepts were experienced long before the Upper Palaeolithic. Indeed, australopithecines probably hallucinated. Be that as it may, the nervous system is a human universal, and we accept that, by the Upper Palaeolithic, it was much the same as it is now. The content of early human mental imagery is, however, more problematic than its existence, because cultural expectations inform the imagery to a considerable extent. For a conservative beginning to an investigation of possible Upper Palaeolithic mental imagery we therefore comment less on culturally informed hallucinations than on a feature of altered states completely controlled by the nervous system.

Under certain circumstances the visual system generates a range of luminous percepts that are independent of light from an external source (e.g. Klüver 1926, 1942; Knoll *et al.* 1963; Horowitz 1964; Oster 1970; Richards 1971; Eichmeier and Höfer 1974; Siegel and Jarvik 1975; Siegel 1977, 1978; Asaad and Shapiro 1986). Although there was interest in these visual percepts in the nineteenth century and at the beginning of this one, it was not until the 1920s that Heinrich Klüver began the systematic analysis of the phenomena. Working under laboratory conditions, Klüver (1926; 1942:177) concluded that these percepts were not just visual 'dust'; they had form. Abstracting redundant form elements from his subjects' reports of altered states of consciousness, he arrived at four groupings of the percepts. Some years later, Horowitz (1975:178), unaware of Klüver's work, similarly abstracted redundant form elements from reports of altered states. He then found that his elements, despite their 'indescribableness' (Klüver 1926:503), corresponded very largely with Klüver's categorization. Other workers (e.g. Knoll 1958, Horowitz 1964, Richards 1971, Eichmeier and Höfer 1974, Siegel 1977) have confirmed these findings and identified further recurring form elements. Their research has shown that these visual phenomena, although complex and diverse, take geometric forms such as grids, zigzags, dots, spirals, and catenary curves. All these percepts are experienced as incandescent, shimmering, moving, rotating, and sometimes enlarging patterns; they also grade one into another and combine in a bewildering way (Klüver 1942:176). Because they derive from the human

ENTOPTIC PHENOMENA		SAN ROCK ART		COSO
		ENGRAVINGS	PAINTINGS	
A	B	C	D	E
I				
II				
III				
IV				
V				
VI				

This table compares six common types of 'entoptic' patterning caused
by drugs with common motifs both from contemporary tribal art (the
San, or African 'Bushmen', and the Coso) and from the cave art of the
Upper Palaeolithic period (facing page). (Lewis-Williams)

PALAEOLITHIC ART				
MOBILE ART		PARIETAL ART		
F	G	H	I	
				I
				II
				III
				IV
				V
				VI

nervous system, all people who enter certain altered states of consciousness, no matter what their cultural background, are liable to perceive
them (Eichmeier and Höfer 1974, Reichel-Dolmatoff 1978*a*).

These geometric visual percepts can be induced by a variety of means.
Under laboratory conditions, electrical stimulation (e.g. Knoll and
Kugler 1959, Knoll *et al*. 1963, Brindley 1973, Eichmeier and Höfer
1974) and flickering light (Young *et al*. 1975) produce them, but,
although flickering fire light may have played a role in the past, we clearly
have to look elsewhere to explain prehistoric experience. Psychoactive
drugs generate the percepts, but fatigue, sensory deprivation, intense
concentration, auditory driving, migraine, schizophrenia, hyperventila-
tion, and rhythmic movement are some other generating factors (Klüver
1942; Horowitz 1965:512–18; Sacks 1970; Siegel and Jarvik 1975). Much
more research will have to be done before it can be established whether
specific geometric forms are associated with particular circumstances
of generation (but *see* Knoll *et al*. 1963).

Nomenclature for these visual percepts poses some problems. Hoping
to avoid a diversionary logomachy, we follow Tyler (1978:1633) in using
entoptic phenomena (from the Greek, 'within vision') to mean visual
sensations derived from the structure of the optic system anywhere
from the eyeball to the cortex. This term covers two classes of geometric
percept that appear to derive from different parts of the visual system –
phosphenes and form constants. *Phosphenes* can be induced by physical
stimulation, such as pressure on the eyeball, and are thus entophthalmic
('within the eye') (Walker 1981). *Form constants* derive from the optic
system, probably beyond the eyeball itself (Knoll *et al*. 1963, Siegel
1977). We distinguish these two kinds of entoptic phenomena from
hallucinations, which have no foundation in the actual structure of the
optic system. Unlike phosphenes and form constants, hallucinations
include iconic visions of culturally controlled items such as animals, as
well as somatic and aural experiences.

. . .

The universality of entoptic phenomena encourages us to construct a
model of the ways in which mental imagery is perceived by people in
certain altered states of consciousness.

The art of many traditional societies is closely connected to the ritual use of drugs. The following analysis focuses on the relationship between the Tukano people of the Amazon and their ritual brew ayahuasca, which contains the psychedelic harmaline.

G. REICHEL-DOLMATOFF

'Drug-induced Optical Sensations and Their Relationship to Applied Art among Some Colombian Indians'

(1978)

The literature on native hallucinatory content abounds with descriptions of the weird imagery produced by advanced harmaline intoxication. It should be kept in mind here that the sphere of hallucinations is one of subjective interpretations in which the person projects a set of pre-established, stored material upon the wavering screen of shapes and colours. Understandably, the mythical scenes seen by the Tukano during the second stage of the drug experience, can be seen only by members of *their* society. But the repetitive luminous patterns perceived during the first stage of the toxic condition represent neurophysiologically an entirely different aspect of the experience and it is this dimension that is of interest to our inquiry.

While engaged in ethnographic field work among the Tukano Indians, I had asked the men to depict the visual images they perceived while under the influence of *Banisteriopsis*. I offered the men a choice of twelve coloured pencils and some sheets of white paper 28 cm × 22 cm, mounted on a wooden tablet. They were all adult males who frequently took *Banisteriopsis*; further, all were non-acculturated Indians who did not live in contact with civilization, none of whom spoke Spanish. The men showed great interest in this task and spent from one to two hours finishing each drawing. For our drawings, they first traced a rectangular frame and then divided the space into convenient quadrants. The colours they selected spontaneously were exclusively red, yellow and blue, on very few occasions adding a shade of hazel brown. There were comments that there was not a good choice of the various tones of the basic colours,

since the Tukano discriminate carefully between a number of shades
of the same pigment, such as clear yellow, orange yellow, reddish yellow,
etc., and evidently would have preferred to execute the drawings in a
wider range than allowed by each of the basic colours. When each
drawing was completed, I recorded on tape the explanation the artist
gave for his work. Sometimes these comments were extremely concise:
others were long and detailed explanations.

Once I had obtained a short series of drawings it became clear that
some of them represented the stage of repetitive geometrical patterns,
while others depicted the stage of figurative imagery seen during hallucination. The Indians themselves readily pointed out this difference.
But, more important still, I noticed that the drawings – mainly those of
the first category – consistently repeated certain design motifs

. . .

I now proceeded to isolate these design motifs by drawing each of them
on a numbered card and showing these around, soliciting comments.
It soon became clear that the drawings contained individual variations
of some twenty well-defined design motifs. As a matter of fact, it seemed
that different people, men belonging to different age-groups, occupying
different social positions, and representing different personality types,
all perceived basically the same geometrical patterns during the first
stage of *Banisteriopsis* intoxication. This observation brought to mind
the possibility of an underlying biological basis, that is, of the question
whether similar brain stimuli would produce similar optical sensations
in different people

. . .

Taken one by one, the native interpretation of the Tukano design
elements appears as follows:

1 Male organ	8 Group of phratries	15 Sun
2 Female organ	9 Line of descent	16 Plant growth
3 Fertilized uterus	10 Incest	17 Thought
4 Uterus as 'passage'	11 Exogamy	18 Stool
5 Drops of semen	12 Ritual box	19 Rattle
6 Mythical canoe	13 Milky Way	20 Cigar holder
7 Exogamic phratry	14 Rainbow	

. . .

The interpretation given to the design motifs revolves almost entirely around the problem of incest, a problem which is all-pervading in the native culture, and the message transmitted by the code insists on the observance of the laws of exogamy. The important point, however, is that the code is extended beyond the narrow confines of individual trance and is applied to the wider physical environment of everyday life. In fact, the designs and patterns perceived under the influence of *Banisteriopsis* are transplanted to the concrete objects of material culture where they come to constitute an art form. Practically all decorative elements that adorn the objects manufactured by the Tukano are said by them to be derived from the photic sensations perceived under the influence of the drug; that is, are based on phosphenes. A closer look at the applied art of the Tukano is most revealing.

The most outstanding examples are the paintings executed on the front part of the longhouses. The walls, made of large pieces of flattened bark, are covered wholly or in part with bold designs painted with mineral colours – occasionally with the admixture of vegetable dyes – and represent the same geometric motifs I have discussed above. Sometimes they are combined with figurative designs of people and animals. When asked about these paintings the Indians simply reply, 'This is what we see when we drink *Banisteriopsis*.'

Further examples are numerous. The bark-cloth aprons used during ritual occasions are painted with phosphene patterns and among some Tukano groups that manufacture bark-cloth masks these, too, exhibit the same designs. One apron shows the sign for exogamy painted prominently over the genital region while others are adorned with the sun, the rainbow, or other designs. The large stamping tubes which the Tukano use to accompany their dances are covered with similar designs showing zigzag lines, rhombs and rows of dots. The gourd rattles are sometimes covered with phosphene patterns. The large drums that were formerly in use were painted with these designs and occasionally a modern beer trough will be adorned with similar patterns

. . .

In summarizing, with the exception of a few more or less realistic designs of animals or houses, the entire art style of the Tukano can be said to be based on drug-induced phosphenes.

The decorative motifs drawn in the sand by this Tukano Indian are representations of the tribe's *ayahuasca* visions (Reichel-Dolmatoff)

*Detached from a traditional culture, attempts to produce 'drug-based
art' are often less satisfactory. Henri Michaux (see p. 80) experimented
with both hashish and mescaline.*

HENRI MICHAUX
Miserable Miracle (Mescaline)

(1956)

When I go out after taking hashish I am a different man. With
different eyes. Hashish points out, chooses, observes and penetrates
like a rigid sword. Without it I look at things the way oxen do,
having like them a slow digestion, an endless digestion of I don't
know what. Such being the case, never quite free of this occupation, I
can only let my eyes wander circularly, unless occasionally a spectacle
more clamorous than usual draws them its way. But never for long,
soon hesitant and staring, my eyes begin their circular contemplation
again.

With Hashish in me I am a falcon. If I give a circular glance it will
be only once, as one makes a general survey, not to be repeated. I am
against dispersion. I look for an object in order to follow a trail. If it is
a face, then through that face I will follow the trail to the ends of the
earth. Nothing can distract me. With a look that thinks, thinks and goes
through the other person's head. Without being in the least excited.
Perhaps it is that inside of the head, that place of metaphysics, of
calculation, which alone makes me regret hashish. For, though known
so slightly, I am definitely giving it up. That place which I can only point
to on my skull, saying, 'it is there, five or six centimetres inside, which
existed then and which had never existed before, and which if not a
faculty is at least a function, and through which, even weakened by the
drug, I know that I am at a centre, that this centre which exists in me
gives me the right (and the facility) to look anyone straight into the eye,
for I go beyond the features. As soon as hashish is extinct in me, it
disappears, and I am obliged to return to the periphery, to the crust,
that other centre having gone to sleep for good.

The drawings I made after taking mescaline, either on the following
day or one or two weeks later, consisted of an enormous number of

very fine parallel lines, very close together with an axis of symmetry and endless repetitions.

The quick vibrating lines I drew endlessly, without thinking, without hesitating, without pausing, by their very appearance gave promise of a 'visionary' drawing.

Very different my drawings after taking hashish. They were clumsy, involved, cut up, prematurely discontinued, always showing unfinished portions. The surfaces were composed of squares and polygons. A great deal was always missing.

In the same way the webs of the Zilla spider that has been drugged with atropine, and benzedrine, nembutal and marihuana (experiment made by Dr Peter Witt of Berne University) are always incomplete, the incompleteness the same for all spiders of the same family, different for each drug used.

Similarly incomplete, as could be expected, are the webs of spiders that have been induced to take the urine of schizophrenics, another proof that the disease is first of all physical, first of all a toxicosis.

Wouldn't it be more appropriate to try the experiment on the psychiatrists, rather than on the spiders?

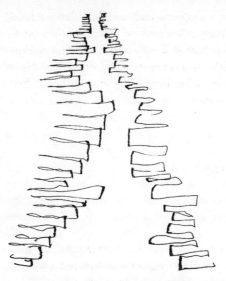

Michaux, drawing under mescaline

Michaux came to regard his attempts at abstract painting under mescaline (top) as a failure. By comparison, microscopic images of mescaline crystals (above) have a striking formal beauty. (EMB-Service for Publishers, Lucerne)

Drugs and music also have a profound and complex relationship in traditional cultures, and by comparison with the visual arts their interaction in modern cultures has been strikingly fertile. The first modern musical forms to become intimately connected with drugs were blues and jazz: here the white jazz musician Mezz Mezzrow describes his first experience of playing while stoned.

MEZZ MEZZROW
'Really the Blues'

(1946)

After I finished the weed I went back to the bandstand. Everything seemed normal and I began to play as usual. I passed a stick of gauge around for the other boys to smoke, and we started a set.

The first thing I noticed was that I began to hear my saxophone as though it was inside my head, but I couldn't hear much of the band in back of me, although I knew they were there. All the other instruments sounded like they were way off in the distance: I got the same sensation you'd get if you stuffed your ears with cotton and talked out loud. Then I began to feel the vibrations of the reed much more pronounced against my lip, and my head buzzed like a loudspeaker. I found I was slurring much better and putting just the right feeling into my phrases – I was really coming on. All the notes came easing out of my horn like they'd already been made up, greased and stuffed into the bell, so all I had to do was blow a little and send them on their way, one right after the other, never missing, never behind time, all without an ounce of effort. The phrases seemed to have more continuity to them and I was sticking to the theme without ever going tangent. I felt I could go on playing for years without running out of ideas and energy. There wasn't any struggle; it was all made-to-order and suddenly there wasn't a sour note or a discord in the world that could bother me. I began to feel very happy and sure of myself. With my loaded horn I could take all the fist-swinging, evil things in the world and bring them together in perfect harmony, spreading peace and joy and relaxation to all the keyed-up and punchy people everywhere. I began to preach my millenniums on my horn, leading all the sinners on to glory.

The other guys in the band were giggling and making cracks, but I couldn't talk with my mouthpiece between my lips, so I closed my eyes and drifted out to the audience with my music. The people were going crazy over the subtle changes in our playing; they couldn't dig what was happening but some kind of electricity was crackling in the air and it made them all glow and jump. Every so often I opened my eyes and found myself looking straight into a girl's face right in front of the bandstand, swinging there like a pendulum. She was an attractive, rose-complexioned chick, with wind-blown honey-coloured hair, and her flushed face was all twisted up with glee. That convulsed face of hers stirred up big waves of laughter in my stomach, waves that kept breaking loose and spreading up to my head, shaking my whole frame. I had to close my eyes fast to keep from exploding with the joy.

It's a funny thing about marihuana – when you first begin smoking it you see things in a wonderful soothing, easygoing new light. All of a sudden the world is stripped of its dirty gray shrouds and becomes one big bellyful of giggles, a spherical laugh, bathed in brilliant, sparkling colours that hit you like a heatwave. Nothing leaves you cold any more; there's a humorous tickle and great meaning in the least little thing, the twitch of somebody's little finger or the click of a beer glass. All your pores open like funnels, your nerve ends stretch their mouths wide, hungry and thirsty for new sights and sounds and sensations; and every sensation, when it comes, is the most exciting one you've ever had. You can't get enough of anything – you want to gobble up the whole goddamned universe just for an appetizer. Them first kicks are a killer, Jim.

. . .

Tea puts a musician in a real masterly sphere, and that's why so many jazzmen have used it. You look down on the other members of the band like an old mother hen surveying her brood of chicks; if one of them hits a sour note or comes up with a bad modulation, you just smile tolerantly and figure, oh well, he'll learn, it'll be better next time, give the guy a chance. Pretty soon you find yourself helping him out, trying to put him on the right track. The most terrific thing is this, that all the while you're playing, really getting off, your own accompaniment keeps flashing through your head, just like you were a one-man band.

You hear the basic tones of the theme and keep up your pattern of improvization without ever getting tangled up, giving out with a uniform sequence all the way. Nothing can mess you up. You hear everything at once and you hear it right. When you get that feeling of power and sureness, you're in a solid groove.

The synergy between marijuana and jazz has been explained on various
levels. For the journalist and spy writer Chapman Pincher, drawing on
the work of the neuroscientist Dr Grey Walter, it works by triggering
an atavistic response in the human brain.

CHAPMAN PINCHER
'Brain Doctor Explains Rhythm and "Reefer" Tie-up'

(*Daily Express*, 28 November 1951)

Is there a link between dope and hot jazz dancing – apart from
the fact that coloured men who peddle reefers can meet susceptible
teenagers at the jazz clubs?

Yes, there is scientific evidence for a much stronger link which involves
the basic nature of the human brain.

URGE TO MOVE

Reefers and rhythm seem to be directly connected with the minute
electric 'waves' continually generated by the brain surface. When the
rhythm of the music synchronizes with the rhythm of the 'brainwaves',
the jazz fans experience an almost compulsive urge to move their bodies
in sympathy. Dope may help the brain to 'tune in' to the rhythm more
sharply, thereby heightening the ecstasy of the dance.

This theory is based on brilliant brain research carried out chiefly by
Dr Grey Walter at the Burden Neurological Institute, Bristol. He has
proved that when some people watch a light flickering at a rate which
matches the rhythm of their 'brainwaves' they undergo a deep emotional
disturbance. Their muscles jerk so violently that the flickering light
sometimes causes convulsions.

Dr Grey Walter suggests that a steadily repeated sound, like the rapid
beating of a drum, may have the same effect if it happens to synchronize
with the 'brainwave' rhythm. He believes that this is why a nicely timed

tune automatically sets us toe-tapping. And why a sustained tom-tom beat will send susceptible dancers into ecstatic movements.

In jungle and in jazz club, dancers close their eyes to enhance the pleasure of the music as they sway. Grey Walter's researches also offer a possible explanation for this.

INCREASED THRILL

They have proved that closing the eyes immediately causes almost the whole of the brain surface to generate special waves at a regular rhythmic rate. The pattern of the 'brainwaves' is also affected by dope. So reefers may increase the thrill of the music by strengthening the jiver's 'rhythm reaction'. It is surely more than a coincidence that primitive peoples dope themselves with narcotic drugs before beginning their frenzied tribal jigs.

The relationship between marijuana and jazz (and also, typically, sex) was cemented by images from popular culture such as this cover illustration for the pulp paperback *Tenement Girl* (reprinted 1995 by Kitchen Sink Press)

For the writer Norman Mailer, both drugs and jazz are quintessential manifestations of the spontaneous 'anti-code' of the Hipster.

NORMAN MAILER
The White Negro

(1957)

The only Hip morality (but of course it is an ever-present morality) is to do what one feels whenever and wherever it is possible, and – this is how the war of the Hip and the Square begins – to be engaged in one primal battle: to open the limits of the possible for oneself, for oneself alone because that is one's need. Yet in widening the arena of the possible, one widens it reciprocally for others as well, so that the nihilistic fulfilment of each man's desire contains its antithesis of human co-operation.

If the ethic reduces to Know Thyself and Be Thyself, what makes it radically different from Socratic moderation with its stern conservative respect for the experience of the past is that the Hip ethic is immoderation, child-like in its adoration of the present (and indeed to respect the past means that one must also respect such ugly consequences of the past as the collective murders of the State). It is this adoration of the present which contains the affirmation of Hip, because its ultimate logic surpasses even the unforgettable solution of the Marquis de Sade to sex, private property, and the family, that all men and women have absolute but temporary rights over the bodies of all other men and women – the nihilism of Hip proposes as its final tendency that every social restraint and category be removed, and the affirmation implicit in the proposal is that man would then prove to be more creative than murderous and so would not destroy himself. Which is exactly what separates Hip from the authoritarian philosophies which now appeal to the conservative and liberal temper – what haunts the middle of the Twentieth Century is that faith in man has been lost, and the appeal of authority has been that it would restrain us from ourselves.

. . . and for the psychiatrist Charles Winick, director of the New York Musician's Clinic and specialist in heroin addiction among jazz musicians, the link between intoxication and inspiration was by no means clear.

CHARLES WINICK
'How High the Moon: Jazz and Drugs'

(*The Antioch Review*, Spring 1961)

What drug use can do for a musician, in addition to making it possible for him to get up on the bandstand at all, is to reinforce his feelings of belonging to a group if the other musicians in the same band are also on drugs. This special emotional contagion of jazz musicians who are 'on' may even be picked up by a musician who has not used drugs and is called a 'contact high'. The more the musician possesses this feeling of group belongingness, the better he is likely to play in a group. Some musician drug users take drugs for the opposite reason: to feel more alone. Marijuana, though it may heighten a musician's sense of humor and whimsy, may also interfere with his time sense. Critic John Hammond has described its effects on time sense as 'devastating'. This is little agreement on the specific effects which heroin has on musicianship, except that the drowsy state it sometimes induces is hardly likely to be musically stimulating. One heroin user said that 'If I'm playing something I know well, like "How High the Moon", heroin helps me to be more creative. But if I'm playing something new, the drug interferes.'

Another rationalization of musician addicts is that their music requires spontaneity and a special alertness which drugs enhance. As one saxophonist said, 'I have to keep alert because the sounds that go by will never come back. A painter or writer can go back and change things, but I can't get back the ten bars that I just played.'

The 1950s, which saw the greatest upsurge in the use of heroin by musicians, also saw considerable publicity about the heroin use of great jazz artists like vocalist Billie Holiday and alto saxophonist Charlie Parker. Some critics speculated on the extent to which the genius of these artists was linked with their drug use. Others noted that some drugs slow down the time sense and allow musicians to perform marvellously fast passages which do not sound fast to them, while some writers discussed how drugs provided otherwise unavailable wings which permitted a soloist to soar, possibly reflecting Parker's nickname of 'Bird'. The best available evidence suggests that opiates do not improve musicianship in any way, although a number of younger musicians may have drifted into drug use through their desire to emulate a musician-addict hero. Such young people may become addicted, but they do not become great artists.

Some musicians were more ready to pay heed to the crutches supplied by drugs than were others, and studies of the musicians who became addicts agree that they were the musicians who had the greatest difficulty in adjusting to the demands of reality. But the musician's ability or inability to adjust to life seems to be quite unrelated to his musical skill or talent. Although many great modern musicians took drugs, there were also many more very poor modern musicians who did so

. . .

Without engaging in special pleading on behalf of drug addict musicians, it is clear that there appears to be a kind of double standard when it comes to the use of drugs by writers and musicians. It is glamorous and interesting when writers and painters take drugs, but degrading and unfortunate when musicians take the same drugs. Law enforcement officials have not arrested noted writers such as Jack Kerouac, Allen Ginsberg, Aldous Huxley, or Norman Mailer, although all these writers have discussed drug use in public print. These writers are presumably carrying on the long and honourable tradition of writer drug use established by Coleridge and De Quincey, and their drug afflatus is regarded as appropriate. A jazz musician who wrote an article for a national magazine on the sensations of drug use, as some of these writers and at least two famous modern painters have done, would undoubtedly receive a visit from police authorities. Jazz drug use is seen as a reinforcement of the legend of the almost contemptible jazzman, while writer and painter drug use is seen as a reinforcement of the writer's and painter's contact with a higher order of inspiration. The contempt with which the jazzman is regarded can be seen in a story which famed trumpeter Dizzy Gillespie tells about being searched for drugs by police in Philadelphia. He refused to be searched and asked the police if they searched violinist Isaac Stern when he played in Philadelphia. Obviously the police applied different standards to Stern and to Gillespie, although both men are great musicians.

'Drug literature' is a term which is used freely and vaguely: does it mean literature about drugs, or literature inspired by drugs – or literature which appeals to readers on drugs? Drugs often appear in literature simply as plot devices or metaphors; by the same token, seemingly innocent texts can often be read as metaphors for drugs.

A text which is classically debated on this level is Alice in Wonderland*: do the hookah-smoking caterpillar, the mushroom and the strange cakes and potions constitute a drug text?*

LEWIS CARROLL
Alice's Adventures in Wonderland

(1865)

There seemed to be no use in waiting by the little door, so she went back to the table, half hoping she might find another key on it, or at any rate a book of rules for shutting people up like telescopes: this time she found a little bottle on it ('which certainly was not here before,' said Alice), and tied round the neck of the bottle was a paper label, with the words 'D R I N K M E' beautifully printed on it in large letters.

It was all very well to say 'Drink me', but the wise little Alice was not going to do *that* in a hurry. 'No, I'll look first,' she said, 'and see whether it's marked "*poison*" or not'; for she had read several nice little stories about children who had got burnt, and eaten up by wild beasts, and other unpleasant things, all because they *would* not remember the simple rules their friends had taught them: such as, that a red-hot poker will burn you if you hold it too long; and that, if you cut your finger *very* deeply with a knife, it usually bleeds; and she had never forgotten that, if you drink much from a bottle marked 'poison', it is almost certain to disagree with you, sooner or later.

However, this bottle was *not* marked 'poison', so Alice ventured to taste it, and, finding it very nice (it had, in fact, a sort of mixed flavour of cherry-tart, custard, pine-apple, roast turkey, toffy, and hot buttered toast), she very soon finished it off.

'What a curious feeling!' said Alice. 'I must be shutting up like a telescope!'

And so it was indeed: she was now only ten inches high, and her face brightened up at the thought that she was now the right size for going through the little door into that lovely garden. First, however, she waited for a few minutes to see if she was going to shrink any further: she felt a little nervous about this; 'for it might end, you know,' said Alice to herself, 'in my going out altogether, like a candle. I wonder what I should be like then?' And she tried to fancy what the flame of a candle looks like after the candle is blown out, for she could not remember ever having seen such a thing.

After a while, finding that nothing more happened, she decided on going into the garden at once; but, alas for poor Alice! when she got to the door, she found she had forgotten the little golden key, and when she went back to the table for it, she found she could not possibly reach it: she could see it quite plainly through the glass, and she tried her best to climb up one of the legs of the table, but it was too slippery; and when she had tired herself out with trying, the poor little thing sat down and cried.

'Come, there's no use in crying like that!' said Alice to herself rather sharply. 'I advise you to leave off this minute!' She generally gave herself very good advice (though she very seldom followed it), and sometimes she scolded herself so severely as to bring tears into her eyes; and once she remembered trying to box her own ears for having cheated herself in a game of croquet she was playing against herself, for this curious child was very fond of pretending to be two people. 'But it's no use now,' thought poor Alice, 'to pretend to be two people! Why, there's hardly enough of me left to make *one* respectable person!'

Soon her eye fell on a little glass box that was lying under the table: she opened it, and found in it a very small cake, on which the words 'EAT ME' were beautifully marked in currants. 'Well, I'll eat it,' said Alice, 'and if it makes me grow larger, I can reach the key; and if it makes me grow smaller, I can creep under the door: so either way I'll get into the garden, and I don't care which happens!'

She ate a little bit, and said anxiously to herself 'Which way? Which way?', holding her hand on the top of her head to feel which way it was growing; and she was quite surprised to find that she remained the same size. To be sure, this is what generally happens when one eats cake; but Alice had got so much into the way of expecting nothing but out-of-the-way things to happen, that it seemed quite dull and stupid for life to go on in the common way.

So she set to work, and very soon finished off the cake.

*Carroll/Dodgson scholars insist that the author never took drugs –
although he was undoubtedly an eccentric self-medicator, taking substances like aconite and arsenic as well as homeopathic remedies, he
was also a virulent anti-smoker. None the less, the drug culture of the
1960s insisted that the book contained a hidden message.*

GRACE SLICK
'White Rabbit'

(1967, from *Surrealistic Pillow*, Jefferson Airplane)

One pill makes you larger
And one pill makes you small
And the ones that mother gives you
Don't do anything at all
Go ask Alice
When she's ten feet tall
And if you go chasing rabbits
And you know you're going to fall
Tell 'em a hookah smoking caterpillar
Has given you the call
Call Alice
When she was just small
When the men on the chessboard
Get up and tell you where to go
And you've just had some kind of mushroom
And your mind is moving low
Go ask Alice
I think she'll know
When logic and proportion
Have fallen sloppy dead
And the White Knight is talking backwards
And the Red Queen's off with her head
Remember what the dormouse said
Feed your head
Feed your head
Feed your head

It now seems likely that, though Dodgson did not take psychoactive drugs himself, he was drawing on a classic work of Victorian drug scholarship.

MICHAEL CARMICHAEL
'Wonderland Revisited'

(1997)

According to his diaries, Dodgson only visited the great Oxford library, the Bodleian, on one occasion, 18 June 1862. Sixteen days later, he told the drug-saturated tale of Wonderland to the three daughters of Dean and Mrs Liddell: Alice, Ina and Edith. Dodgson's visit to the Bodleian coincides perfectly with Wasson's suggestion that he had been influenced by the books of Mordecai Cooke, which were both on deposit at the library at the time of Dodgson's singular visit.

While performing the research for this essay, I examined the Bodleian copies of Cooke's two books. The physical condition of the earlier one, *The Seven Sisters of Sleep*, provides important evidence for Wasson's theory. At first glance, the Bodleian copy of *The Seven Sisters of Sleep* appeared to be unread, for the pages were joined together at the top. For a regular reader at the Bodleian it is uncommon to find unopened volumes from the nineteenth century, although I have found several. The books were originally deposited in uncut form, and many are still unread to the present day. However, on closer examination, I discovered that certain pages had been opened by an earlier reader. The first pages of the book that contained the table of contents had been torn apart quite carelessly, the tops of their pages are jagged and broken, apparently pulled apart rapidly and forcibly by hand as some reader had all too eagerly wished to examine the table of contents. The other signatures in the book are intact and uncut, except for the one containing the ultimate chapter, 'The Exile of Siberia'. Here the tops of the pages are smoothly cut, as if they have been carefully and deliberately severed, coolly and specifically selected for their subject matter. Was Charles Dodgson the first reader to open these few pages in the Bodleian copy of *The Seven Sisters of Sleep*? The question is pertinent, for the chapter deals with the use of magic mushrooms as drugs of vision and ecstasy by the tribal shamans in Siberia, and Dodgson was fascinated by Russia. The Crimean War made a deep and vivid impression on him in the mid-1850s. His diaries resound with notes about the war in Sebastopol, Balaklava and the Malakoff Tower. He viewed an exhibition of Crimean photographs in Ripon and made a note of the signing of the peace. In later years, he invented a game for children he called 'The Ural Mountains'. The only journey Dodgson ever undertook outside of Britain was to Russia. Dodgson was a fully qualified Russophile, and Cooke's chapter on Siberian mushroom shamanism would have drawn his immediate attention. Dodgson would have been immediately attracted to Cooke's *The Seven Sisters of Sleep* for two more obvious reasons: he had seven sisters and he was a lifelong insomniac.

Cooke's Seven Sisters of Sleep *does indeed provide clues to many of Alice's extravagant and hallucinatory experiences.*

MORDECAI COOKE
The Seven Sisters of Sleep

(1860)

The most singular circumstance connected with the history of this fungus is the place it occupies as a substitute for these narcotics known in other parts of the world, and which an ungenial northern climate fails to produce. What the coca is to the Bolivian, and opium to the Chinese – the areca to the Malay, and hashish to the African – the tobacco to the inhabitants of Europe and America, and the thorn-apple to those of the Andes – is the fly agaric to the natives of Siberia and Kamchatka. Why it has been called by this name has arisen from its use as a fly poison. Never having seen those dipterous insects while under its influence, we cannot detail the symptoms it produces.

This poisonous fungus has some resemblance to the one generally eaten in this country, yet there are also striking points of difference. As, for instance, the gills are white instead of pinkish red, inclining to brown, and the cap or pileus, which is rather flat, is generally of a livid red colour, sprinkled with angular lighter coloured worts. These are distinctions broad enough to prevent any one having the use of his eyes, and who has ever seen the edible mushroom being deceived into belief that the fungus thus briefly described is identical with the delicacy of our English tables.

These fungi are collected by those who indulge in them narcotically, during the hot, or rather summer months, and afterwards hung up to dry in the open air. Or they may be left to ripen and dry in the ground, and are afterwards collected. When left standing until they are dried, they are said to possess more powerful narcotic properties than when dried artificially. The juice of the whortleberry in which this substance has been steeped, acquires thereby the intoxicating properties of strong wine.

The method of using this singular substance is to roll it up in the form of a bolus and swallow it without any mastication, as one would swallow a large pill. It is swallowed thus on principle, not that its flavour would be unpleasant, as compound colocynth might be when masticated, but because it is stated to agree ill with the stomach when that operation is performed. Nature is jealous of her rights, and it would appear from experience, that the gastronomic regions expect to receive all other supplies well triturated, except these – amanita and pill colocynth – which are both expected equally alike to arrive at the regions below without mutilation.

A day's intoxication may thus be procured at the expense of one good-sized bolus, compounded of one large or two small toadstools; and this intoxication is affirmed to be, not only cheap, which is a consideration, but also remarkably pleasant. It commences an hour or so after the bolus has been swallowed.

The effects which this singular narcotic produces are, some of them, similar to that produced by intoxicating liquors, others resemble the effects of hashish. At first, it generally produces cheerfulness, afterwards giddiness and drunkenness, ending occasionally in the entire loss of consciousness. The natural inclinations of the individual become stimu-lated. The dancer executes a *pas d'extravagance*, the musical indulge in a song, the chatterer divulges all his secrets, the oratorical delivers himself of a philippic, and the mimic indulges in caricature. Erroneous impressions of size and distance are common occurrences, equally with the swallower of amanita and hemp. The experiences of M. Moreau with hashish are repeated with the fungus-eaters of Siberia; a straw lying in the road becomes a formidable object, to overcome which, a leap is taken sufficient to clear a barrel of ale, or the prostrate trunk of a British oak.

Alice and the White Rabbit: 'Erroneous impressions of size and distance'
inspired by mushroom hallucinations?

Does taking drugs help writers? The British poet Thom Gunn found that producing poetry inspired by his experiences with LSD was a profound challenge.

THOM GUNN
The Occasions of Poetry: Essays in Criticism and Autobiography

(1982, 1985)

When I returned to San Francisco it was with half thoughts of ultimately moving back to London. But San Francisco in mid-1965 was only a little behind London in the optimism department and was prepared to go much further. It was the time, after all, not only of the Beatles but of LSD as well. Raying out from the private there was a public excitement at the new territories that were being opened up in the mind. Golden Gate Park, the scene of so many mass trips and rock concerts, seemed like

> The first field of a glistening continent
> Each found by trusting Eden in the human.

We tripped also at home, on rooftops, at beaches and ranches; some went to the opera loaded on acid, others tried it as passengers on gliders, every experience was illuminated by the drug. (The best account of these years in San Francisco is to be found in issue no. 207 of the *Rolling Stone*, a brilliant history put together ten years later.) These were the fullest years of my life, crowded with discovery both inner and outer, as we moved between ecstasy and understanding. It is no longer fashionable to praise LSD, but I have no doubt at all that it has been of the utmost importance to me, both as a man and as a poet. I learned from it, for example, a lot of information about myself that I had somehow blocked from my own view. And almost all of the poems that were to be in my next book, *Moly*, written between 1965 and 1970, have in some way however indirect to do with it.

The acid experience was essentially non-verbal. Yet it was clearly important, and I have always believed that it should be possible to write poetry about any subject that was of importance to you. Eventually a friend, Belle Randall, and I decided that it was time to stop generalizing the origin of the acid poem. (Her book that resulted from this decision was *101 Different Ways of Playing Solitaire*, not published until 1973.) By 1968 taking the drug was no longer an unusual experience, probably hundreds of thousands had had at least one experience with it, and many more knew about it without having taken it, so to write about its effects was not any more to be obscure or to make pretentious claims to experience closed to most readers.

Metre seemed to be the proper form for the LSD-related poems, though at first I didn't understand why. Later I rationalized about it thus. The acid trip is unstructured, it opens you up to countless possibilities, you hanker after the infinite. The only way I could give myself any control over the presentation of these experiences, and so could be true to them, was by trying to render the infinite through the finite, the unstructured through the structured. Otherwise there was the danger of the experience's becoming so distended that it would simply unravel like fog before wind in the unpremeditated movement of free verse. Thomas Mann, speaking about how he wrote *Doctor Faustus*, tells of 'filtering' the character of the genius-composer through the more limited but thus more precise consciousness of the bourgeois narrator. I was perhaps doing something like Mann.

Gunn described his poem 'Being Born' as 'an anthology of things I'd noticed on acid'. The title refers to his sensation of two people standing slightly behind him, who he interprets as 'the doctor and midwife when I was being born'.

THOM GUNN
'Being Born'
(1970)

BEING BORN

The tanker slips behind a distant ridge
And, on the blue, a formal S of smoke
Still hangs. I send myself out on my look.
But just beyond my vision, at the edge

To left and right, there reach or seem to reach
Margins, vague pillars, not quite visible,
Or unfleshed giant presences so tall
They stretch from top to bottom, sky to beach.

What memory loosed, of man and boundary blended?
One tug, one more, and I could have it here.
– Yes that's it, ah, two shapes begin to clear:
Midwife and doctor faintly apprehended.

I let them both almost solidify,
Their quiet activity bit by bit outlined,
Clean hand and calm eye, but still view behind,
Bright crinkling foam, headland, and level sky.

I think of being grabbed from the warm sand,
Shiny red bawling newborn with clenched eyes,
Slapped into life; and as it clarifies
My friends recede, alas the dwindling land.

Must I rewrite my childhood? What jagg'd growth
What mergings of authority and pain,
Invading breath, must I live through again?
Are they the past or yet to come or both?

Both. Between moving air and moving ocean
The tanker pushes, squat and purposeful,
But elsewhere. And the smoke. Though now air's pull
Begins to suck it into its own motion.

There is a furnace that connects them there.
The metal, guided, cuts through fall and lift,
While the coils from it widen, spread, and drift
To feed the open currents of the air.

The literary philosopher Walter Benjamin found that hashish turned him into an 'enraptured prose-being'.

WALTER BENJAMIN
'Hashish in Marseilles'

(1979)

To begin to solve the riddle of the ecstasy of trance, one ought to meditate on Ariadne's thread. What joy in the mere act of unrolling a ball of thread. And this joy is very deeply related to the joy of trance, as to that of creation. We go forward; but in so doing we not only discover the twists and turns of the cave, but also enjoy this pleasure of discovery against the background of the other, rhythmical bliss of unwinding the thread. The certainty of unrolling an artfully wound skein – is that not the joy of all productivity, at least in prose? And under hashish we are enraptured prose-beings in the highest power.

A deeply submerged feeling of happiness that came over me afterward, on a square off the Cannebière where rue Paradis opens on to a park, is more difficult to recall than everything that went before. Fortunately I find on my newspaper the sentence 'One should scoop sameness from reality with a spoon.' Several weeks earlier I had noted another, by Johannes V. Jensen, which appeared to say something similar: 'Richard was a young man with understanding for everything in the world that was of the same kind.' This sentence had pleased me very much. It enabled me now to confront the political, rational sense it had had for me earlier with the individual magical meaning of my experience the day before. Whereas Jensen's sentence amounted, as I had understood it, to saying that things are as we know them to be, thoroughly mechanized and rationalized, the particular being confined today solely to nuances, my new insight was entirely different. For I saw only nuances, yet these were the same. I immersed myself in contemplation of the sidewalk before me, which, through a kind of unguent with which I covered it, could have been, precisely as these very stones, also the sidewalk of Paris. One often speaks of stones instead of bread. These stones were the bread of my imagination, which was suddenly seized by a ravenous hunger to taste what is the same in all places and countries.

And yet I thought with immense pride of sitting here in Marseilles in a hashish trance; of who else might be sharing my intoxication this evening, how few. Of how I was incapable of fearing future misfortune, future solitude, for hashish would always remain. The music from a nearby nightclub that I had been following played a part in this stage. G. rode past me in a cab. It happened suddenly, exactly as, earlier, from the shadows of the boat, U. had suddenly detached himself in the form of a harbour loafer and pimp. But there were not only known faces. Here, while I was in the state of deepest trance, two figures – citizens, vagrants, what do I know? – passed me as 'Dante and Petrarch'. 'All men are brothers.' So began a train of thought that I am no longer able to pursue. But its last link was certainly much less banal than its first and led on perhaps to images of animals.

. . . while Alethea Hayter's survey of opium-using writers – De Quincey, Coleridge, Poe, Wilkie Collins and others – suggests that their drug use took from them more than it gave.

ALETHEA HAYTER
Opium and the Romantic Imagination: Addiction and Creativity in De Quincey, Coleridge, Baudelaire and Others

(1968)

We know that De Quincey took opium. We know what he afterwards wrote. We do not know what he would have written if he had never taken it. It can be no more than a hypothesis that the action of opium, though it can never be a substitute for innate imagination, can uncover that imagination while it is at work in a way which might enable an exceptionally gifted and self-aware writer to observe and learn from his own mental processes.

But it could only do so at a price which no writer of integrity would ultimately be prepared to pay. I am not referring to moral integrity, but to the poet's responsibility to his own art. One of the most obvious effects of opium addiction on a writer's powers is that it induces indolence, absence of feeling, a state in which the power to observe is detached from the power to sympathize with what is observed. At its very outset, this state of mind can be useful to a poet; there are times when he needs detachment. But in the long run it is deadly. The dislocation of objects and events from the feelings which they normally arouse is in the end destructive of poetic truth. In *Dejection* Coleridge gave, once for all, the classic description of this creeping death of the imaginative impulse, but Crabbe and Keats can also be seen fighting against it, and Poe and Collins yielding to it, and to what comes in its train – the tendency that Coleridge called 'histrionism', the resort to violent attitudes because you no longer have normal feelings. Nearly all the opium-addicted writers indulged in descriptions of violence, gruesomeness, insanity, extremes of fear. The action of opium, by its exaggeration and distortion of normal feelings, may give to one who takes it unusual insights into the mental experience of the wicked, the insane, the terrified, the tortured, the dying, which may be useful and enlightening to a writer; but it only enables him to observe, not to sympathize with, these mental experiences. He feels himself to be a pariah; he recognizes the other pariahs; but he cannot hold out a hand even to them. He is insulated from his fellow-men, and has renounced the obligation of commitment.

Nor is he any longer committed to the physical world in which he lives. Landscapes, which once to him were beautiful in themselves and part of a significant whole, are now only an expression of his mood. No identities are stable and separate, they combine and engraft on each other. There are masks and disguises everywhere, and under the mask there may be only another mask, or nothing at all. Many of these writers felt that they had been endowed with an exceptional insight into the secret of the universe, and could reveal its philosophical framework for the enlightenment of mankind; but the great work could never be finished, because the power to hold things together had gone, everything disintegrated, fell away into fragments. It did not always seem so to them themselves. Among the powers that opium damaged was the power to detect damage; judgment and self-criticism do not make their absence felt by him who has lost them.

It is the great plans that are destroyed. Writers can still write, and in fragments write well, when they have been addicted to opium for many years; and this is not necessarily only during withdrawal periods, though these do in some cases provide the energy to commit to paper the imaginative creations which may otherwise stay uselessly imprisoned in the mind. But the holding together has gone, the great luminous images which shed light and pattern across all the wide tracts of a writer's imagination do not radiate any more. The images are still there, but some are darkened, some are luridly spotlit, all are enclosed. The effect of what Baudelaire called the *'paysage opiacé'* is produced by blotting out some of the features of a normal landscape of imagery – the groups of people, the flowing streams, the roads, the cottages, the woods, the sun – and highlighting the solitary figure, the stagnant pools, the cliffs, the castles, the stone faces and slimy claws that show for a moment at the mouths of caves. It is not another planet, it is our own, but in a light of eclipse. The foregoing pages have shown that certain images – pariahs, harlot-ogresses, quicksands, petrified landscapes, freezing cold, drowned or buried temples, watching eyes – do recur in the works of the opium-addicted writers. Some of these images – the fairly obvious poppy, the honey-dew, the temptress, the buried temple – may be conscious or unconscious equivalents for opium itself. Some – the ice-cold, the quicksands, the petrifaction, the floating lovers – may be connected with physical symptoms produced by opium dosage or withdrawal. Some – the idea of the outcast, the images of watching eyes and hybrid shape-changing creatures – may express the addict's isolation and suspicion. None of the images is peculiar to the writing of addicts, and none of the addict-writers use only these images and no others; but they form a recognizable pattern.

Anais Nin, who took LSD in the 1950s, felt on reflection that it had offered nothing new or valuable to her writing.

ANAÏS NIN
'The Diary of Anaïs Nin 1947–1955'

(1955)

After my experience with LSD I began to examine whether it was an unfamiliar world, inaccessible except to the chemical alterations of reality.

I found the origin of most of the images either in my work or in literary works by other writers.

In *House of Incest*, written in 1935, objects become liquefied and I describe them as seen through water. There is a reference to Byzantium and I was brought up on volumes of *Voyages Autour du Monde*, which had images of Cambodia, Thailand, Bali, India, and Japan, and which remained forever in my memory. I have listened to countless recordings of Balinese music, tapes made by Colin McFee.

Images of split selves appear in *House of Incest*.

The image of loneliness on another planet is derived from my frequent reading of *The Little Prince* by Antoine de Saint-Exupéry.

In *House of Incest* there is mention of crystals, precious stones: 'The muscovite like a bride, the pyrite, the hydrous silica, the cinnabar, the azurite of benefic Jupiter, the malachite, all crushed together, melted jewels, melted planets.'

The sensation of becoming gold is one I had many times when sunbathing on the sands; the sun's reflection came through my closed eyelids, and I felt myself becoming gold.

I could find correlations all through my writing, find the sources of the images in past dreams, in reading, in memories of travel, in actual experience, such as the one I had once in Paris when I was so exalted by life that I felt I was not touching the ground, I felt I was sliding a few inches away from the sidewalk.

Therefore, I felt, the chemical did not reveal an unknown world. What it did was to shut out the quotidian world as an interference and leave you alone with your dreams and fantasies and memories. In this way it made it easier to gain access to the subconscious life. But obviously, by way of writing, reveries, waking dreams, and night dreams, I had visited all those landscapes. The drug added a synthesis of color, sound, image, a simultaneous fusion of all the senses which I had constantly aspired to in my writing and often achieved.

I reached the fascinating revelation that this world opened by LSD was accessible to the artist by way of art. The gold sun mobile of Lippold could create a mood if one were receptive enough, if one let the image penetrate the body and turn the body to gold. All the chemical did was to remove resistance, to make one permeable to the image, and to make the body receptive by shutting out the familiar landscape which prevented the dream from invading us.

What has happened that people lose contact with such images, visions, sensations, and have to resort to drugs which ultimately harm them? They have been immured, the taboo on dream, reverie, visions, and sensual receptivity deprives them of access to the subconscious. I am grateful for my natural access. But when I discuss this with Huxley, he is rather irritable: 'You're fortunate enough to have a natural access to your subconscious life, but other people need drugs and should have them.'

This does not satisfy me because I feel that if I have a natural access others could have it too

. . .

I will not be just a tourist in the world of images, just watching images passing by which I cannot live in, make love to, possess as permanent sources of joy and ecstasy.

A study performed in 1966 of the value of psychedelic drugs in creative endeavours offers a series of concise arguments for and against their usefulness.

W. HARMAN ET AL.
Psychedelic Agents in Creative Problem-solving: A Pilot Study

(1966)

TABLE 1

SOME REPORTED CHARACTERISTICS OF THE PSYCHEDELIC EXPERIENCE

Those Supporting Creativity	Those Hindering Creativity
1 Increased access to unconscious data.	1 Capacity for logical thought processes may be diminished.
2 More fluent free association; increased ability to play spontaneously with hypotheses, metaphors, paradox, transformations, relationships, etc.	2 Ability to consciously direct concentration may be reduced.
3 Heightened ability for visual imagery and fantasy.	3 Inability to control imaginary and conceptual sequences.
4 Relaxation and openness.	4 Anxiety and agitation.
5 Sensory inputs more acutely perceived.	5 Outputs (verbal and visual communication abilities may be constricted).
6 Heightened empathy with external processes, objects, and people.	6 Tendency to focus upon 'inner problems' of a personal nature.
7 Aesthetic sensibility heightened.	7 Experienced beauty may lessen tension to obtain aesthetic experience in the act of creation.
8 Enhanced 'sense of truth', ability to 'see through' false solutions and phony data.	8 Tendency to become absorbed in hallucinations and illusions.
9 Lessened inhibition, reduced tendency to censor own thoughts by premature negative judgment.	9 Finding the best solution may seem unimportant.
10 Motivation may be heightened by suggestion and providing the right set.	10 'This-worldly' tasks may seem trivial, and hence motivation may be decreased.

(from *Altered States of Consciousness*, edited by Charles T. Tart, Harper & Row, San Francisco, 1969)

5

Storming Heaven: Drugs and Pleasure

Pleasure was probably the simple reason why mankind first started to use drugs in prehistory, and the same simple reason probably accounts for most of their use today. Mankind is not alone: many animals also use drugs for this reason (see p. 189).

The immediate and desirable alteration of brain chemistry has always made elaborate processes and rituals for drug-taking worthwhile, however bizarre they may seem to outsiders. The Classical historian Herodotus recorded with amazement the process whereby the Scythians – nomads from the homeland of cannabis in Central Asia – contrived to inhale the plant's smoke.

HERODOTUS
The Histories

(*c.* 450 BC)

Afer a burial the Scythians go through a process of cleaning themselves; they wash their heads with soap, and their bodies in a vapour-bath, the nature of which I will describe. On a framework of three sticks, meeting at the top, they stretch pieces of woollen cloth, taking care to get the joins as perfect as they can, and inside this little tent they put a dish with red-hot stones in it. Now, hemp grows in Scythia, a plant resembling flax, but much coarser and taller. It grows wild as well as under cultivation, and the Thracians make clothes from it very like linen ones – indeed, one must have much experience in these matters to be able to distinguish between the two, and anybody who has never seen a piece of cloth made from hemp, will suppose it to be of linen. They take some hemp seed, creep into the tent, and throw the seed on to the hot stones. At once it begins to smoke, giving off a vapour unsurpassed by any vapour-bath one could find in Greece. The Scythians enjoy it so much that they howl with pleasure.

*The association of cannabis with pleasure began in the distant past
and has continued unbroken to the present. In Rabelais's medieval
compendium of sensual delights,* Gargantua and Pantagruel, *it appears
in the guise of 'the herb Pantagruelion'.*

FRANÇOIS RABELAIS
The Histories of Gargantua and Pantagruel

(1532–4)

Pantagruelion is prepared at the autumn equinox in different
ways according to the fancies of the people and to national preferences.
Pantagruel's first instructions were to strip the stalk of its leaves and
seeds; to soak it in still – not in running – water for five days, if the
weather is fine and the water warm, and for nine to twelve if the weather
is cloudy and the water cold; then to dry it in the sun, and afterwards
in the shade, remove the outside, separate the fibres – in which, as has
been said, lies all its use and value – from the woody part, which is
useless except to make a fire blaze, as kindling, or for blowing up pigs'
bladders to amuse children. Sometimes also gluttons will find a sly use
for them, as syphons to suck up new wine through the bung-hole

. . .

Pantagruelion owes its name also to its virtues and peculiarities. For as
Pantagruel has been the exemplar and paragon of perfect jollity – I don't
suppose that any one of you boozers is in any doubt about that – so in
Pantagruelion I recognize so many virtues, so much vigour, so many per-
fections, so many admirable effects, that if its full worth had been known
when, as the Prophet tells us, the trees elected a wooden king to reign
over them and govern them, it would no doubt have gained the majority
of their votes and suffrages. Shall I go further? If Oxylus, son of Oreius,
had begotten it on his sister Hamadryas, he would have taken more delight
in its worth alone than in his eight children, so celebrated by our mytho-
logists, who have caused their names to be eternally remembered

. . .

Arabians, Indians, and Sabaeans,
Cease your praise, sing no more paeans
To incense, myrrh or ebony.
Come here a nobler plant to see.
We'll give you seed to take away;
And if it grow with you, then say
A million prayers of thanks to Heaven;
And swear the realm of France, that's given
The sacred Pantagruelion's
The happiest beneath the sun.

For the psychologist Moreau de Tours (see p. 19) cannabis, in the form
of hashish, produced the quintessence of pleasure.

JACQUES-JOSEPH MOREAU DE TOURS
Hashish and Mental Illness

(1845)

It is really *happiness* that hashish gives, and by that I mean
mental joy, not sensual joy as one might be tempted to believe. This is
indeed very curious, and one can draw strange conclusions – this one
among others, that all joy, all contentment, even though its cause is
strictly mental, deeply spiritual, and highly idealistic, could well be in
reality a purely physical sensation, developed physiologically, exactly
like those caused by hashish. At least, if one relies on inner feelings,
there is no distinction to be made between these two orders of sensations,
in spite of the diversity of the causes to which they are related – for the
hashish user is happy, not in the manner of the glutton, of the ravenous
man who satisfies his appetite, or even of the hedonist who gratifies his
desires, but in the manner, for example, of the man who hears news
that compounds his joys, of the miser counting his treasures, of the
gambler whom luck favours, or the ambitious man whom success
intoxicates.

*. . . and Géza Csáth (see p. 90) insisted that the levels of pleasure attained
with the use of drugs such as opium were worth any price.*

GÉZA CSÁTH
'Opium'

(1910, translated 1980)

Pleasure erases contours, dissolves senselessness, freeing us from
the shackles of space, halting the rattling of the clock's seconds: it lifts
us on its sultry undulations to the highest reaches of Life.

There to remain, if but for moments, trembling and fearful of coming
down – misery indeed. Yet most people count themselves rewarded
with the pittance of those few moments. What else is there for them?
They haven't the strength or the courage to risk themselves in a splendid,
enduring pleasure that rocks them to eternity. This risk is cheap, absurdly
small. True, ten hammering hours of malicious, murderous daylight go
tediously by; but for those fourteen evening and night hours we experience a portion of eternity's mystery and timeless wonder.

In that time we recognize life's deepest meaning; the opacity, the
darkness is made bright. Like the lips of fresh and gentle girls, sound
like kisses showers our bodies. In our spine, in our skull, colour and
line buzz new yet ancient and clear. And now, *no longer resembling* the
colour and line to which we are accustomed, they reveal the grand
secrets hidden in forms. That primitive and so very flawed knowledge
of Life we had gained through sight, hearing, smell, taste and touch is
now improved, and made whole. We are given the chance to learn the
truth of Life inherent in each of us, all of truth, perfected, beyond the
faculties of our senses. A truth inexpressible in words or by concepts
and judgments, just as the senses cannot recognize it. What right have
I to say I know the weight of a cube, when I have merely seen but never
lifted it? The same is true of one who has only seen, heard, smelled,
tasted, touched: he has no right to say he's lived. Pleasure alone can
give us knowledge of things and God's joy. Yet may we say that God's
joy endures for a moment only? Yes, for that is what He doles out to
fools and cowards. But those who, desirous of more, deserve more, they
have a chance to steal from eternity – through noble, heroic daring.

They must forgo the capacity to see and hear well. Opium, horrible and blessed connection of pleasure, destroys our organs and senses. The healthy appetite and the bourgeois sensation of feeling good and tired have to be sacrificed. The eyes water, the ears ring. Objects, printed words, people look faded. Sounds and words wander randomly in the tiny mechanisms of the organs of hearing.

Stop those miserable, inferior little contraptions!

In some quiet little room where sounds die on thick carpeting and stained glass scatters the lamp's low flickering flame – lie down there on your back. Shut your eyes. And the tiny opium pipe will lead you to where we live for the sake of Life alone and nothing more. That is after all the only be-all and end-all. And even our miserly God gave each one of his pitiable worms a few seconds of life, just to live to go on living to procreate. And the new worm gets his share of a second, too.

So costly an item is the essence of Life that whole generations and centuries can be given but a single hour of it.

Whoever agrees to this also agrees to die before he's ever even been born. However, those who can grow to be men, who have taken things into account as befits their pride, should seize fourteen hours of it a day, every day. Those fourteen hours are equivalent to eight thousand years in the lives of four hundred generations. But let's call it only five thousand. Hence in one single day I live five thousand years. In one single year I live about two million years. Suppose you pick up on opium as a strong, well-developed adult and take good care of your health – best left to a skilled doctor – why, then you can live for ten years. And then at twenty million years of age you can let your head fall on the icy pillow of eternal annihilation.

As for those who don't wish to pay the price, who don't desire twenty million years of life eternal – let them live a hundred years increasing and multiplying.

The reaction of cats to catnip and other plants suggests that the physical pleasure produced by drugs can resemble and even surpass sexual ecstasy.

RONALD K. SIEGEL

Intoxication: Life in Pursuit of Artificial Paradise

(1989)

Cats are attracted to catnip purely for reasons of chemical pleasure. Catnip (*Nepeta cataria*) is a perennial herb with downy leaves and a strong mint odour. It is native to such diverse locales as Scandinavia, Kashmir, Canada, and New Jersey. Today it is widely cultivated throughout the world. Surprisingly, there is no overlap in the distribution of the catnip plant and its namesake. Yet when placed near catnip, cats will seek the plant and return to it each day. The behaviour is illustrative of our own attraction to drugs that may be alien to our immediate environment but that, once introduced, evoke strong natural feelings. Unlike the birds seeking berries, the cats are exhibiting deliberate intoxications.

When cats encounter the plant, their first reaction is to sniff. To humans, fresh catnip has the odour of mint mixed with fresh-cut grass or alfalfa. In the dried plant, or in commercial cat toys, the alfalfa odour predominates. Upon reaching the plant source, the cat commences to lick and sometimes chew the leaves, in the second stage of the response. The chewing is often interrupted when the cat momentarily stares into space with a blank expression, then quickly shakes its head from side to side. In the third stage the cat will usually rub against the plant with its chin and cheek. Last, there is a 'head over' roll with rubbing of the entire body. Extremely sensitive cats may also flip from side to side by rolling over on their backs. The four-stage reaction runs its fixed course in approximately ten minutes.

Biologists have referred to this intoxication as an example of animal addiction to pleasure behaviour. The nature of the pleasurable intoxication becomes increasingly evident when high doses of catnip in the form of concentrated extracts are offered to the animals. The subsequent reactions are intense: cats head-twitch violently, salivate profusely, and show other signs of central nervous system excitation. One sign is sexual stimulation. Males have spontaneous erections while females adopt mating stances, complete with vocalization and 'love-biting' of any available object.

The similarity of the catnip response to the normal sexual behaviour of cats is striking. The presentation of catnip results in a rolling pattern of behaviour that is exhibited by oestrous females during the course of normal sexual displays. These displays have prompted naturalists to speculate that catnip once served the evolutionary function in the wild of preparing cats for sex, a natural springtime aphrodisiac

. . .

Matatabi, which the Japanese call a pleasure plant, does the same trick for cats even better. This plant contains secondary compounds closely related in chemical structure and behavioural activity to nepetal-actones. Concentrated *matatabi* chemicals, in doses unavailable to the cats in the natural plant, were placed on cotton balls and presented to the large cats at the Osaka Zoo. After an initial exposure, the cats became so eager for more that they would ignore whatever else they were doing – eating, drinking, or even having sexual intercourse – whenever the chemicals were made available. They displayed a very intense 'catnip' response, then rolled on their backs where they stayed for some time 'in complete ecstasy'.

. . . and, given that sex and drug use are not mutually exclusive, it is no surprise that they have been practised together across cultures and throughout history. In contemporary culture, their iconography frequently overlaps – a pattern recognizable even in early silent cinema like D. W. Griffiths' Broken Blossoms.

MAREK KOHN
Dope Girls: The Birth of the British Drug Underground

(1992)

*B*roken Blossoms is the tragic story of Cheng Huan (played by Richard Barthelmess), a pacific Chinese poet who comes to England; his purpose to bring Oriental spiritual enlightenment to a continent that has plunged itself into the barbarity of war. Its brutalization is underlined at one point by a casual reference to 'only 40,000 dead this week' – a remarkably sharp directorial sally, especially since a state of war still technically obtained during the period in which the film was made. Western brutality is personified in the figure of Battling Burrows, an East End prizefighter who terrorizes and beats his daughter Lucy, played by Lillian Gish.

Cheng Huan settles in Limehouse, where contact between the races is shown to have a corrupting effect. A magnificently composed establishing scene . . . shows white women in an opium den, surrounded by Chinamen and other men of colour. Opium dissolves the natural barriers between the races; the focus is unequivocally upon the willing absorption of the women into this smoky promiscuity.

A series of close-ups show, first, white women seated with examples of different races; then the woman at the centre of the composition is shown reclining alone. Her eyelids close, her lips part and her head tilts back in voluptuous abandonment, the cause emphasized by cuts to the Chinese man with his pipe in the foreground of the tableau. In the middle of this company, her solitary, self-gratifying pleasure is more shocking still than the intercourse – the social form implying the possibility of the sexual – between the other women and the men. Griffith shrewdly identified an aspect of drugtaking that remains an unspoken source of distaste for outsiders, the attainment of ecstatic sensual states in company.

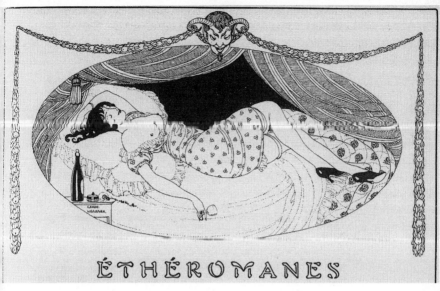

ÉTHÉROMANES

Eroticized images of drug-taking; an 'ether maniac' from turn-of-the-century Paris. (Mary Evans Picture Library)

*Despite this legacy, the serious-minded pioneers of the 1960s drug
culture were slow to appreciate the age-old association of sex and drugs.*

TIMOTHY LEARY
Flashbacks: A Personal and Cultural History of an Era

(1983)

I was at that time a successful robot – respected at Harvard,
clean-cut, witty, and, in that inert culture, unusually creative. Though
I had attained the highest ambition of the young American intellectual,
I was totally cut off from body and senses. My clothes had been
obediently selected to fit the young professional image. Even after one
hundred drug sessions I routinely listened to pop music, drank martinis,
ate what was put before me.

I had 'appreciated' art by pushing my body around to 'sacred places',
but this tourism had nothing to do with direct aesthetic sensation.
My nervous system was cocooned in symbols; the event was always
second-hand. Art was an academic concept, an institution. The idea
that one should live one's life as a work of art had never occurred to
me.

After we took psilocybin, I sat on the couch in Flora Lu's Elysian
chamber, letting my right cerebral hemisphere slowly open up to direct
sensual reception. Flora Lu and Maynard started teaching me eroticism –
the yoga of attention. Each moment was examined for sensual possibility.
The delicious grace of moving one's hand, not as part of a learned
survival sequence, but for kinaesthetic joy.

I was wearing the silk shirt and velvet trousers that Flora Lu, true to
her promise to be my fashion coordinator, had left on my bed while I
showered. Flora Lu was wearing light blue silk. Maynard was a Floren-
tine noble garbed in tight-fitting velvet pants. In a Moroccan caftan
Malaca was soft, touchable.

A fire burned gently in the hearth. The air was scented with incense.
His sensitized ears now as big as the Arecibo Dish, Maynard swayed
with pleasure. Flora Lu floated around the room, her face transfigured

with delight. Malaca blossomed into a flower of great beauty, her classic features now stylized with the dignity of an Egyptian frieze.

My eyes connected with hers. We rose as one and walked to the sun porch. She turned, came to me, entwined her arms around my neck.

We were two sea creatures. The mating process in this universe began with the fusion of moist lips producing a soft-electric rapture, which irradiated the entire body. We found no problem manoeuvring the limbs, tentacles, and delightful protuberances with which we were miraculously equipped in the transparent honey-liquid zero-gravity atmosphere that surrounded, bathed, and sustained us.

This was my first sexual experience under the influence of psychedelics. It startled me to learn that in addition to being instruments of philosophic revelation, mystical unity and evolutionary insight, psychedelic drugs were very powerful aphrodisiacs.

Malaca was upstairs taking a bubble bath. Maynard dozed on the sofa. I stood by the glass doors in the dawn, aware that my sunrise-watching index had risen dramatically since initiating this research into brain-change.

Flora Lu carried in a tray containing a silver coffee pot, a silver pitcher of cream, two porcelain cups, and a bowl of apples, bananas, and shiny green grapes.

She placed the tray on a low table and rode gravity down to a sitting position on the rug. 'I want to continue the discussion we were having last night.'

I felt a flush of warmth in my body, as my face muscles softened into a smile. 'Yes, I remember.' The secret-of-the-universe business.

We had been sitting harmoniously in front of the fire when Flora Lu leaned towards me. 'It's all Sex, don't you see?'

It had all become clear. Black jazz combos playing the boogie. Swedish blondes disrobing on a tropical beach. Tanned slim Israeli boys belly dancing to frenzied drums. Soft laughter from dark corners and behind bushes. The real secret of the universe was that everyone knew it but me.

A few days after this session I asked Aldous Huxley what he thought about the erotogenic nature of psychedelic drugs. His immediate reaction was agitation. 'Of course this is true, Timothy, but we've stirred up enough trouble suggesting that drugs can stimulate aesthetic and religious experiences. I strongly urge you not to let the sexual cat out of the bag.'

My first reaction to the aphrodisiac revelation was to have a good laugh at my own expense. We had been running around the land offering mystic visions and instant personality-change to priests, prisoners, and professors, and all the time we were unwittingly administering the key (if used in the right circumstances) to enhanced sex. What an inhibited square I had been. Why did it take so long for me to stumble on this fact? We had long recognized that these drugs tremendously intensified bodily sensations – taste, smell, touch, colours, sounds, motion, breathing. And we knew that in the right setting strong empathetic connections formed between people. By programming set and setting toward the philosophic, spiritual, or scientific, we had steered ourselves perversely away from an otherwise inevitable heightening of sensuality and affection.

The correlation between drug use and sexual arousal was established by the psychologist Charles Tart in the first government-funded study of the effects of cannabis.

CHARLES T. TART
On Being Stoned: A Psychological Study of Marijuana Intoxication

(1971)

Given the common American stereotype of the 'sex-crazed dope fiend', it is interesting to see what effects on sexuality are perceived by marijuana users themselves.

MAJOR EFFECTS

Desire for Sex

A common effect is '*My sexual drive goes up when stoned; I have more need for sex*' (18%, 21%, 28%, 21%, 12%). This may begin to occur at the Moderate to Strong levels of intoxication (11%, 25%, 32%, 8%, 2%). Users of Psychedelics experience this at lower levels of intoxication ($p.<0005$), as does the Therapy and Growth group ($p<.05$, overall).

The converse effect '*I have much less sexual drive when stoned; it's difficult to arouse me even in a situation which would normally arouse me*' is rare (42%, 34%, 15%, 5%, 2%). When it occurs, it is at the strong levels and higher (6%, 11%, 17%, 13%, 7%). The Professionals experience this loss of sexual need at lower levels of intoxication ($p<.05$).

A very common effect is '*I have no increase in sexual feelings unless it's a situation that I would normally be sexually aroused in, and then the sexual feelings are much stronger and more enjoyable*' (7%, 11%, 27%, 23%, 24%). Users of Psychedelics report this more frequently ($p<.05$) than Non-users. It generally occurs at Moderate to Strong levels (17%, 28%, 27%, 8%, 2%).

QUALITIES OF ORGASM

One of the factors that enhance love-making when intoxicated on marijuana is the characteristic effect '*Sexual orgasm has new qualities, pleasurable qualities, when stoned*' (6%, 9%, 22%, 27%, 28%). This occurs somewhat less often, albeit still very frequently, for the Meditators ($p<.01$, overall) and the Professionals ($p<.01$). Most users experience these new qualities of orgasm by the Strong level of intoxication (8%, 21%, 37%, 8%, 8%).

Among the various qualities potentially going into orgasm enhancement that my informants are able to describe, one or several of the following may be experienced as part of an orgasm when intoxicated: (1) prolongation of orgasm (possibly an effect of time slowing); (2) feelings of energy flowing and/or exploding or erupting in the body; (3) feelings of energy interchange with one's sexual partner, both flows before orgasm and explosive interchanges through the genitals and whole body during orgasm; (4) absolutely total immersion in the orgasm, no distractions of any sort; (5) the orgasm taking place as ecstatic sensations through most of the body rather than being confined to the genital area; (6) merging of identity with one's sexual partner during orgasm, with a sharing of sensation and joy; (7) feelings that the energy interchange during orgasm balances and replenishes each partner's own vital energies, rather than depleting them – more so than when not intoxicated; (8) greater awareness of the bodily feelings leading up to orgasm, with a consequent ability to time one's movements in a way that will maximize the pleasurable qualities of the orgasm; (9) the ego temporarily disappearing, the body taking over, the orgasm happening rather than being produced; and (10) the feeling that the orgasm (and shared feelings with the sexual partner) are happening on a much vaster, wider scale than those consciously experienced, that this is an event of much greater magnitude or significance than the ego is able to sense or comprehend

. . .

SUMMARY

For practically all experienced users, marijuana intoxication greatly intensifies the sensations experienced in sexual intercourse. A minority feel that this takes something important away from sexual intercourse, namely, contact with their sexual partner as they become immersed in their own intensified sensations. For the great majority, however, marijuana seems to be the ideal aphrodisiac. Sex is generally desired more, but with others who would be likely sexual partners anyway; there is usually no drive toward sex unless the overall situation seems right to the user. Desire is then intensified, sexual sensations enhanced, and feelings of greater contact, responsiveness, sharing, desire to give, and empathy with one's sexual partner are often experienced.

While many aspects of human experience, particularly when intoxicated on marijuana, are difficult to describe, my informants and the user-respondents indicate this is particularly true for sexual experience. So much is beyond words. The descriptions above deal only with some of the partially describable aspects.

Drugs are also enjoyed in combination with other sensual pleasures such as food. Gertrude Stein's lover Alice B. Toklas famously included a recipe for 'haschich fudge' in her cookbook, apparently unaware that the substance was illegal.

ALICE B. TOKLAS
'Haschich Fudge'
(1954)

HASCHICH FUDGE
(which anyone could whip up on a rainy day)

This is the food of Paradise – of Baudelaire's Artificial Paradises: it might provide an entertaining refreshment for a Ladies' Bridge Club or a chapter meeting of the DAR. In Morocco it is thought to be good for warding off the common cold in damp winter weather and is, indeed, more effective if taken with large quantities of hot mint tea. Euphoria and brilliant storms of laughter; ecstatic reveries and extensions of one's personality on several simultaneous planes are to be complacently expected. Almost anything Saint Theresa did, you can do better if you can bear to be ravished by *'un évanouissement reveillé'*.

Take 1 teaspoon black peppercorns, 1 whole nutmeg, 4 average sticks of cinnamon, 1 teaspoon coriander. These should all be pulverised in a mortar. About a handful each of stoned dates, dried figs, shelled almonds and peanuts: chop these and mix them together. A bunch of *canibus sativa* can be pulverized. This along with the spices should be dusted over the mixed fruit and nuts, kneaded together. About a cup of sugar dissolved in a big pat of butter. Rolled into a cake and cut into pieces or made into balls about the size of a walnut, it should be eaten with care. Two pieces are quite sufficient.

Obtaining the *canibus* may present certain difficulties, but the variety known as *canibus sativa* grows as a common weed, often unrecognized, everywhere in Europe, Asia and parts of Africa; besides being cultivated as a crop for the manufacture of rope. In the Americas, while often discouraged, its cousin, called *canibus indica*, has been observed even in city window boxes. It should be picked and dried as soon as it has gone to seed and while the plant is still green.

Perhaps the strangest combination of drug and food is the Japanese cult of eating toxic fugu, *or puffer-fish.*

WADE DAVIS
The Serpent and the Rainbow
(1985)

The subtleties of safely preparing puffer fish were quite unknown to the first European explorers to reach the Orient, and as a result they have left some of the most vivid accounts of just what these toxins are capable of. During his second circumnavigational voyage, Captain James Cook ignored a warning from the two naturalists he had on board and ordered the liver and roe of a puffer dressed for his supper. Cook insisted that he had safely eaten the fish elsewhere in the Pacific, and then in the unassuming way of a captain in the Royal Navy, he invited the two naturalists to eat with him. Fortunately, the three men merely tasted the morsel. Nevertheless, between three and four in the morning they were 'seized with an extraordinary weakness in all our limbs attended with a numbness or sensation like that caused by exposing one's hands or feet to a fire after having been pinched much by frost.' Cook wrote, 'I had almost lost the sense of feeling; nor could I distinguish between light and heavy bodies . . . a quart pot full of water and a feather being the same in my hand.'

. . .

While Cook and the rest of the Europeans were having their diffi-culties on the high seas, the Japanese had adopted the Chinese passion for the puffer fish and carried its preparation to the level of art. The ardour with which the Japanese consumed their *fugu* fish bewildered early European observers. Engelbert Kaempfer, a physician attached to the Dutch embassy in Nagasaki at the turn of the eighteenth century, noted that 'the Japanese reckon [this] a very delicate fish, and they are fond of it, but the Head, Guts, bones and all the garbage must be thrown away, and the flesh carefully wash'd and clean'd before it is fit to eat. And yet many people die of it . . .' He also observed that the fish was so dangerous and yet so popular that the emperor had been obliged to issue a special decree forbidding his soldiers to eat it. Curiously, though Kaempfer seems to have witnessed many individuals eating and enjoying the puffer, he concludes, 'the poison of this sort is absolutely mortal, no washing nor cleaning will take it off. It is therefore never asked for, but by those who intend to make away with themselves.' This Dutchman, like countless generations of Western visitors who came after him, missed the point of the puffer experience completely. As the Japanese explain in verse, 'Those who eat *fugu* are stupid. But those who don't eat *fugu* are also stupid.'

Today the Japanese passion for puffers is something of a national institution. In Tokyo alone puffers are sold by over eighteen hundred fish dealers. Virtually all the best restaurants offer it, and to retain some semblance of control the government actually licenses the specially trained chefs who alone are permitted to prepare it. Generally the meat is eaten as sashimi. Thus sliced raw, the flesh is relatively safe. So are the testes, except that they are sometimes confused with the deadly ovaries by even the most experienced chefs. Yet many connoisseurs prefer a dish known as *chiri*, partially cooked fillets taken from a kettle containing toxic livers, skins, and intestines. Lovers of *chiri* are invariably among the hundred or more fatalities that occur each year.

The Japanese prefer and pay premium prices for four species of puffer, all in the genus *Fugu*, and all known to be violently poisonous. Why would anyone play Russian roulette with such a creature? The answer, of course, is that *fugu* is one of the few substances that walks the line between food and drug. For the Japanese, consuming *fugu* is the ultimate aesthetic experience. The refined task of the *fugu* chef is not to eliminate the toxin, it is to reduce its concentration while assuring that the guest still enjoys the exhilarating physiological aftereffects. These include a mild numbing or tingling of the tongue and lips, sensations of warmth, a flushing of the skin, and a general feeling of euphoria. As in the case of so many stimulants, there are those who can't get enough of a good thing. Though it is expressly prohibited by law, certain chefs prepare for zealous clients a special dish of the particularly toxic livers. The organ is boiled and mashed and boiled again and again until much of the toxin is removed. Unfortunately, many of these chefs succumb to their own cooking. It was such a dish that caused the controversial death in 1975 of Mitsugora Bando VIII, one of Japan's most talented Kabuki actors, indeed, an artist who had been declared a living national treasure by the Japanese government. He, apparently, like all of those who eat the cooked livers, was among those who, in the words of one *fugu* specialist, enjoy 'living dangerously'.

The fugu *cult illustrates another effect of the pleasure produced by drugs: that the means used to ingest them can often seem unspeakably repellent to the outside observer. A notorious example is the* Amanita *or fly agaric mushroom parties traditional in Siberia.*

JOHN G. BOURKE
Scatological Rites of All Nations

(1891, foreword by Freud 1913)

The most singular effect of the *Amanita* is the influence it possesses over the urine. It is said that from time immemorial the inhabitants have known that the fungus imparts an intoxicating quality to that secretion, which continues for a considerable time after taking it. For instance, a man moderately intoxicated today will by the next morning have slept himself sober; but (as is the custom) by taking a cup of his urine he will be more powerfully intoxicated than he was the preceding day. It is therefore not uncommon for confirmed drunkards to preserve their urine as a precious liquor against a scarcity of the fungus.

The intoxicating property of the urine is capable of being propagated, for every one who partakes of it has his urine similarly affected. Thus, with a very few *Amanitae*, a party of drunkards may keep up their debauch for a week. Dr Langsdorff mentions that by means of the second person taking the urine of the first, the third of the second, and so on, intoxication may be propagated through five individuals.

In *Letters from a Citizen of the World*, Oliver Goldsmith speaks of 'a curious custom' among the Tartars of Koraki. The Russians who trade with them carry thither a kind of mushroom. These mushrooms the rich Tartars lay up in large quantities for the winter; and when a nobleman makes a mushroom feast all the neighbours around are invited. The mushrooms are prepared by boiling, by which the water acquires an intoxicating quality, and is a sort of drink which the Tartars prize beyond all other. When the nobility and the ladies are assembled, and the ceremonies usual between people of distinction over, the mushroom broth goes freely round, and they laugh, talk *double-entendres*, grow fuddled, and become excellent company. The poorer sort, who love mushroom broth to distraction as well as the rich, but cannot afford it at first hand, post themselves on these occasions round the huts of the rich, and watch the opportunity of the ladies and gentlemen as they come down to pass the liquor, and holding a wooden bowl, catch the delicious fluid, very little altered by filtration, being still strongly tinctured with the intoxicating quality. Of this they drink with the utmost satisfaction, and thus they get as drunk and as jovial as their betters.

"Happy nobility!" cried my companion, "who can fear no diminution of respect unless seized with strangury, and who when drunk are most useful! Though we have not this custom among us, I foresee that if it were introduced, we might have many a toad-eater in England ready to drink from the wooden bowl on these occasions, and to praise the flavour of his lordship's liquor. As we have different classes of gentry, who knows but we may see a lord holding the bowl to the minister, a knight holding it to his lordship, and a simple squire drinking it double distilled from the loins of knighthood?"'

*Localized conditions can often produce bizarre manifestations of rec-
reational drug use, such as the 'ether craze' in nineteenth-century Ulster.*

DAVID R. NAGLE, MD
'Anesthetic Addiction and Drunkenness:
A Contemporary and Historical Survey'

(1968)

About 1840 a Catholic priest, Father Matthew, led a great
temperance crusade throughout England, Scotland, and Ireland. It was
one of the most successful that ever occurred; thousands took the
pledge. In Draperstown, Northern Ireland, there lived an alcoholic
practitioner named Kelly who was carried away by the good Father's
eloquence. Aghast at the pleasure he had given up, but not wishing to
break his pledge, he cast about for a substitute. He had prescribed ether
by mouth on occasion and knew of its pleasant effects. After a few
personal experiments he imparted the knowledge to his friends and
patients who had also taken the pledge.

Meanwhile the crusade died down; and matters might have ended with
this small circle, except for the matter of taxes. The British government in
1855 placed an onerous tax upon ethyl alcohol and the beverages which
contained it. Following this, an efficient constabulary put an end to
home distillation of Poteen.

A combination of British ingeniousness and Irish thirst found a
loophole in the law. Methylated (in America, denatured) alcohol bore
no tax. Proper distillation of it with sulfuric acid would produce diethyl
ether. The London distillers did not work too hard at it; as much as
twenty per cent alcohol was present in some samples. This 'methylated
ether' was then shipped by the *tons* (!) to Draperstown and the surrounding area. It was preferred in some ways, and especially among the poor,
to the now-expensive whiskey. The drunk was quick and cheap, and
could be achieved several times a day without hangover. If arrested for
drunkenness, the offender would be sober by the time the police station
was reached.

In 1878 Sir Benjamin Ward Richardson wrote a charming essay on his travels through this area of Ireland. He noted that the main street of Draperstown smelled like his surgery. He also described the proper method of drinking: first, rinse the mouth with cold water; then down about a tablespoonful of ether, followed quickly with a glass of cold water. An old toper could finish off a three-ounce wine glass full of ether at a swig without the aid of water (Richardson, 1878).

Everyone who discussed this particular phenomenon admitted that there appeared to be less chronic damage than with alcohol. Principle hazards were chronic gastritis, death from overdosage, and burns from smoking while drinking.

By 1890 the pressure of temperance societies, aided by an article by the editor of the *British Medical Journal* (Hart, 1890), and loss of tax revenue, caused a Parliamentary committee to investigate (Select Committee on British and Foreign Spirits, 1890–1891). Subsequently, regulations limiting the sale of this ether were imposed. Nevertheless, in 1910, Caldwell reported that the practice was still prevalent in the area (Caldwell, 1910). According to a survey done by R. A. Gailey (unpublished) the practice seems to have died out in the 1920s. It was replaced by beverages that were cheaper and more easily available.

. . . or the reported outbreak of cordite-drinking among British troops during the Boer War.

"MAD DRUNK" WITH CORDITE.

TERRIBLE HABIT OF SOLDIERS IN SOUTH AFRICA.

The South African war and the weariness of life on the "illimitable veldt" are responsible for the discovery of a new and extraordinary form of intoxication.

Some British soldiers discovered that by eating cordite they could get all the excitement of the most powerful narcotic—and all the terrible after-effects, too. Cordite consists roughly of about 58 parts of nitroglycerine, 37 parts gun cotton, and five-parts of mineral jelly.

Each cartridge contains 60 cylindrical strands of cordite, and when Major Jennings, D.S.O., learned that the men were eating these (says the "British Medical Journal") he experimented on himself by sucking a strand. He found that it tasted sweet, pleasant, and pungent, but it resulted in giving him the most racking, splitting headache he ever had in his life, and it lasted for 36 hours.

Dissolved in tea, cordite produces an almost immediately exhilarating effect "inciting to almost demoniacal actions." If many persons have partaken of the beverage all begin talking at once, each seemingly anxious to inform the other of everything that has happened to him since his birth.

This condition is followed by heavy sleep and stupor, lasting five to twelve hours, according to the quantity taken. To awaken the subject it is often necessary to slap his face, punch or shake him, and awakening is accompanied by severe dull, boring headache, muscular twitchings, and protrusion of the eyes.

It is as an addition to beer that cordite appears to produce its worst effects. It then excites a quarrelsome, destructive mania in an otherwise peacefully disposed individual, and produces immediate intoxication in a man who can commonly consume as much as four or five pints of beer without exhibiting a trace of having done so. If taken in quantity insufficient to produce sleep it makes him not only quarrelsome, but brings out the worst traits in his character.

A possible clue to the inception of this habit is given by the fact that a large number of the men seem to have used cordite as a means of lighting pipes in default of matches.

Traditionally, the intoxicant of choice in Western military culture has been alcohol.

RICHARD HOLMES
'Rum and Blood'

(1985)

Some of the French knights at Agincourt had been drinking heavily on the eve of the battle, Corporal Shaw of the Life Guards was fighting drunk when he hewed nine Frenchmen through steel and bone at Waterloo, and some of the soldiers who advanced on the morning of July 1916 were fortified by more than *esprit de corps*. During the Falklands War Lieutenant David Tinker testified, half-seriously, to the therapeutic effects of alcohol. 'The best thing to do is to have a few wets before an attack,' he advised. 'I'd had a drink before the Exocet attack and the pulse rate stayed very normal.' Drink and drugs are time-honoured ways of palliating stress, and their use is infinitely more widespread than bland official histories might suggest. The very expression 'Dutch courage' has military origins, dating from the predisposition of English soldiers in the Low Countries to fortify themselves with a nip or two of genever.

There are four main aspects to the question of alcohol and drug use in armies. Firstly, both drugs and drink have an entirely legitimate function in helping overwrought men to sleep. Alcohol is more useful in this context than is often recognized: Rick Jolly made a plea for 'the traditional use of alcohol' to help stressed men sleep, and Frank Richardson found rum useful for the same purpose. Major J. R. Phillips, a regimental medical officer in 1940, was short of drugs: 'there was, however, an ample supply of alcohol, an excellent sedative, which proved most effective'. Alan Hanbury-Sparrow, on the receiving end, was utterly frank. 'Certainly strong drink saved you,' he acknowledged. 'For the whole of your moral forces were exhausted. Sleep alone could restore them, and sleep, thanks to this blessed alcohol, you got.'

Secondly, soldiers in garrison in both peace and war tend to overindulge in alcohol as a means of making an unbearable existence more tolerable. Brigadier Richard Simpkin declared: 'every army I know of

– except the Swedish, Swiss and Israeli forces – conspires to make its conscripts' life so wretched that they are fully occupied in coming to terms with it or in using drink or drugs to distance themselves from it'. Jean Morvan recounted the spirited performance of a First Empire officer who habitually drank two bottles of wine with his lunch. He then had a well-deserved nap, enjoyed another bottle in bed, had dinner, and then took a short walk and another drink before turning in. On a more serious note, drink and drugs play an important part in crime in most armies: one-third of law violations by Soviet military personnel are carried out in a state of drunkenness.

Communal drinking also assists in the small-group bonding process. In the Anglo-Saxon hall thanes boasted over their drinking-horns about the deeds they would perform in battle. When Earl Byrhtnoth's men faced destruction at the Battle of Maldon in 991, they were reminded of the vows they had made in happier times, and encouraged to live up to them. 'Remember the times,' exhorted Aelfwine,

> when we spoke at the mead-drinking, when on the bench we uttered boasting, heroes in hall, about hard strife . . . Thanes shall not reproach me among the people, that I wish to leave this army, to seek my home, now that my prince lies low, hewn down in battle.

Tired as they were by their march to Hastings in 1066, King Harold's men still spent much of the night before the battle drinking. A Norman chronicler gave a slightly bewildered version of the cries of 'drink-wassail' that rang out in the Saxon camp as Harold's host prepared for its last battle. Stuart Mawson noticed 'a subtle parade of manhood, an unconscious swagger in the manner of drinking' the night before the drop on Arnhem. Samuel Janney, who served with the 1st Infantry Division in Vietnam in 1968, was initiated into his platoon by a drinking party in the field. 'That was my platoon,' he said. 'And that was the first time I'd gotten loaded with them. I'd probably been in the unit for two weeks at that point. It makes a big difference being part of the group. They definitely initiated me.'

It is with the fourth aspect of alcohol and drug use – as a means of mitigating the stresses of battle – that we are most concerned. To a degree, at least, this use has been officially approved. The infantry divisions of Saint-Hilaire and Vandamme, given the crucial task of seizing the Pratzen at Austerlitz, were also given triple rations of brandy, nearly half a pint per man: small wonder that, as a French officer observed, 'the troops now burst with eagerness and enthusiasm'. Wheeler watched Sergeant Butley serving out the rum ration under fire at Badajoz in 1812, saving for himself the ration of those who were killed before they could drink it. Major O'Hare of the 95th chatted with Captain Jones of the 52nd as they waited in the dark to assault the fortress. O'Hare was depressed and fatalistic, and Jones tried to cheer him up. ' "Tut, tut, man! I have the same sort of feeling, but I keep it down with a drop of the cratur," answered the Captain, as he handed his calabash to the Major.' Wheeler and his comrades insulated themselves against the rain the night before Waterloo by stocking up with liquor: they were, he recalled, 'wet and comfortable'. For many years British soldiers enjoyed a rum ration, and care was often taken to issue it shortly before battle.

Officially supplied drugs are not generally used for the same purpose: they are more often employed to help soldiers cope with lack of sleep. Benzedrine was widely used during and after the Second World War. At least 10 per cent of Second World War American troops took amphetamines at some time or other, and in 1947 one-quarter of the prisoners in US military jails were 'heavy and chronic users' . . . The French army made widespread use of Maxiton: many of the garrison of Dien Bien Phu were able to stay on duty for days on end with its assistance.

. . . but the Vietnam War saw a cultural shift to the use of marijuana and heroin.

DAN BAUM
Smoke and Mirrors: The War on Drugs and the Politics of Failure

(1996)

In May 1971, two congressmen stepped off a plane in D.C. bearing grim tidings. Robert Steele, Republican of Connecticut, and Morgan Murphy, Democrat of Illinois, had just come from visiting the troops in Vietnam, where, they reported, a horrifying number were addicted to heroin. As many as 15 percent – maybe 40,000 men – were hooked on smack. 'The soldier going to South Vietnam today runs a far greater risk of becoming a heroin addict than a combat casualty,' Steele told reporters.

. . .

Now the press was on the story. 'As common as chewing gum,' *Time* said of drugs in Vietnam. The *New York Times* estimated that as many as a quarter of the privates fighting in Vietnam – some 60,000 men – were hooked on smack. ABC News aired a one-hour special, 'Heroes and Heroin', that showed soldiers handing little packets to each other and then snorting up. Heroin made even the increasingly rapid withdrawal from Vietnam a problem. 'The spectre of weapons-trained, addicted combat veterans joining the deadly struggle for drugs [in the streets of America] is ominous,' reported *Time*. The article went on to quote Iowa senator Harold Hughes: 'Within a matter of months in our large cities, the Capone era of the '20s may look like a Sunday school picnic by comparison.'

Krogh flew to Vietnam. He took no entourage, only a set of fatigues and a pass to travel wherever he wanted.

He flew all over the country, from the DMZ to the southern Delta, visiting twelve firebases. Krogh was thirty-one. By himself, in fatigues, and calling himself 'a member of the White House staff', he looked like a harmless underling, not the man in charge of national drug policy. What amazed him was how candid the men were. Krogh would sit with them in their bunkers as they passed joints back and forth or cracked out vials of heroin, which they bragged was 90 percent pure and which they usually snorted, smoked in cigarettes, or mixed with alcohol and drank. Nobody was inhibited even when officers were around. There didn't even seem to be a 'drug culture' among the troops he could delineate from the straight culture. Everybody smoked pot, and a lot of the men were using heroin.

The heroin problem Krogh was seeing was created largely by the Pentagon itself. The army had figured out in 1968 that a lot of its troops in Vietnam were smoking pot. The army then began an all-out campaign to cut off the supply – with pot-sniffing dogs, searches of men's billets, and mass arrests for possession. It also endeavoured to reduce demand through a 'reefer madness'-style propaganda campaign on Armed Forces Radio. Marijuana use declined, but when the Pentagon sent a researcher to study the campaign's effects two years later, he reported that the real results of the army's anti-marijuana campaign were disastrous. 'Human ingenuity being what it is – and the desire for an intoxicant in Vietnam being what it was – many soldiers simply switched' to heroin, which was odourless, far less bulky than pot and, in Vietnam, extremely inexpensive. Within two years field officers would miss the good old days when their troops merely smoked pot. One commanding officer told the Pentagon researcher, 'If it would get them to give up the hard stuff, I would buy all the marijuana and hashish in the Delta as a present.'

The worst drug in America – the most feared, the most taboo – has long been heroin. By clamping down hard on marijuana, the army not only created a big health problem in its ranks, it also pushed its soldiers across a line. If thousands of soldiers could casually accept heroin as 'normal', what chance did the army have of controlling any kind of drug use?

Even casual use of drugs for pleasure is often accompanied by elaborate ritual, associated not just with the drugs but also with the tools and accessories of their use. The anthropologist Claude Lévi-Strauss recorded the meticulous ceremony which still surrounds the drinking of maté *tea across large areas of South America.*

CLAUDE LÉVI STRAUSS
Tristes Tropiques

(1955)

Twice a day – at eleven thirty in the morning and seven in the evening – everybody would assemble under the pergola surrounding the living quarters for the ritual of the *chimarrão*, the imbibing of maté through a pipe. It is well known that the maté is a shrub of the same family as our holly-oak; the twigs are lightly roasted in the smoke of an underground fire, then reduced to a coarse greenish powder which keeps for a long time in casks. I am referring to the genuine maté; the product sold under this name in Europe has usually undergone such noxious transformations that it bears no resemblance whatever to the real thing.

There are several ways of drinking maté. If, in the course of an expedition, we were so exhausted that we longed for the immediate comfort it could provide, we would simply throw a large handful into cold water, which was then quickly brought to the boil but removed from the heat – this was an essential point – at the first sign of bubbling; otherwise the maté would lose all its flavour. This method, the reverse process to making an infusion, produces what is called *cha de maté*, a dark green liquid, almost oily like a cup of strong coffee. When we were short of time, we made do with *téréré*: cold water is poured on to a handful of powder and then sucked up through a pipette. Those who dislike the bitter taste can, like Paraguayan ladies, choose *maté doce*: the powder is mixed with sugar and caramelized over a hot fire; boiling water is then poured on to it and the liquid is passed through a sieve. But I know of no maté lover who does not infinitely prefer the method of the *chimarrão*, as it was practised at the *fazenda*; it is at once a social rite and a private vice.

The company sits in a circle around a little girl, the *china*, who is equipped with a kettle, a stove and the *cuia*. The latter may be a gourd, the orifice of which has been edged with silver, or sometimes, as at Guaycurus, a zebu's horn carved by a peon. The receptacle is two-thirds full of powder, which the little girl gently soaks with boiling water. Once the mixture forms a paste, she takes the silver tube, the lower end of which is bulb-shaped and pierced with holes, and carefully makes a cavity for it. This allows the pipette to rest at the bottom, in a tiny space where the liquid can collect, while the tube has just enough play not to break up the paste, but not so much that the water does not mix in properly. The *chimarrão* is now ready and has only to be filled with liquid before being offered to the master of the house; after sucking two or three times on the pipette, he hands back the receptacle and the same operation is performed for all the participants, the men first, and then the women, if there are any present. The instrument goes the rounds until there is no more water left in the kettle.

The first mouthfuls produce a delightful sensation – for the regular maté drinker at least, since the beginner is likely to scald himself – made up of the somewhat viscous contact with the hot silver, and the foaming water enhanced with a thick froth: it is at once bitter and fragrant, like a whole forest concentrated in a few drops. Maté contains an alkaloid similar to those in coffee, tea and chocolate, and its soothing and invigorating effect is perhaps to be explained by the amount and the semi-raw state of the medium. After a few rounds, the maté loses its flavour, but careful prodding with the pipette can reveal still-unexplored nooks and crannies which prolong the pleasure with tiny explosions of bitterness.

This ritual is seen by some as a practical means of protection against the more dangerous aspects of drug use.

ANDREW WEIL
The Natural Mind

(1973)

Ritual seems to protect individuals and groups from the negative effects of drugs, possibly by establishing a framework of order around their use. At least, people who use drugs ritually tend not to get into trouble with them, whereas people who abandon ritual and use drugs wantonly tend to have problems. We can see this protective function of ritual in our own society with our uses of alcohol. Americans who lay down a ritual for drinking – for example, people who drink only after 6 p.m., only with others present, only with food present, and only for a specified period before supper for the purpose of promoting social intercourse – are not the people who get into trouble with alcohol. Americans who get into trouble with alcohol are those who begin to use it without ritualistic rules and forms; uncontained by ritual, their drug use becomes unstable and begins to disrupt their lives.

I see the same principle at work among people I know who use marihuana. Those who use it ritually – that is, in groups as a recreational intoxicant or before going to a movie or before eating a good meal – do not have their lives taken over by their drug use. But those who dispense with ritual and smoke marihuana whenever they feel like it begin to get into a worse and worse relationship with the drug. I remember also that when I lived and worked in the Haight–Ashbury district of San Francisco, the people I met who were in the very worst relationships with drugs (usually with amphetamines, barbiturates, alcohol, and heroin) were always the people who had done away with rules entirely and used drugs according to no logical plan.

Probably, the effectiveness of ritual is independent of its content. I do not think it matters much what rules one makes for using drugs as long as one makes rules. If a rationale is needed for these rules, any rationale will do as long as it is consistent with prevailing beliefs. In Indian societies ritual is often explained in terms of respect for the god or spirit supposed to dwell within the magic plant. In American society, ritual may be understood as 'good social form'. In either case, the principle works to protect users from the negative potential of drugs.

One aspect of Indian ritual that deserves special emphasis is the use of altered states of consciousness for positive ends. That is, drug-induced states are not entered for negative reasons (such as escape from boredom or anxiety); rather, they are entered because they can be of positive usefulness to individuals and the tribe. I stress this point because it contrasts sharply with practices in the United States. Very many Americans take drugs for negative reasons or no reasons at all, and, again, I suspect this difference is a key factor in our having a drug problem. The principle that positive application of altered consciousness is protective is apparent among amphetamine users in our country. People who take amphetamines in order to use the stimulation they trigger for positive ends – for example, students who take them only to study for exams – do not tend to get into trouble with amphetamines. The people who do get into trouble with amphetamines are those who begin to take them just because they like the feeling of stimulation. Just liking the feelings drugs provide without using those feelings for positive purposes seems to me to be the beginning of most bad relationships with drugs – that is, patterns of use destined to become more and more unstable and more and more dominating of the user's life.

This principle should be intuitively obvious because drug experiences are rarely pleasant when one's set is couched in negative terms. The person who expects a joint of marihuana or a tab of acid to undo a pre-existing depression often has the drug backfire on him by intensifying his negative mental state. I have seen this pattern again and again among users of all drugs in this country and have experienced it myself. On every occasion that I have smoked marihuana or taken a hallucinogen out of boredom or in order to escape depression, I have experienced exactly the opposite result. Consequently, when patients or friends ask my advice about trying drugs like marihuana or hallucinogens for the first time, I urge them not to do so unless they can phrase their expectations in positive terms.

. . . but for many the ritual and accessories of drug use are fetishized to the point where much of the pleasure is invested in them rather than the drug. This fetishism perhaps reaches its literary high point in the decadent, opiated writings of the pseudonymous French author Claude Farrere.

CLAUDE FARRERE
Black Opium

(1929)

In my layout, I have five pipes.

For the reason that China, the source of opium, the source of wisdom, is familiar with five primitive virtues.

My first pipe is of brown shell, with a black earthenware bowl and two muzzles of light-coloured shell.

It is old and precious.

The stem is thick, and opaque or diaphanous according to the marbling of the shell. The *knob*, which holds the fingers while one is smoking, is an amber-hued projecture, finely carved in the form of a diminutive fox. The bowl is hexagonal, and is fastened in the middle by a silver fang.

In the centre of it, the coagulated opium-ash, the dross, bitter and rich in morphine, has been gradually deposited in the form of thin black pellicles. Therein resides the soul of by-gone pipefuls, the soul of dead intoxications. And the shell, progressively penetrated by the dross, retains among its molecules the vestiges of the years which have flown.

Those are Japanese years. For my first pipe was in Kiou-Siou, the Japanese island of turtles. And in the convex mirror of the wide stem, I can see the whole of Japan reflected.

The fox which forms the knob is not a fox. It is the *Kitsoune* of legend, the fairy beast which undergoes a metamorphosis at will. And so it is, when I take the shell pipe in my hands, I never fail to examine the knob, to see if it may not, mysteriously, have changed form. If it were to undergo such a change, some fine day, I should not be greatly surprised. The *Kitsoune* of my pipe must, indeed, be a famous beast, and one wise in sorcery, to have been selected as a model by the artist who did this carving.

. . .

The shell pipe knows many Japanese stories, and sometimes tells them to me in a low voice, during the winter evenings, while the opium is budding and crackling above the lamp.

My second pipe is wholly of silver, with a bowl of white porcelain.

It is old and precious.

The extremely long stem is not a thick but a fragile one. This is in order that the pipe may not be too heavy in the smoker's hands. The knot is a massive silver projecture, carved in the form of a rat. And the bowl, carefully polished, is as round as a little snowball.

The whole length of the pipe has been engraved by the artist with marvelous Chinese ornaments. For my second pipe is Chinese – Cantonese. It speaks to me of that south of China, where I once passed some very charming years.

Coiled about the silver pipe are flowers, leaves and grasses. The flowers are the beautiful hibiscus in bloom; the leaves are leaves of wild mint; and the grasses are rice-stalks. All this exhales a delicious odor of the China of Kwang-tung, with its cool lanes, its fertile rice-fields and its pretty villages squatting in groves of trees.

Coiled about the silver pipe are men and women. The men are, alternately, labourers and pirates; and both groups are courteous and impassive. The women are the daughters of Pak-Hoi, of Now-Chow or of Hainan. Their soft skin gleams like amber-colored satin. Their hands and feet would make the most noble of our marquises jealous. Ot-Che, my mistress, where are you? It is your memory that haunts me now, the memory of your fingers so expert in handling the needle, as I dream on amid the black smoke, the silver pipe resting in my hands.

My third pipe is of ivory, with a white-jade bowl and two muzzles of green jade.

It is older and more precious than the first two.

It is carved in the form of an elephant's tusk. It is very thick, and so heavy that one guesses it to have been made for the men of old, who were more robust than we. The knot is of bark, and is in the form of a rustically carved ape. The square bowl gleams like milk which has been turned green by the adding of a little pistachio, while opaque serpentine veins twine about the middle of the transparent jade.

The ivory pipe was formerly white, white as the western race, which conquers the elephants beyond the mountains. But the patient dross has yellowed and then browned it, little by little, until it is today like the opium-smoking oriental race. Thus, the souls of the two rival races mingle – in the ivory pipe.

Fertile India, swarming from the Ganges to the Deccan; wise Thibet, crouched upon her snowy steppes; nomadic Mongolia, where the gawky camels trot; China, countless and divine, China, imperial and philosophic: the ivory pipe mysteriously evokes the whole of Asia.

For it is old, older than many civilizations. I happen to know that an Occidental Queen – Persian, Tartar, Scythian? – presented it, one historic day, to the Chinese Emperor who had come to visit her, all of thirty centuries ago. I used to know the name of the Queen and the name of the Emperor, but the disdainful opium has swept them from my memory, and all that I can remember is the noble and peace-inspiring tale of those great rulers who came, one hastening to anticipate the other, across the breadth of their empires, to exchange, across frontiers which were no more, vows of concord which were like to vows of love. Thirty times a hundred years . . . Ivory pipe, how many imperial mouths have pressed you to them since that time? How many Majesties, clad in yellow silk, have sought in your cradling kiss forgetfulness of their sorrows and of their cares, forgetfulness of the ruin and injuries which, growing each day more bitter, were falling upon the Sacred Empire of the Hoang-Ti's. And if I behold you now tarnished and blackened, is that merely the mourning which you wear, mourning for all the wise centuries that have died to make way for this century of ours, so light and frivolous?

I do not know of what it is my fourth pipe is made. It is my father's pipe, and he died from smoking it.

It is a murderous pipe. It is saturated with dross, saturated in all its pores and in all its fibers. Ten poisons, all of them ferocious ones, lie ambushed in its black cylinder, which is like the trunk of a venomous cobra. – Morphine, codeine, narcotine – what others? My father died from having smoked too much, and the opium, evaporating in this pipebowl of his, takes on the mysterious odour of death.

It is a funeral pipe. Wholly black, on account of the dross, and plated with gold-chasings, which shine like coffin-trappings. I dare not bring it near my mouth, – not as yet. But often, I gaze upon it – as one gazes upon a tomb which stands ajar – with desire and with dizziness.

My father died from having smoked it, – my father whom I loved. Between life and death – life ugly and futile, death serene and prolific in marvelous intoxications – he chose death. When the day shall have come, I shall do as he did.

And I shall seek, upon the black gold-plated pipe, the cold taste of paternal lips, – seek it devoutly.

And now, the lamp is lighted, the mats are on the floor, and the green tea is steaming in the cups without handles.

And here is my fifth pipe, all ready for me. It is not old, and it is not precious. I purchased it of the coffin-maker for six taels. It is a plain brown bamboo, finished off with a red-earth bowl. The bamboo knob is sufficient to give a grip to the fingers.

It has no gold nor jade nor ivory. No prince, no queen has smoked. It does not evoke, in magic fashion, poetically distant provinces nor centuries of past glory.

But all the same, it is the one which I prefer above all the others. For it is this one that I smoke – not the others; they are too sacred. – It is this one which, each evening, pours an intoxicating draft for me, opening for me the dazzling door to clear-headed pleasures, bearing me triumphantly away, out of life and to those subtle spheres which opium-smokers know: those philosophic and beneficent spheres where dwell Hwang-Ti, the Sun-Emperor; Kwong-Tsu, the Perfectly Wise; and the God without a Name who was the first of smokers.

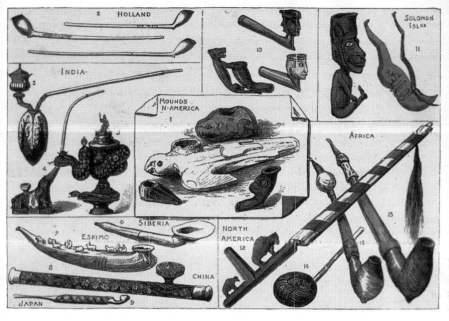

Rituals of pleasure: an engraving of pipes and accessories from 1892.
(Wellcome Trust)

6
Over the Edge: Drugs and Madness

Drugs and madness are connected on many levels. On a metaphorical level, they often represent each other; on a literal level, they are often causally connected. Drugs can be used to provoke madness, or to treat it – or both. Drugs have long been seen as paths to madness; in today's neurochemical model, madness is created by the brain's internal drugs.

Almost any psychoactive drug can trigger some manifestations of madness: even 'caffeine psychosis' has now been recognized by American courts. Marijuana, despite its apologists' claims, can produce psychotic effects, as in the case of the therapist Ann Shulgin ('Alice'), wife of the chemist Alexander (see p. 73).

ANN SHULGIN
Tihkal

(1997)

My first experiment with marijuana was when I was in my twenties, and it was a disastrous one. I found my awareness chopped into ten-second segments, separated by a wall of amnesia that clanged down, just as I had managed to remember who I was, where I was, and what was happening. After the wall had cut me off, I would begin the entire process of identifying myself and my reality all over again.

CLANG:

'Who am I?'
'I'm Alice.'
'Oh, yes, that's right. Well, where am I?'
'Sitting on my couch, in my home.'
'What am I doing?'
'I've taken marijuana, and I'm trying to make sense out of all this.'

CLANG:

'Who am I?'
'My name is Alice.'

And so on and so on, for hours. When I finally came out of it, I resolved never to touch the stuff again.

But, of course, people are resilient and forgetful. In my thirties, for a while, I had a boyfriend called Steven who was brilliant, arrogant and extremely controlling, and he decided that the circumstances of my first experiment with pot – mind-set perhaps – must have been wrong in some way, and he insisted that I should take it once more, with him. 'I promise you,' he said firmly. 'This time it will be a wonderful experience. Just leave it to me!'

He took me outside, had me sit down under the trees at the back of the house, gave me a marijuana cigarette and watched while I went through the usual coughing and recovery. He kept telling me to inhale, and inhale again. 'Come on, come on! I want you to give this stuff a real try, this time. Trust me, Alice. Just breathe it in, that's my girl!'

So I kept inhaling until I began to feel very dizzy. When I said I'd had enough, that's it, he let me stop. He patted my head approvingly, took the cigarette out of my fingers and finished it himself, while I sat and saw the world split into one, two, three, four levels of vision, four levels of reality, four versions of Alice watching sunlight flowing over branches and twigs, wild plants and brown-edged leaves in the dry riverbed below.

I sat cross-legged, feeling the intense push of wave after wave of sensation, wondering if it would ever mellow out, slow down, stop coming at me. It was impossible to relax, because I had to stay braced against the next surge. I didn't enjoy the feeling. I knew it wasn't dangerous or hostile, just very strong, and it made me uncomfortable.

Suddenly there was a fifth and a sixth level, and I turned to Steven and said, 'I want to go in, please. Things are getting complicated.'

Inside the house, seated on my couch, I counted a final total of eight levels, and wondered which was the real one, the one I had been living in before smoking the marijuana.

Looking at the eight levels or tracks from the outside, which I could occasionally do, was like seeing an eight-story apartment building with the outer wall removed. I hoped that one of the apartments was my normal world. The other apartments looked similar, but here and there a piece of furniture – so to speak – was out of place, or a door didn't have the right shape, and everything kept shifting into something else. So I had to look carefully, to feel out every thought-form and all the not-quite-right versions of myself, if I was to sort it all out and bring an end to the loud confusion.

I glanced at my friend, seated across from me in an armchair, eyes closed, smiling, and became aware of a growing suspicion that he had known all this would happen – the fracturing, splitting –

Wonder if this is how paranoia feels. I've got a sense that there's a secret agenda somewhere, that I'm being set up, betrayed, by somebody or something. I've got to get out. Got to find my way out.

And on several of the eight levels or tracks, some versions of me decided, quite coldly and finally, that I'd had enough of this relationship with Steven, that it was time to stop being the classic approval-seeking victim; time to grow up and move on.

By the time the defensive mental scrambling had begun to clear, hours had gone by. The reality track that I belonged to had settled in, friendly and familiar, while the others slowly faded and thinned until finally, I was myself, I was where I belonged, and anxiety had been replaced by a lovely, simmering anger.

The drugs which simulate madness most acutely are the tropane alkaloids
– toxic, amnesiac delirants found in datura, deadly nightshade and
henbane. Their effects are so disorientating that they are difficult to
describe; one of the best recent accounts is by the pseudonymous 'Medlar
Lucan'.

MEDLAR LUCAN & DURIAN GRAY
The Decadent Gardener
(1996)

MEDLAR LUCAN ON HENBANE
(*HYOSCYAMUS NIGER*)

A few years ago, Durian, Heinrich and I took a house in Slovenia
with no intention other than idling away the summer. It was a peasant
house with a small garden and along one side of the house there grew
in abundance a plant which I recognized as henbane, *Hyoscyamus niger*.
I watched the plant with an interest bordering on obsession throughout
the summer, as I waited for its seeds to ripen. When this occurred I
collected a quantity and set about preparing them.

I discovered that there are two ways of experiencing henbane. One
is to make a sort of paste from the seeds and to rub it into an area of
the chest close to the heart. The other is to roast the seeds and inhale
the fumes. Feeling unconvinced about the first method, I decided to
start with the second. I took a handful of the flat, greyish seeds and
placing them on a metal plate, I heated them slowly from below using
a spirit stove. I watched with anticipation and unease as the seeds began
to swell. Shortly after, their shells burst and the fumes began to rise. I
inhaled deeply . . . It was not long (although I cannot say how long)
before it became clear that the fumes were beginning to penetrate my
consciousness. The first effects were physical – I began to feel very
unsteady on my feet. My head was aching and I experienced a sickening
dizziness. Also my mouth and throat became parched, to the point
where I could barely swallow, let alone speak. I began to feel frightened.
One might have thought that this was related to having taken the

henbane, that it was a fear of poisoning or death. But it could not have been, as I no longer had any idea how I had got into this state. No, it was just a vague, unspecific terror.

I remember looking in a mirror and this increased my anxiety. My face had swollen and become livid. The flesh on my head had grown much heavier and I could feel the bulk of it weighing about my cheeks, distorting the shape of my face. My eyes stared out at me, enlarged and black. I had trouble fixing my gaze on the mirror as it kept moving back and forth.

Soon not just the mirror but the entire room was on the move. I had to clutch hold of something to stop myself from sliding rapidly first to the left then to the right. My senses were diminishing. Sounds began to fade and the objects in the room began to darken. My peripheral vision became lost in a grey fog, I was drenched in perspiration by now and as the darkness deepened, sight was replaced by a series of terrifying hallucinations.

A thin stone column with an elaborately carved capital suddenly presented itself to my sight. It stood in front of me and was looking at me. I tried to move my head to avoid its gaze but found I was unable to. My body no longer responded to my wishes. I was paralysed. The gaze of the column became unbearable. I was overcome with a terrible sense of shame and terror towards this. My whole body seemed to be shaking uncontrollably.

As I stood there, unable to move, the column slowly dissolved and reformed in the shape of a grotesque infant. Its face was hideously contorted in a silent scream. It appeared to be in great pain, but I felt no sorrow or pity for it. I knew that it bore me ill-will and I desperately wanted to escape its malevolence. There was something deeply violent and almost satanic about it.

At this point, a whole host of images crowded around me – weird animals, talking plants, a cloud of tiny black insects, demented voices whispering urgently to me, as if semi-human creatures were trying to crawl inside my ears. It was as if I was inhabiting the world of a medieval text, a bestiary of madness. All the time I was trying to move, to escape, but my legs refused to respond. A wave of sickness rose up in me, to the point where I was sure I would collapse, although at the same time I knew that this would not bring me unconsciousness. The grotesque visions would continue to haunt me.

The next stage which I remember was both the most horrifying and

also the most exultant. Between the waves of nausea, I experienced
moments of profound well-being. These were accompanied by a feeling
of bodily disintegration. Although I was paralysed, it appeared that parts
of my body were beginning to detach themselves and take on a separate
existence. My head was stretching upwards and at any moment would
be parted from my body. Simultaneously, a sensation of flight began to
take hold of me. With this came a relaxation. As I experienced the terror
of my dissolving body, I abandoned myself to my hallucinations and I
was soon at one with them, drifting through a gloomy sky and over a
strange, crepuscular landscape. This was little short of euphoric. The
terror had lifted and I accepted the horror of the images which presented
themselves as a matter of course.

When I returned to consciousness, I was totally disoriented. Durian
and Heinrich must have carried me to my bed, where I lay for some
days languishing in deep gloom. My body was racked with discomfort
and the nausea remained with me. Even several days later I was still
unsteady and found it difficult to walk or take hold of objects.

This account is inevitably sketchy and incoherent. One consequence
of henbane narcosis is memory failure, so all that I was left with are
one or two particular hallucinations and a general sense of the physical
effects. This may be for the best. I shudder to think what nightmarish
images I have forgotten.

*Occasionally the effects of these drugs produce mass hysteria, as in this
recent report of a datura craze in Colombia.*

ANNE PROENZA
The Tree that Drives Colombians Mad
(1994)

A particularly insidious drug extracted from the tree *Datura
arborea* is being exploited by criminals in Colombia. Anne Proenza
reports from Bogotá.

When the Spanish discovered and invaded the savannah around
Bogotá in the 17th century they found the area covered with *Datura
arborea*, a small tree with spectacular bell-shaped flowers. Legend has
it that when they discovered the effects it had on anyone or any animal
that rested for a moment beneath its branches they nicknamed it 'the
tree that drives people mad'.

Today the *borrachero* (the common name for the tree) is still sending
people out of their minds. In the seventies Colombian criminals discovered a way of extracting an alkaloid called scopolamine (or hyoscine)
from part of its fruit. They used the alkaloid to make a devastating drug
which has a 'hypnotic' effect on people and causes them to lose their
memory.

Since then, the use of *burundanga* (the popular Colombian name for
the drug and all its variants) has been on the increase. Two months
ago, under its influence, a senator and his wife spent a whole night
withdrawing large amounts of money from their various banks' cash
dispensers and gave it to thieves. The couple then opened up their flat
and handed over their most precious possessions to the gang.

But that was a relatively banal case of how the drug can be used for
criminal purposes. Every weekend, 15–20 victims are admitted to the
emergency ward of Bogotá's Kennedy Hospital with absolutely no
recollection of what has happened to them. It usually turns out they
have been robbed of their money and jewellery, and sometimes raped.

The drug responsible, made from scopolamine and/or benzodiazepine
(a synthetic substance which goes into many tranquillisers such as
lorazepam and clonazepam, and which has similar effects to scopolamine

when administered in high doses), seems to be a Colombian speciality that is only rarely used outside the country's borders.

'A few isolated cases have been reported in Venezuela,' says Dr Camilo Uribe of the Bogotá Toxicology Clinic. 'There was also a case at a Spanish airport, but the people responsible were a Colombian couple.' He thinks that burundanga is responsible for over 80 per cent of the poisoning cases that the casualty departments of Colombian hospitals have to deal with.

Dr Uribe says it is an ideal drug for criminals: 'The victim does what he or she is told, then forgets both what happened and who the attackers were. It's a perfect form of chemical "hypnosis" which allows all sorts of crimes. Rape and sexual abuse are the most common, but it can also lead to some more serious crimes. Some people use it as a kind of truth serum like sodium pentothal, which was tried out during the second world war.'

He recalls the case of a young American woman who went home in a state of utter confusion on a Monday, convinced that the weekend had only just begun. A hospital examination revealed she had been raped by at least seven different men. She could remember nothing.

And then there was the case of a well-known diplomat, who vanished on a Friday evening after having a drink at a swish Bogotá bar. He resurfaced the following Tuesday, when he was arrested by customs officers at Santiago airport in Chile in the company of a woman he did not know – and in possession of two kilos of cocaine.

Scopolamine, an alkaloid similar to the atropine which is found in several plants of the *Solanaceae* (nightshade) family, and more especially in daturas, acts directly on the central nervous system. It is used in medicine, for example in some antispasmodic drugs.

It blocks neurotransmission and thus prevents the mechanism of memorisation. The effect of the drug on the brain is comparable to that of a power cut on a computer: all the data so far memorised is lost for ever. The result is no ordinary amnesia, but an anterograde lacunar form with irreversible aftereffects (the victim is unable to remember new information).

What Dr Uribe describes as 'a new burundanga', apparently, the work of 'highly skilled chemists', made its appearance in 1985. It would seem to be the result of combining scopolamine with benzodiazepine. Its effects are ideally suited to criminal purposes: the victim becomes totally suggestible, and remains both awake and quite calm.

Dr Pablo Tizo of the Institute of Forensic Medicine, which analyses the 140-odd complaints registered each month in Bogotá, says that criminals are now quite prepared to use pure benzodiazepine.

'For several years now, scopolamine has mostly been replaced by benzodiazepine, which is much easier to procure than scopolamine since it is present in over 15 medical products found in pharmacies,' he says. 'What's more, it produces similar effects to scopolamine when the dose exceeds two milligrams: loss of memory and a form of somnolence that does not prevent the victim from hearing what he or she is being told or from carrying out orders such as signing a cheque or handing over keys. Within a quarter of an hour, the victim is at the mercy of the aggressor. Moreover, benzodiazepine is never fatal, as scopolamine can be in some cases.'

Whether made of scopolamine (a natural substance) or benzodiazepine (an artificial substance), burundanga has to be administered orally in order to have an effect. It takes the form of a white or yellow powder which has the advantage, for the criminal, of being perfectly soluble and remaining odourless and tasteless.

Blood and urine analysis can prove the presence of one or other of the drugs in the organs for about three days after ingestion. 'Benzodiazepine has no aftereffects, apart from psychological ones,' says Dr Tizo, 'and the only cure is to get the patient to rest and to drink a lot of water to eliminate the drug.'

Scopolamine, on the other hand, has more serious medical consequences. Dr Uribe says that there is only one antidote, physostigmine, and that in the absence of any treatment major psychiatric disorders may occur four or five months later.

There is only one way for Colombians to avoid the dreaded effects of burundanga, and that is to mistrust any stranger who offers them something to drink or eat. Most cases of poisoning occur in nightspots or during public events.

The toxicology department of the Institute of Forensic Science has a display case filled with all the potential traps – sweets, chewing gum and pieces of chocolate containing the poison, some slightly cloudy *aguardiente* (the local spirit), and an unopened can of Coca-Cola into which the poison had been injected through a tiny hole.

Datura arborea still grows wild in Colombia and elsewhere in South America. For the past few years, there has been intensive farming of the tree in Ecuador to meet the needs of the pharmaceutical industry.

It would seem that some of the substances produced find their way illegally into Colombia. Paradoxically, a superb specimen of the 'tree that drives people mad' is to be found in the courtyard of the Institute of Forensic Science in Bogotá.

Visions of madness: A nineteenth-century ether-induced hallucination. (Mary Evans Picture Library)

But can we always be sure that it is the drug which is inducing the madness, and not the madness which is inventing the drug?

ANTONIO MELECHI
'The Case of Dr Johnson'

(1997)

In the early 1950s, Dr Donald Johnson published two deeply paranoic booklets on the subject of hallucinogenic drugs and mental health. In the first of these, *Indian Hemp: A Social Menace* (1952), Johnson argued that the grain or extract of hemp provided the perfect means 'to discredit you personally . . . to remove you for some time from your affairs, and perhaps permanently from the place where you are living' – in which time 'your enemy, who will have laid his plans, will be consolidating in uninterrupted fashion his control over your finances . . . or your wife.' As far as Johnson was concerned, there were countless psychiatric patients who were nothing more than hapless victims of hemp poisoning, effectively being held hostage by the institutions in which they were sectioned. In *The Hallucinogenic Drugs* (1953), Johnson reiterated the same fears – adding LSD to the list of substances that could produce insanity in the unsuspecting victim – and called upon his fellow medical practitioners to recognise this possibility when treating the manifestly psychotic.

Donald Johnson's career as a drugs commentator is of particular significance to this brief history because not only did his involvement in the issue of hallucinogenic drugs anticipate the work of Aldous Huxley, but if Johnson can be believed – and there is good reason for some doubt – his writings were based on personal experience. Furthermore, Johnson's experience revealed to him not only the diabolical aspects of drug psychosis, but, like Huxley, Johnson also had intimations of another reality, of the transfigured universe invoked in the writings of the mystics, and it was this transcendental realm which Johnson struggled to address in his work.

According to Johnson, he and his wife Betty were poisoned in October 1950, shortly after they were called back to their Oxfordshire hotel, The Marlborough Arms Inn. Over the course of a weekend, the Johnsons experienced a growing and unaccountable sense of anxiety which quickly escalated into full-blown paranoia. As the hotel staff became increasingly concerned with the Johnsons' strange behaviour, husband and wife were admitted to Warneford Psychiatric Hospital in Oxford. In a matter of days, Mrs Johnson had recovered enough for her to return home to the care of relatives. Meanwhile her husband remained in a 'state of mental excitement', At times believing himself to be undergoing clandestine training for a high-ranking position in the U N or the Commonwealth, Johnson also began to suspect that he and his wife had been victims of foul play: 'I felt that I had been poisoned and continued to say so until I saw that no notice was being taken. I had no idea what the poisoning agent was: at that time I still shared the general ignorance in regard to Indian Hemp.'

Soon after his discharge, Johnson set out to establish if the psychosis he had suffered over a period of four weeks could, as he suspected, have been drug-related. A visit to a Harley Street doctor and friend indicated that the symptoms he described were consistent with poisoning by a combination of hemp, opium and datura, and this satisfied him that his suspicions had been founded. Further evidence arrived in September 1951, when the *Sunday Graphic* published a series of articles which sought to alert its readership to the impending danger of the 'reefer craze' becoming 'the greatest social menace this country has known.'

Convinced that hemp had been used to poison him and his wife, Johnson set out to track down his mysterious nemesis. Finding no immediate evidence to implicate his hotel staff or guests, he was quickly distracted from his enquiries by an article in *The Lancet* which reported the outbreak of mass mania in the French town of Pont Saint Esprit, where four people had died, 15 had gone insane and 200 had fallen ill. The consensus of medical opinion favoured the theory that the epidemic was most probably a form of erysipelas caused by an ergot fungus in the local bread – a throwback to the medieval outbreaks of ergotism known as St Anthony's Fire – but Johnson was struck by the similarity between his own psychosis and the outward symptoms of the mania, and in its wake he set out to investigate. From the accounts which he managed to glean from doctors and townsfolk at Pont Saint Esprit, Johnson was left in little doubt that the town had been the victim of a case of mass poisoning by hemp – which he had found to be growing in outlying rural *départements*. Returning home with this even more alarming evidence of the hazards of hemp madness, Johnson set about informing medical practitioners and the general public of the grave dangers which hallucinogenic drugs posed to the nation's sanity.

Drugs and madness are artfully confused in the amphetamine-fuelled author Philip K. Dick's novel A Scanner Darkly. *Into the paranoid world of the undercover narcotics detective, Dick introduces a fictional drug called 'Substance D' which has the gradual effect of separating the brain hemispheres. The split lives of Bob Arctor/Fred, the undercover protagonist, become divorced to the point where he ends up arresting himself*

PHILIP K. DICK
A Scanner Darkly

(1977)

Item. What an undercover narcotics agent fears most is not that he will be shot or beaten up but that he will be slipped a great hit of some psychedelic that will roll an endless horror feature film in his head for the remainder of his life, or that he will be shot up with a mex hit, half heroin and half Substance D, or both of the above plus a poison such as strychnine, which will nearly kill him but not completely, so that the above can occur: lifelong addiction, lifelong horror film. He will sink into a needle-and-a-spoon existence, or bounce off the walls in a psychiatric hospital or, worst of all, a federal clinic. He will try to shake the aphids off him day and night or puzzle forever over why he cannot any longer wax a floor. And all this will occur deliberately. Someone figured out what he was doing and then got him. And they got him this way. The worst way of all: with the stuff they sell that he was after them for selling.

Which, Bob Arctor considered as he cautiously drove home, meant that both the dealers and the narks knew what the street drugs did to people. On that they agreed.

. . .

As he drove, Arctor ruminated about other ironic agreements in the minds of narcotics agents and dealers. Several narcotics agents that he had known had posed as dealers in their undercover work and wound up selling like hash and then, sometimes, even smack. This was a good cover, but it also brought the nark a gradually increasing profit over and above his official salary plus what he made when he helped bust and seize a good-sized shipment. Also, the agents got deeper and deeper into using their own stuff, the whole way of life, as a matter of course; they became rich dealer addicts as well as narks, and after a time some of them began to phase out their law-enforcement activities in favor of full-time dealing. But then, too, certain dealers, to burn their enemies or when expecting imminent busts, began narking and went that route, winding up as sort of unofficial undercover narks. It all got murky. The drug world was a murky world for everyone anyhow.

. . .

To himself, Bob Arctor thought, *How many Bob Arctors are there?* A weird and fucked-up thought. Two that I can think of, he thought. The one called Fred, who will be watching the other one, called Bob. The same person. Or is it? Is Fred actually the same as Bob? Does anybody know? I would know, if anyone did, because I'm the only person in the world that knows that Fred is Bob Arctor. *But*, he thought, *who am I? Which of them is me?*

. . .

He found himself confronting an all-white room with steel fixtures and steel chairs and steel desk, all bolted down, a hospital-like room, purified and sterile and cold, with the light too bright. In fact, to the right stood a weighing scale with a sign HAVE TECHNICIAN ONLY ADJUST. Two deputies regarded him, both in full uniform of the Orange County Sheriff's Office, but with medical stripes.

'You are Officer Fred?' one of them, with a handle-bar mustache, said.

'Yes, sir,' Fred said. He felt scared.

. . .

'Do you take Substance D?' the left-hand medical deputy said.

'That question,' the other said, 'is moot because it's taken for granted that in your work you're compelled to. So don't answer. Not that it's incriminating, but it's simply moot.' He indicated a table on which a bunch of blocks and other riff-raff colorful plastic objects lay, plus peculiar items that Officer Fred could not identify. 'Step over here and be seated, Officer Fred. We are going to administer, briefly, several easy tests. This won't consume much of your time, and there will be no physical discomfort involved.'

'What this is about,' the left-hand medical deputy said, as he seated himself and produced a pen and some forms, 'stems from a recent departmental survey showing that several undercover agents working in this area have been admitted to Neural Aphasia Clinics during the past month.'

'You're conscious of the high factor of addictiveness of Substance D?' the other deputy said to Fred.

'Sure,' Fred said. 'Of course I am.'

'We're going to give you these tests now,' the seated deputy said, 'in this order, starting with what we call the BG or –'

'You think I'm an addict?' Fred said.

'Whether you are an addict or not isn't a prime issue, since a blocking agent is expected from the Army Chemical Warfare Division sometime within the next five years.'

'These tests do not pertain to the addictive properties of Substance D but to – Well, let me give you this Set-Ground Test first, which determines your ability readily to distinguish set from ground. See this geometric diagram?' He laid a drawn-on card before Fred, on the table. 'Within the apparently meaningless lines is a familiar object that we would all recognize. You are to tell me what the . . .'

. . .

'. . . object is and point to it in the total field.'

I'm being Mutt-and-Jeffed, Fred thought. 'What is all this?' he said, gazing at the deputy and not the diagram.

. . .

The seated deputy said, 'In many of those taking Substance D, a split between the right hemisphere and the left hemisphere of the brain occurs. There is a loss of proper gestalting, which is a defect within both the percept and cognitive systems, although *apparently* the cognitive system continues to function normally. But what is now received from the percept system is contaminated by being split, so it too, therefore, fails gradually to function, progressively deteriorating. Have you located the familiar object in this line drawing? Can you find it for me?'

. . .

'Are you getting any cross-chatter?' one of the deputies asked him suddenly.

'What?' he said uncertainly.

'Between hemispheres. If there's damage to the left hemisphere, where the linguistic skills are normally located, then sometimes the right hemisphere will fill in to the best of its ability.'

'I don't know,' he said. 'Not that I'm aware of.'

'Thoughts not your own. As if another person or mind were thinking. But different from the way you would think.'

The paradigmatic location of madness in the modern drug world is the crack-dealer's den.

JERRY STAHL
Permanent Midnight
(1995)

The real passion for my dealer was freebasing. The first occasion when he invited me to share his pursuit, I felt every bit as transfixed and terrified as any other novice standing in the open doorway of cultdom.

It wasn't the drug that spooked me, it was the look on Jésus' face.

As I watched him tiptoe about the apartment, ducking past the windows, bending over the stove to stir up the cocaine and baking soda like some psychotic master chef, arranging everything to a compulsive T, the thought jumped up and gripped me by the throat: *He might as well be planning a murder.*

For the occasion, Jésus invited over Felix, a lumbering, jug-eared tattoo victim he knew from the joint. Six-foot-five of solid muscle, Felix was simultaneously frightening and ludicrous looking. It's as if Prince Charles's head had been randomly transplanted on the body of Lou Ferrigno: the Hulk with the face of a basset hound.

Felix, who turned out to be half Latino, did not talk a lot. He didn't have to. You kind of got the message without a lot of verbal interference. Before he showed up, Jésus had told me he collected for a Mexican loan shark on Brooklyn Avenue. He said he was a little strange. 'But then,' he added in the first hint of levity since we'd made plans to freebase, 'so are you, right, amigo? That's why I figured you'd be friends.' He figured wrong.

For the most part, between hits – when Felix wasn't pulling out a .357 and I wasn't pretending not to be scared shitless – we smoked and sat, sat and smoked, in complete silence. Occasionally, though, I'd bolt upright, look wildly around me, and slump back down again. I didn't know enough about the drug I was doing to know if no time had passed or if it was the middle of the night already.

Everything that was happening, everything that had happened, had become so frightening, I could absorb it only by sitting where I was, putting my leather jacket on to kill the chill that wouldn't go away, and staying glued to the Home Shopping Channel. That was, I learned, as much a part of this whole savage ritual as the pipe, the cooking, or the minute-but-powerful minitorch.

Jésus had positioned himself more or less permanently beside his front window. There, every second or so, he would risk a peek, peeling the blind back a hair to glue one eye at the street.

'Oh shit, OH SHIT!' he shouted. 'Oh SHIT – THEY'RE COMING!'

'Who's coming?'

'The fucking cops man. *Listen* . . . OH SHIT! Can't you hear? Can't you hear the fucking choppers? They – ARE – COMING! *THEY ARE COMING, MAN!!*'

And I did listen. They *were* out there. Helicopters. I heard them. Lots of helicopters, taking off from somewhere, flying somewhere else. Not here, that was certain. Not descending like an outtake from *Apocalypse Now* to round up Jésus and me. No, I was sure of that. But, because I was sure, I was even more scared. More scared than he was, because I was sitting there in a room, with a guy who *did* believe they were after him. Who believed, after he did enough base, after he crossed whatever line there was left for him to cross, that every footstep, every car horn, distant shout, or flushing toilet – every noise in the universe had a threat behind it. And with enough rock in your system, you could hear every noise in the universe.

*Can madness itself be a drug? In author Terry Southern's short story
'The Blood of a Wig', the protagonist is offered the blood of a schizophrenic patient.*

TERRY SOUTHERN
'The Blood of a Wig'

(1967)

It was just about then he sprung it – first giving me his look of
odd appraisal, then the sigh, the tired smile, the haltering deference:
'Listen, man . . . you ever made red-split?'

'I beg your pardon?'

'Yeah, you know – *the blood of a wig.*'

'No,' I said, not really understanding, 'I don't believe I have.'

'Well, it's something else, baby, I can tell you that.'

'Uh, well, *what* did you call it – I'm not sure I understood . . .'

'"Red-split," man, it's called "red-split" – it's schizo-juice . . . *blood*
. . . the blood of a wig.'

'Oh, I see.' I had, in fact, read about it in a recent article in the *Times*
– how they had shot up a bunch of volunteer prisoners (very normal,
healthy guys, of course) with the blood of schizophrenia patients – and
the effect had been quite pronounced . . . in some cases, manic; in other
cases, depressive – about 50/50 as I recalled.

'But that can be a big bring-down, can't it?'

He shook his head sombrely. 'Not with *this* juice it can't. You know
who this is out of?' Then he revealed the source – Chin Lee, it was, a
famous East Village resident, a Chinese symbolist poet, who was presently residing at Bellevue in a straitjacket. 'Nobody,' he said, 'and I
mean *nobody*, baby, has gone anywhere but *up*, *up*, *up* on *this* taste!'

I thought that it might be an interesting experience, but using caution
as my watchword (the *Times* article had been very sketchy) I had to
know more about this so-called red-split, blood of a wig. 'Well, how
long does it, uh, you know, *last?*'

He seemed a little vague about that – almost to the point of resenting
the question. 'It's a *trip*, man – four hours, six if you're lucky. It all
depends. It's a question of *combination* – how your blood makes it with

his, you dig?' He paused and gave me a very straight look. 'I'll tell you this much, baby, it *cuts acid and STP* . . .' He nodded vigorously. 'That's right, cuts both them. *Back*, *down*, and *sideways*.'

'Really?'

He must have felt he was getting a bit too loquacious, a bit too much on the old hard-sell side, because then he just cooled it, and nodded. 'That's right,' he said, so soft and serious that it wasn't really audible.

'How much?' I asked, finally, uncertain of any other approach.

'I'll level with you,' he said, 'I've got this connection – a ward attendant . . . you know, a male nurse . . . has, what you might call *access* to the hospital pharmacy . . . does a little trading with the guards on the fifth floor – that's where the *monstro*-wigs are – "High Five" it's called. That's where Chin Lee's at. Anyway, he's operating at cost right now – I mean, he'll cop as much M, or whatever other hard-shit he can, from the pharmacy, then he'll go up to High Five and trade for the juice – you know, just fresh, straight, uncut wig-juice – 90 c.c.'s, that's the regular hit, about an ounce, I guess . . . I mean, that's what they hit the wigs for, a 90 c.c. syringeful, then they cap the spike and put the whole outfit in an insulated wrapper. Like it's supposed to stay at body temperature, you dig? They're very strict about that – about how much they tap the wig for, and about keeping it fresh and warm, that sort of thing. Which is okay, because that's the trip – 90 c.c.'s, "piping hot", as they say.' He gave a tired little laugh at the curious image. 'Anyway the point is, he never knows in front what the *price* will be, my friend doesn't, because he never knows what kind of M score he'll make. I mean like if he scores for half-a-bill of M, then that's what he charges for the split, you dig?'

To me, with my Mad Ave savvy, this seemed fairly illogical.

'Can't he hold out on the High Five guys?' I asked, '. . . you know, tell them he only got half what he really got, and save it for later?'

He shrugged, almost unhappily. 'He's a very ethical guy,' he said, 'I mean like he's pretty weird. He's not really interested in narcotics, just *changes*. I mean, like he lets *them* do the count on the M – they tell him how much it's worth and that's what he charges for the split.'

'That *is* weird,' I agreed.

'Yeah, well it's like a new market, you know. I mean, there's no established price yet, he's trying to develop a clientele – can you make half-a-bill?'

While I pondered, he smiled his brave tired smile, and said: 'There's one thing about the cat, being so ethical and all – he'll never burn you.'

. . . and in Fear and Loathing in Las Vegas, *Hunter S. Thompson conjures the possibility of getting high on an extract from the human pineal gland.*

HUNTER S. THOMPSON
Fear and Loathing in Las Vegas: A Savage Journey to the Heart of the American Dream
(1971)

I tossed him the kit-bag. 'Be careful,' I muttered. 'There's not much left.'

He chuckled. 'As your attorney,' he said, 'I advise you not to worry.' He nodded toward the bathroom. 'Take a hit out of that little brown bottle in my shaving kit.'

'What is it?'

'Adrenochrome,' he said. 'You won't need much. Just a little *tiny* taste.'

I got the bottle and dipped the head of a paper match into it.

'That's about right,' he said. 'That stuff makes pure mescaline seem like ginger beer. You'll go completely crazy if you take too much.'

I licked the end of the match. 'Where'd you get *this*?' I asked. 'You can't buy it.'

'Never mind,' he said. 'It's absolutely pure.'

I shook my head sadly. 'Jesus! What kind of monster client have you picked up *this* time? There's only one source for this stuff . . .'

He nodded.

'The adrenalin glands from a *living* human body,' I said. 'It's no good if you get it out of a corpse.'

'I know,' he replied. 'But the guy didn't have any cash. He's one of these Satanism freaks. He offered me human blood – said it would make me higher than I'd ever been in my life,' he laughed. 'I thought he was kidding, so I told him I'd just as soon have an ounce or so of pure adrenochrome – or maybe just a fresh adrenalin gland to chew on.'

I could already feel the stuff working on me. The first wave felt like a combination of mescaline and methedrine. Maybe I should take a swim, I thought.

'Yeah,' my attorney was saying. 'They nailed this guy for child molesting, but he swears he didn't do it. "Why should I fuck with *children*?" he says; "They're too *small*!" ' He shrugged. 'Christ, what could I say? Even a goddamn werewolf is entitled to legal counsel . . . I didn't *dare* turn the creep down. He might have picked up a letter opener and gone after my pineal gland.'

'Why not?' I said. 'He could probably get Melvin Belli for that.' I nodded, barely able to talk now. My body felt like I'd just been wired into a 220 volt socket. 'Shit, we should get us some of that stuff,' I muttered finally. 'Just eat a big handful and see what happens.'

'Some of what?'

'Extract of pineal.'

He stared at me. 'Sure,' he said. 'That's a *good* idea. One *whiff* of that shit would turn you into something out of a goddamn medical encyclopedia! Man, your head would swell up like a watermelon, you'd probably gain about a hundred pounds in two hours . . . claws, bleeding warts, then you'd notice about six huge hairy tits swelling up on your back . . .' He shook his head emphatically. 'Man, I'll try just about anything; but I'd never in hell touch a pineal gland.

'Last Christmas somebody gave me a whole Jimson weed – the root must have weighed two pounds; enough for a *year* – but I ate the whole goddamn thing in about twenty minutes!'

I was leaning toward him, following his words intently. The slightest hesitation made me want to grab him by the throat and force him to talk faster. 'Right!' I said eagerly. 'Jimson weed! What happened?'

'Luckily, I vomited most of it right back up,' he said. 'But even so, I went blind for three days. Christ I couldn't even walk! My whole body turned to wax. I was such a mess that they had a haul me back to the ranch house in a wheelbarrow . . . they said I was trying to talk, but I sounded like a raccoon.'

'Fantastic,' I said. But I could barely hear him. I was so wired that my hands were clawing uncontrollably at the bedspread, jerking it right out from under me while he talked. My heels were dug into the mattress, with both knees locked . . . I could feel my eyeballs swelling, about to pop out of the sockets.

'Finish the fucking story!' I snarled. 'What *happened*? What about the *glands*?'

He backed away, keeping an eye on me as he edged across the room. 'Maybe you need another drink,' he said nervously. 'Jesus that stuff got right on *top* of you, didn't it?'

I tried to smile. 'Well . . . nothing worse . . . no, this *is* worse . . .' It was hard to move my jaws; my tongue felt like burning magnesium. 'No . . . nothing to worry about,' I hissed. 'Maybe if you could just . . . shove me into the pool, or something . . .'

'Goddamnit,' he said. 'You took too *much* You're about to explode. Jesus, look at your *face!*'

I couldn't move. Total paralysis now. Every muscle in my body was contracted. I couldn't even move my eyeballs, much less turn my head or talk.

'It won't last long,' he said. 'The first rush is the worst. Just ride the bastard out. If I put you in the pool right now, you'd sink like a goddamn stone.'

Death. I was sure of it. Not even my lungs seemed to be functioning. I needed artificial respiration, but I couldn't open my mouth to say so. I was going to *die*. Just sitting there on the bed, unable to move . . . well at least there's no pain. Probably, I'll black out in a few seconds, and after that it won't matter.

My attorney had gone back to watching television. The news was on again. Nixon's face filled the screen, but his speech was hopelessly garbled. The only word I could make out was 'sacrifice'. Over and over again: 'Sacrifice . . . sacrifice . . . sacrifice . . .'

I could hear myself breathing heavily. My attorney seemed to notice. 'Just stay relaxed,' he said over his shoulder, without looking at me. 'Don't try to fight it, or you'll start getting brain bubbles . . . strokes, aneurisms . . . you'll just wither up and die.' His hand snaked out to change channels.

It was after midnight when I finally was able to talk and move around . . . but I was still not free of the drug; the voltage had merely been cranked down from 220 to 110. I was a babbling nervous wreck, flapping around the room like a wild animal, pouring sweat and unable to concentrate on any one thought for more than two or three seconds at a time.

My attorney put down the phone after making several calls. 'There's only one place where we can get fresh salmon,' he said, 'and it's closed on Sunday.'

'Of course,' I snapped. 'These goddamn Jesus freaks! They're multiplying like rats!'

He eyed me curiously.

'What about the Process?' I said. 'Don't they have a place here? Maybe a delicatessen or something? With a few tables in back? They have a fantastic menu in London. I ate there once; incredible food . . .'

'Get a grip on yourself,' he said. 'You don't want to even *mention* the Process in this town.'

'You're right,' I said. 'Call Inspector Bloor. He knows about food. I think he has a *list*.'

'Better to call room service,' he said. 'We can get the crab looey and a quart of Christian Brothers muscatel for about twenty bucks.'

'No!' I said. 'We *must* get out of this place. I need air. Let's drive up to Reno and get a big tuna fish salad . . . hell, it won't take long. Only about four hundred miles; no traffic out there on the desert . . .'

'Forget it,' he said. 'That's *Army territory*. Bomb tests, nerve gas – we'd never make it.'

We wound up at a place called The Big Flip about halfway downtown. I had a 'New York steak' for $1.88. My attorney ordered the 'Coyote Bush Basket' for $2.09 . . . and after that we drank off a pot of watery 'Golden West' coffee and watched four boozed-up cowboy types kick a faggot half to death between the pinball machines.

'The action never stops in this town,' said my attorney as we shuffled out to the car. 'A man with the right contacts could probably pick up all the fresh adrenochrome he wanted, if he hung around here for a while.'

*During the nineteenth century, the idea developed that drugs could be
used to treat various forms of mental illness.*

JACQUES-JOSEPH MOREAU DE TOURS
Hashish and Mental Illness

(1845)

As soon as I was able to appreciate its effects not from the
reports of those who had used it but by myself, I thought of the
advantages that could be derived from it, first of all in the study of
madness and perhaps also in the treatment of this illness.

One of the effects of hashish that struck me most forcibly and
which generally gets the most attention is that manic excitement always
accompanied by a feeling of gaiety and joy inconceivable to those who
have not experienced it. I saw in it a means of effectively combatting
the fixed ideas of depressives, of disrupting the chain of their ideas, of
unfocusing their attention on such and such a subject. It was perhaps
no less appropriate to arouse the drowsy intelligence of mute (*stupides*)
psychotics or even to return a little energy and resiliency to the
demented.

Were my conjectures mistaken? I am led to believe so, without,
however, considering the matter closed. I administered hashish, either
in the form of *dawamese* or extract of butter, in gradually larger doses
to the demented, depressives, and mute psychotics. In the demented,
the results (I am speaking here only of the physiological action) were
almost nil, despite an increase in the dosage; it was the same with the
mutes. Two depressives felt a rather strong *excitement* after five or six
hours, with all the characteristics of gaiety and garrulousness that we
know. One of them in particular, who for more than nine months had
not pronounced more than ten words a day, tormented as he constantly
was by imaginary terrors and fixed ideas, could not stop talking, laughing,
and doing silly things for an entire evening. Something worthy of note
is that I rarely found any relationship between his words and the thoughts
that usually preoccupied him. Be that as it may, when the *excitement*
passed, he soon regressed to his previous state.

. . .

Must we conclude from what has just been said that there is nothing to expect from hashish in the treatment of depression? Certainly not. These therapeutic attempts are quite imperfect. With such limited results, we cannot judge the action of any medication. Possessing only a small amount of hashish, I had to use it sparingly. Many depressives, particularly the demented, seem to resist its action to the extent that very strong doses never suffice to excite them. I cannot tell if, through repeated attempts they might eventually overcome the rigidity of their ideas, or if, by occasionally coming out of their reveries, they might finally manage to break the chain of their thoughts.

The use of LSD as an aid to psychiatric treatment came into vogue in the 1950s, shortly after Hofmann first synthesized the drug (see p. 55).

JAY STEVENS
Storming Heaven: LSD and the American Dream

(1989)

By 1956 the question 'what's in the unconscious?' had fragmented into a host of subsidiary questions as therapists realized that the Dark Room, like a grandmother's attic, was crammed with treasure. In this trunk, Jungian archetypes; in that one, lovely Freudian neuroses that could be tracked all the way back to the moment when the patient, standing in her cradle barely one year old, had watched her parents making love. Instead of having to walk, the therapist could fly. And while that presented a new set of problems – for one thing, LSD sessions lasted a wearying three to four hours – it didn't diminish the excited feeling that they were on the edge of Something Big. Whenever LSD researchers got together the conversation quickly turned anecdotal, as one eye-widening story followed another: '. . . and suddenly I found myself giving birth to myself. I could actually feel myself floating around in the amniotic fluid, then I was flushed down the vaginal canal, thinking "this is it, I've died and now I'm being reborn."'

It was like belonging to an elite fraternity. 'When you made contact,' remembers Oscar Janiger, 'it was like two people looking at each other from across the room, and with a sort of nod of the head ... like "Welcome brother, you have now entered the Mysteries." That's all. That was your ticket of admission. Nothing else. That knowing look.'

Oscar Janiger was a Beverley Hills psychiatrist who preferred research to analysis, although he did just enough of the latter to pay for the leisure to indulge in the former.

. . .

Janiger, Bivens, and their wives took the LSD at Janiger's vacation home at Lake Arrowhead. A short while into the experiment Bivens's wife had disappeared into a bedroom. She returned a few minutes later wearing a purple sweater, skintight vermillion pants, yellow ballet slippers, and a long mauve scarf. And then, an intimation of things to come, she began to dance.

Driving back to Los Angeles, Janiger felt like Moses coming down from the mountain, except in his case what he lacked was the tablets – or ampoules. I've got to get my hands on some more LSD, he thought. I'll go crazy if I can't figure out an experiment that will satisfy Sandoz. But what kind of an experiment? Janiger had no interest in experimental lab work, giving LSD to snails and fish and making voluminous notes on their reactions. Nor was he interested in the Lab Madness rigmarole of personality and intelligence tests. After puzzling over the problem for several weeks, he arrived at a simple solution: why not just give LSD to volunteers and let them do whatever they wanted? Provide them with paper, pencils, typewriter, tape recorder, and leave them alone – a completely naturalistic study. Much to his surprise, Sandoz agreed, and within a few weeks he had his own supply of LSD.

. . .

One of Janiger's counterparts was Sidney Cohen, a psychiatrist attached to the Los Angeles Neuropsychiatric Hospital, which was part of the Veterans Administration. Cohen had obtained his first LSD fully intending to pursue the model psychoses work of Max Rinkel and the other Lab Madness researchers, but his own personal experience with the drug had caused him to change direction.

'I was taken by surprise,' he recollected a few years later at an LSD symposium. 'This was no confused, disoriented delirium, but something quite different. Just what it was I could not say.' It refused to be Englished. Or easily psychologized. 'Though we have been using the available measuring instruments, the check lists, the performance tests, the psychological batteries, and so forth, the core of the LSD situation remains in the dark, quite untouched by our activities,' he confessed.

. . .

But however cautious he might have been about LSD's ultimate utility, Sidney Cohen was instrumental in turning on not only his colleagues, mostly psychiatrists and psychologists, but a few writers and scientists as well. During one stretch his office was full of analysts from the Rand Corporation, the semi-secret think tank located in Santa Monica. One of them, Herman Kahn, took LSD and lay on the floor murmuring 'wow' every few minutes. Later he claimed he had spent the time profitably reviewing bombing strategies against mainland China.

One of the psychologists whom Cohen introduced to LSD was a man named A. Wesley Medford. With a friend, a cancer specialist and radiologist named Mortimer Hartman, Medford began spending his weekends experimenting with the drug. Gradually others joined in, until their private weekend investigations resembled what in left political circles would have been called a cell – a cell not of the class wars, but the consciousness wars. All sorts of crazy things started happening to the Wesley group. Astral projection. Past lives. Telepathy over vast spaces. Enhanced intelligence. The sense that they could link up into a multiple mind, a Group Mind. Although all the experiments that they designed to test these newfound powers failed – remember Weir Mitchell with his poems and psychology papers – it didn't dampen the group's ardour, and the rest of the LSD research community watched in bemused fascination as the Wesley group grew in intensity and then came apart amid denunciations and recriminations. It seemed LSD also enhanced some of the negative personality traits that make it difficult for people to get along with each other.

Wesley returned to his former practice, warning that LSD was uncontrollable. But not Hartman. LSD had lit a fire under Hartman; he couldn't leave it alone. Teaming up with a psychiatrist named Arthur Chandler, who had joined the Wesley group late in the game, Hartman opened an office in Beverly Hills and launched a five-year therapeutic study that had Sandoz's blessing.

. . .

Of all the actors, writers, musicians, and directors who passed through Chandler and Hartman's portals, the most famous was Cary Grant. Grant took LSD more than sixty times, and although he was considered one of Hollywood's most private stars, he found his enthusiasm for the drug hard to contain. It finally overflowed during the filming of the movie *Operation Petticoat*. The scene was appropriately bizarre. There was Grant sitting on the deck of the pink submarine that was *Petticoat*'s principal set. He had an aluminium sheet attached to his neck to facilitate his tan and he was chatting with two reporters, both of whom were prepared for the usual hour of teeth pulling that an interview with Grant required. But today Cary was totally relaxed, a condition he attributed to the insights he had achieved using an experimental mind drug called LSD.

'I have been born again,' he told the astonished reporters. 'I have been through a psychiatric experience which has completely changed me. I was horrendous. I had to face things about myself which I never admitted, which I didn't know were there. Now I know that I hurt every woman I ever loved. I was an utter fake, a self-opinionated bore, a know-all who knew very little.

'I found I was hiding behind all kinds of defences, hypocrisies and vanities. I had to get rid of them layer by layer. The moment when your conscious meets your subconscious is a hell of a wrench. With me there came a day when I saw the light.'

Although Grant, his lawyers, and MGM all tried to kill the story, it appeared in print on April 20, 1959, and while it didn't alter Grant's popularity one iota, it was an enormous shot in the pocketbook for LSD therapists like Chandler and Hartman. Suddenly everyone in Hollywood wanted to be born again.

One of its most successful results was the redesign of mental hospitals.

P. G. STAFFORD AND B. H. GOLIGHTLY
LSD: The Problem-Solving Psychedelic

(1967)

Perhaps the outstanding instance of creative problem solving lending itself to therapeutic implementation occurred when Kyoshi Izumi, a prominent architect, was asked to design a mental hospital in Canada and decided to take LSD in search of better insight into the problem. In his words:

Psychiatrists talk one language and I talk another. They knew what they wanted but someone had to translate their wishes into architecture. To me there was really no other way. If I were to really understand the fears and problems of the schizophrenic, I would have to look at things the way they did.

Consequently, when he took LSD, Izumi paid extensive visits to old mental institutions in an attempt to see them through the eyes of derangement. He found himself terrified by literally dozens of standard hospital accoutrements and features which had always been taken for granted as adequate. The tiles on the wall glistened, eerily, thereby projecting hideous fantasies that sprang at him from the cracks. The recessed closets seemed to yawn like huge, dark cavities, threatening to swallow him alive. The raised hospital beds, too high for a patient to sit on and at the same time touch the floor, were like crags jutting out over abysses. There was no privacy, and the time sense was nil, due to the absence of clocks, calendars or any other measuring device which might help a patient find his bearings. The bars on the windows were a constant reminder of incarceration. But worst of all were the long, endless corridors leading into more of Nowhere which, nevertheless, had to be traversed.

After his LSD insights, Mr Izumi was able to design what has been called 'the ideal mental hospital'. The first was built in Yorkton, Saskatchewan, and five others have been modeled upon it elsewhere in Canada. There is a similarly inspired hospital in Haverford, Pa., and because commendation has been made for this outstanding architectural advancement by the Joint Information Service of the American Psychiatric Association, it is possible that the present outdated hospitals will give way to new ones resembling Izumi's designs.

The Yorkton hospital consists of small, cottage-like clusters of rooms, thirty to a unit, joined together by underground passageways. Seen from the air, the entire structure resembles a Maltese cross. There are many windows, low and unbarred, eliminating the old, dismal barnlike aspect of mental hospitals. The walls are painted in pleasant, flat colors, and each patient has his own room in one or another of the clusters, rather than a bed in an austere, nearly bare ward. The beds are low to the floor, and the rooms are furnished with regard to making it easier to define the floor as a mere floor, not a pit. Also, the furniture is comfortable and not unlike that with which the patient is familiar at home. The closet problem has been solved by installing large, movable cabinets which the patient can clearly see possess both a back and a front. Clocks and calendars abound, while floor tiles are sparingly used. The emphasis throughout puts patient needs foremost, without sacrificing utility.

*. . . while its most terrifying application was as a 'mind-control agent'
in the CIA programme known as MKULTRA.*

JOHN MARKS

The Search for the 'Manchurian Candidate'

(1991)

Dr Harris Isbell, whose work the CIA funded through Navy
cover with the approval of the Director of the National Institutes of
Health, published his principal findings, but he did not mention how
he obtained his subjects. As Director of the Addiction Research Center
at the huge Federal drug hospital in Lexington, Kentucky, he had access
to a literally captive population. Inmates heard on the grapevine that if
they volunteered for Isbell's program, they would be rewarded either
in the drug of their choice or in time off from their sentences. Most of
the addicts chose drugs – usually heroin or morphine of a purity seldom
seen on the street. The subjects signed an approval form, but they were
not told the names of the experimental drugs or the probable effects.
This mattered little, since the 'volunteers' probably would have granted
their informed consent to virtually anything to get hard drugs.

Given Isbell's almost unlimited supply of subjects, TSS officials used
the Lexington facility as a place to make quick tests of promising but
untried drugs and to perform specialized experiments they could not
easily duplicate elsewhere. For instance, Isbell did one study for which
it would have been impossible to attract student volunteers. He kept
seven men on LSD for 77 straight days. Such an experiment is as
chilling as it is astonishing – both to lovers and haters of LSD. Nearly
20 years after Dr Isbell's early work, counterculture journalist Hunter
S. Thompson delighted and frightened his readers with accounts of
drug binges lasting a few days, during which Thompson felt his brain
boiling away in the sun, his nerves wrapping around enormous barbed
wire forts, and his remaining faculties reduced to their reptilian ante-
cedents. Even Thompson would shudder at the thought of 77 days
straight on LSD, and it is doubtful he would joke about the idea. To

Dr Isbell, it was just another experiment. 'I have had seven patients who have now been taking the drug for more than 42 days,' he wrote in the middle of the test, which he called 'the most amazing demonstration of drug tolerance I have ever seen'. Isbell tried to 'break through this tolerance' by giving triple and quadruple doses of LSD to the inmates.

Filled with intense curiosity, Isbell tried out a wide variety of unproven drugs on his subjects. Just as soon as a new batch of scopolamine, rivea seeds, or bufontenine arrived from the CIA or NIMH, he would start testing. His relish for the task occasionally shone through the dull scientific reports. 'I will write you a letter as soon as I can get the stuff into a man or two,' he informed his Agency contact.

No corresponding feeling shone through for the inmates, however. In his few recorded personal comments, he complained that his subjects tended to be afraid of the doctors and were not as open in describing their experiences as the experimenters would have wished. Although Isbell made an effort to 'break through the barriers' with the subjects, who were nearly all black drug addicts, Isbell finally decided 'in all probability, this type of behaviour is to be expected with patients of this type.'

. . .

Sid Gottlieb and his colleagues at MKULTRA soaked up pools of information about LSD and other drugs from all outside sources, but they saved for themselves the research they really cared about: operational testing. Trained in both science and espionage, they believed they could bridge the huge gap between experimenting in the laboratory and using drugs to outsmart the enemy. Therefore the leaders of MKULTRA initiated their own series of drug experiments that paralleled and drew information from the external research. As practical men of action, unlimited by restrictive academic standards, they did not feel the need to keep their tests in strict scientific sequence. They wanted results now – not next year. If a drug showed promise, they felt no qualms about trying it out operationally before all the test results came in. As early as 1953, for instance, Sid Gottlieb went overseas with a supply of a hallucinogenic drug – almost certainly LSD. With unknown results, he arranged for it to be slipped to a speaker at a political rally, presumably to see if it would make a fool of him.

These were freewheeling days within the CIA – then a young agency whose bureaucratic arteries had not started to harden. The leaders of MKULTRA had high hopes for LSD. It appeared to be an awesome substance, whose advent, like the ancient discovery of fire, would bring out primitive responses of fear and worship in people. Only a speck of LSD could take a strong-willed man and turn his most basic perceptions into willowy shadows. Time, space, right, wrong, order, and the notion of what was possible all took on new faces. LSD was a frightening weapon, and it took a swashbuckling boldness for the leaders of MKULTRA to prepare for operational testing the way they first did: by taking it themselves. They tripped at the office. They tripped at safehouses, and sometimes they traveled to Boston to trip under Bob Hyde's penetrating gaze. Always they observed, questioned, and analysed each other. LSD seemed to remove inhibitions, and they thought they could use it to find out what went on in the mind underneath all the outside acts and pretensions. If they could get at the inner self, they reasoned, they could better manipulate a person – or keep him from being manipulated.

The men from MKULTRA were trying LSD in the early 1950s – when Stalin lived and Joe McCarthy raged. It was a foreboding time, even for those not professionally responsible for doomsday poisons. Not surprisingly, Sid Gottlieb and colleagues who tried LSD did not think of the drug as something that might enhance creativity or cause transcendental experiences. Those notions would not come along for years. By and large, there was thought to be only one prevailing and hard-headed version of reality, which was 'normal', and everything else was 'crazy'. An LSD trip made people temporarily crazy, which meant potentially vulnerable to the CIA men (and mentally ill, to the doctors). The CIA experimenters did not trip for the experience itself, or to get high, or to sample new realities. They were testing a weapon; for their purposes, they might as well have been in a ballistics lab.

Despite this prevailing attitude in the Agency, at least one MKULTRA pioneer recalls that his first trip expanded his conception of reality: 'I was shaky at first, but then I just experienced it and had a high. I felt that everything was working right. I was like a locomotive going at top efficiency. Sure there was stress, but not in a debilitating way. It was like the stress of an engine pulling the longest train it's ever pulled.' This CIA veteran describes seeing all the colours of the rainbow growing out of cracks in the sidewalk. He had always disliked cracks as signs of imperfection, but suddenly the cracks became natural stress lines that measured the vibrations of the universe. He saw people with blemished faces, which he had previously found slightly repulsive. 'I had a change of values about faces,' he says. 'Hooked noses or crooked teeth would become beautiful for that person. Something had turned loose in me, and all I had done was shift my attitude. Reality hadn't changed, but I had. That was all the difference in the world between seeing something ugly and seeing truth and beauty.'

At the end of this day of his first trip, the CIA man and his colleagues had an alcohol party to help come down. 'I had a lump in my throat,' he recalls wistfully. Although he had never done such a thing before, he wept in front of his co-workers. 'I didn't want to leave it. I felt I would be going back to a place where I wouldn't be able to hold on to this kind of beauty. I felt very unhappy. The people who wrote the report on me said I had experienced depression, but they didn't understand why I felt so bad. They thought I had had a bad trip.'

Despite some spectacular successes, the risks of LSD therapy turned out to be high, and many of its effects disturbing.

RONALD SANDISON
'LSD Therapy'

(1997)

Consider the following 'snapshots' from a patient undergoing LSD therapy in our clinic. She was a married woman, 29 years of age, of German birth. She wrote:

I began to see a face on the wall, it was a man with one eye and he had a moustache. He sometimes smiled at me cynically and sometimes looked very grim and threatening. I tried to connect him with something which had happened to me a long time ago. It was then that he got mixed up with Hitler and I saw nothing else but swastikas. For one brief moment it was my father's face. Then I remembered one man in particular. He was a German officer. Then I remembered the incident connected with that man.

The patient goes on to describe how this officer took her to his flat one evening and seduced her. She continues:

The thing that bothered me most under LSD was that I was being forced against my will without showing the slightest resistance. As I pondered over this Hitler appeared again and I saw the connection. He too, in a subtle way, together with his powerful personality, made me do things against my will without me resisting. Then I had a feeling of falling down deeper and deeper and yet I felt detached just as if I were watching it all happen.

There followed a series of reductive and unpleasant sessions, of which the following is an example:

There was a huge image of Hitler on the wall like a big shadow in which I could see many other hostile faces. I wanted to get away from these hostile men and tried to hide in a corner. Then I saw skulls and crossbones on the wall and suddenly I felt the flesh falling off my bones and I was a skeleton, I think only from the waist down. I remember my teeth falling out and when I tried to bite I was biting on my gums.

In the next series of treatments the degradation persisted; she saw herself, for example, as a prostitute stabbed and lying in the gutter, she became depressed and suicidal. She describes the tenth LSD treatment as follows:

There is tremendous confusion within me. There is no harmony. The muddled faces had terrific mouths and tried to swallow me up. I felt that they would swallow me up only as long as they were in a such a muddle and it was therefore necessary to find order in this confusion. I then found that there was some order insofar as there were two sides to it each opposing the other and pulling in opposite directions. I tried to find out about the two parts and discovered that they must be the good and evil in me.

The patient then had a dream. In the beginning part of the dream she meets her lover and feels very happy but she is unable to make love to him. She goes on:

I tried to find out why I could not make love to him and suddenly something inside me said: 'Because you have not picked up the five stones from the bottom of the sea. You did not do it for your parents either, that is why you could not love them.' I felt as if all my problems had been solved, or at least that I now knew what I had to do.

In the next LSD treatment she decided to investigate this. She wrote:

I feel I must overcome my fear and go to the bottom of the sea. Then I started going down under the water but I met alligators who were waiting for me and I could feel their teeth in my body. I went down under the water again and as I went deeper my fear grew less. I could see the stones, but they were now only four in number. It was as if the fifth had represented fear which has now gone. I came closer and closer and suddenly it was as if I were looking in a mirror. These four stones formed a face. I cannot describe its ugliness and horribleness. At the same time the face was beautiful. I could not say what piece was ugly and what piece was beautiful, for in it were both extremes completely merging and forming a whole. I felt that these were my anchors and on these I had to build up my personality. I knew too that this was the same in all of us and everything alive. I had a feeling that what I had just seen was part of God.

. . . but some of its early practitioners, such as the Czech therapist Stanislav Grof, still feel its potential value remains unexplored.

STANISLAV GROF
LSD Psychotherapy

(1980, 1994)

THE FUTURE OF LSD PSYCHOTHERAPY

LSD is a unique and powerful tool for the exploration of the human mind and human nature. Psychedelic experiences mediate access to deep realms of the psyche that have not yet been discovered and acknowledged by mainstream psychology and psychiatry. They also reveal new possibilities and mechanisms of therapeutic change and personality transformation. The fact that the spectrum of the LSD experience appears puzzling to most professionals and cannot be accounted for by the existing theoretical frameworks does not mean that the effects of LSD are totally unpredictable. The safe and effective use of this drug requires a fundamental revision of the existing theory and practice of psychotherapy. However, it is possible to formulate basic principles for LSD-assisted psychotherapy which maximize its therapeutic benefits and minimize the risks.

It is very difficult at this point to predict the future of LSD psychotherapy. The fact that it can be used safely and effectively does not automatically mean that it will be assimilated by mainstream psychiatry. This issue is complicated by many factors of an emotional, administrative, political and legal nature. However, we should clearly differentiate between the future of LSD psychotherapy and its contribution to the theory and practice of psychiatry. I mentioned earlier in this volume that LSD is a catalyst or amplifier of mental processes. If properly used it could become something like the microscope or the telescope of psychiatry. Whether LSD research continues in the future or not, the insights that have been achieved in LSD experimentation are of lasting value and relevance.

. . .

It is true that psychedelic experimentation has its dangers and pitfalls. But ventures into unexplored areas are never without risk. Wilhelm Conrad Roentgen, the discoverer of x-rays, lost his fingers as a result of his experiments with the new form of radiation. The mortality-rate of the early pilots who paved the way for today's safe jet travel was allegedly 75 percent. The degree of risk is directly proportional to the significance of the discovery, and its potential; thus the invention of gunpowder involved a different level of risk from the development of nuclear energy. LSD is a tool of extraordinary power; after more than twenty years of clinical research I feel great awe in regard to both its positive and negative potential.

. . .

LSD entered the scene at the time of the psychopharmacological revolution, when new tranquillizers and antidepressants had their early triumphs and generated excessive hope for easy chemical solutions to most of the problems in psychiatry. At present much of the original enthusiasm in this area has tapered off. While appreciating the humaniz-ation of the mental hospitals and pacification of psychiatric wards which has brought their atmosphere close to that of general hospitals, it is becoming increasingly obvious that tranquillizers and antidepressants are, by and large, only symptomatic remedies. They do not solve the problems and in more serious cases lead to a life-long dependence on maintenance medication. In addition, there is an increasing number of professional papers that emphasize the dangers of massive use of these drugs – irreversible neurological symptoms of tardive dyskinesia, degenerative changes in the retina, or actual physiological addiction with a withdrawal syndrome.

We should also mention important social forces that might play a role in the future changes of policy toward psychedelic research. Many of the young persons who are in or will be moving into various positions of social relevance – as lawyers, teachers, administrators, or mental health professionals – had intense exposure to psychedelics during their student years. Those individuals who had experiences themselves, or had the opportunity to observe the process in close friends and relatives, will have formed an independent image and will not be dependent on second-hand sources for information.

7

The Algebra of Need:
Drugs and Addiction

The concept of metabolic addiction, as opposed to simply over-indulgence or moral weakness, evolved throughout the course of the nineteenth century – mostly with reference to alcohol, for the abuse of which various terms including 'dipsomania' and 'alcoholism' were coined. The clinical descriptions of the 'morbid cravings' for opium and morphine in the 1870s began the process of bringing drug use under close medical supervision for the first time.

But the experience of craving for, tolerance of and dependence on opiates was not new, and had been described in detail by writers such as De Quincey (see p. 11).

THOMAS DE QUINCEY
Confessions of an English Opium Eater

(1822)

It will occur to you often to ask, why did I not release myself from the horrors of opium, by leaving it off, or diminishing it? To this I must answer briefly: it might be supposed that I yielded to the fascinations of opium too easily; it cannot be supposed that any man can be charmed by its terrors. The reader may be sure, therefore, that I made attempts innumerable to reduce the quantity. I add, that those who witnessed the agonies of those attempts, and not myself, were the first to beg me to desist. But could not I have reduced it a drop a day, or by adding water, have bisected or trisected a drop? A thousand drops bisected would thus have taken nearly six years to reduce; and that way would certainly not have answered. But this is a common mistake of those who know nothing of opium experimentally; I appeal to those who do, whether it is not always found that down to a certain point it can be reduced with ease and even pleasure, but that, after that point, further reduction causes intense suffering. Yes, say many thoughtless persons, who know not what they are talking of, you will suffer a little low spirits and dejection for a few days. I answer, no; there is nothing like low spirits; on the contrary, the mere animal spirits are uncommonly raised: the pulse is improved: the health is better. It is not there that the suffering lies. It has no resemblance to the sufferings caused by renouncing wine. It is a state of unutterable irritation of stomach (which surely is not much like dejection), accompanied by intense perspirations, and feelings such as I shall not attempt to describe without more space at my command.

The opium addict in his East End 'den', in a Victorian engraving after
Gustave Doré. Many expressions such as 'opium den' and 'drug fiend'
were first coined in the late nineteenth century. (Wellcome Trust)

The contemporary image of the urban junkie and the horrors of 'cold turkey' was established in novels like Nelson Algren's Man With The Golden Arm.

NELSON ALGREN
The Man with the Golden Arm

(1959)

'Let me tell you how everythin' is.' He sounded like a man talking on and on for dread of something that will move through his brain the moment the tongue ceases its babble.

'I can see how everythin' is awright,' Sparrow assured him.

'No, you can't see. Nobody can. Nobody knows, just junkies. Just junkies know how everythin' is. Sit down, Solly – *please.*'

The light was fading in his eyes now, they were sinking into his head and the freshness the drug had brought to his cheeks had turned into a dull putty-gray. He said 'please' like a man begging for a dime and just the way he said it left Sparrow feeling that he himself had just swallowed a mouthful of dust. 'If it'll do you good to talk,' he thought with the taste of dust on his tongue, 'I'll listen this one time. Because I knew you when you were the best sport I knew my whole life. What's your story, cousin?' he offered aloud.

Frankie coughed into his palm. 'It's like this, Solly. You put it down for months 'n months, you work yourself down from monkey to zero. You beat it. You got it beat at last.' He was talking low and breathlessly, like one who fears that, if he doesn't get his story told quickly it will never be told at all; like one who believes he is the only one who knows. Really knows. '*You know* you got it beat. You got it beat so stiff when the fixer says, "It ain't gonna cost you a dime this time, I got some new stuff I just want to try," you tell him, "Try it yourself." 'n give him the laugh. When he tells you, innocent-like. "The hypo is in the top drawer over there, help yourself any time," just to put it in your head how easy it'd be, you turn him down flat. Because gettin' fixed is the one thing you'll never need again all your life.

'Three weeks later you wake up, it's dark out but not like night 'n it ain't morning neither – it's just Fix Time. It's comin' on like a wave way out there, bigger 'n bigger 'n comin' right at you till it's big as this hotel, it hits you 'n you're gone. You're so sick you're just turnin' around down there under that wave not carin' who knows, your mother 'r your sister 'r your buddy 'r your wife – anythin' just so's you can stop drownin' for a minute.

'Nobody can stand gettin' that sick 'n live, Solly. You have to puke 'n you can't. You just heave 'n heave 'n sweat 'n heave 'n still nothin' happens – then somebody turns on the faucet in the sink or the bathtub down the hall 'n just the sound of water runnin' rolls your whole stomach over on top of itself 'n you got to puke 'r die.

'Then you don't even know no more *where* you're sick – if you think just for one second, "It's my poor gut" – it starts bustin' your brains out the back on your head just to show you. So you think it's your head 'n it slams you a dirty one in the stones – it's here 'n it's there 'n you're shaggin' it in a dream, tryin' to pin it down to some place you can feel it so you can fight it.

'But it won't stay still 'n you can't get hold 'n if you don't pin it in a minute you're dead' – he brushed the buffalo-coloured shag of hair out of his eyes – 'that's all. There ain't no "will power" to it like squares like to say. There ain't that much will power on God's green earth. If you had that much will power you wouldn't be a man, you'd be Jesus Christ.'

. . . and the experience of the modern addict has been charted by opiate-addicted writers like William Burroughs. For Burroughs, opiates are a 'virus', and addiction 'a disease of exposure'.

WILLIAM BURROUGHS
The Naked Lunch

(1959)

Junk is the ideal product . . . the ultimate merchandise. No sales talk necessary. The client will crawl through a sewer and beg to buy . . . The junk merchant does not sell his product to the consumer, he sells the consumer to his product. He does not improve and simplify his merchandise. He degrades and simplifies the client. He pays his staff in junk.

Junk yields a basic formula of 'evil' virus: *The Algebra of Need*. The face of 'evil' is always the face of total need. A dope fiend is a man in total need of dope. Beyond a certain frequency need knows absolutely no limit or control. In the words of total need: *'Wouldn't you?'* Yes you would. You would lie, cheat, inform on your friends, steal, do *anything* to satisfy total need. Because you would be in a state of total sickness, total possession, and not in a position to act in any other way. Dope fiends are sick people who cannot act other than they do.

The medical establishment has never been unanimous about the subjective experience which addiction entails, and the medical seriousness of withdrawal. For some it is all in the mind of the addict.

DAVID P. AUSUBEL
'Causes and Types of Narcotic Addiction: A Psychosocial View'

(1961)

Let us examine first the addict's own view of the cause of drug addiction. According to him, all human beings are equally susceptible to addiction. The unlucky victim need only have the misfortune to be introduced to the drug as the result of abnormal curiosity, chance encounters with addicts and narcotic peddlers, or prolonged illness. Then, once he is caught in the 'iron grip' of physical dependence on the drug he is allegedly powerless to help himself. He is obliged to continue using more narcotics 'just to stay normal', that is, to avoid the 'unbearable' symptoms that ensue when the drug is discontinued.

This dangerously distorted account of the causes of drug addiction is a great comfort to the addict. It puts his illness in the most favourable possible light and also absolves him of all responsibility. Unfortunately, however, he has not only successfully deluded himself, but has also managed, with the unwitting co-operation of the mass media, to foist his understandably biased view on a credulous American public. Physical dependence and withdrawal symptoms are genuine physiological phenomena, and association with confirmed addicts or drug peddlers *is* the typical way in which candidate addicts are introduced to narcotics. But neither factor explains *why* an individual becomes a drug addict.

. . .

How credible is the physical dependence explanation? In the first place, although the symptoms of withdrawal are distressing, they are generally no worse than a bad case of gastrointestinal influenza, and, in any event, largely disappear within 10 days. Thus, unless other potent satisfactions were derived from the narcotic habit, it is difficult to believe that any individual would be willing to pay the fantastic price of the drug and risk imprisonment and social ostracism merely to avoid a moderately severe 10-day illness. Second, every year thousands of persons with serious fractures, burns and surgical conditions receive opiates long enough to develop physiological dependence, but are nevertheless able to break this dependence quite easily. Third, the dosage of morphine (or equivalent) required to prevent withdrawal symptoms is never more than one to two grains daily. Hence, why will drug addicts take up to 20 grains a day if they take the drug, as they claim to, 'just to feel normal'? Fourth, withdrawal symptoms can be adequately prevented and relieved if morphine is taken hypodermically. Therefore, why will addicts run the risk of thrombophlebitis and septicaemia by injecting the drug 'main-line' – or directly into their veins – with crude, homemade syringes? The answer to both third and fourth questions is that the large dose and the 'main-line' route increase the 'kick' or euphoric effect. Fifth, new, synthetic opiate-like drugs have been developed which have all of the analgesic and euphoric properties of opiates, but for which withdrawal symptoms are minimal. Nevertheless, the evidence is conclusive that addiction develops just as rapidly for these drugs as for other opiates.

Last, if physical dependence were a significant causal factor in drug addiction, how could we explain the fact that at least 75 percent of all addicts discharged from federal hospitals start using the drug almost immediately after release? By the time of release, it is at least a year since physical dependence was broken. If addicts are really so terrified by withdrawal symptoms, why should they start developing the habit all over again after suffering the symptoms once and then escaping their clutches?

*. . . while for the heretical 'anti-psychiatrist' Thomas Szasz, addiction is
merely the construct of a medical profession seeking a spurious clinical
basis for their moral judgements.*

THOMAS SZASZ
Ceremonial Chemistry

(1974)

Ever since pharmacology and psychiatry became accepted as
modern medical disciplines – that is, since about the last quarter of
the nineteenth century – chemists and physicians, psychologists and
psychiatrists, politicians and pharmaceutical manufacturers, all have
searched, in vain of course, for non-addictive drugs to relieve pain, to
induce sleep, and to stimulate wakefulness. This search is based on the
dual premises that addiction is a condition caused by drugs, and that
some drugs are more, and others less, 'addictive'. This view epitomizes
the confusion between the pharmacological effects of drugs and their
practical uses.

When a drug deadens pain, induces sleep, or stimulates wakefulness,
and when people know that there are drugs that do these things,
then some persons may – depending on their personal and social
circumstances and desires – develop an interest in using such drugs. Why
many people habitually use such drugs, and countless other substances,
need not for the moment concern us here, other than to note that the
reason cannot be said to be because the drugs are 'addictive'. It is the
other way around: we call certain drugs 'addictive' because people like
to use them – just as we call ether and gasoline 'flammable' because
they are easily ignited. It is therefore just as absurd to search for
non-addictive drugs that produce euphoria as it would be to search for
non-flammable liquids that are easy to ignite.

Our contemporary confusion regarding drug abuse and drug addiction
is an integral part of our confusion regarding religion. Any idea or act
that gives men and women a sense of what their life is about or for –
that, in other words, gives their existence meaning and purpose – is,
properly speaking, religious. Science, medicine, and especially health
and therapy are thus admirably suited to function as quasi-religious

ideas, values, and pursuits. It is necessary, therefore, to distinguish between science as science, and science as religion (sometimes called 'scientism').

Since the use and avoidance of certain substances has to do with prescriptions and prohibitions, with what is legal or licit and illegal or illicit, the so-called 'problem' of drug abuse or drug addiction has two aspects: religious (legal) and scientific (medical). Actually, however, since the factual or scientific aspects of this subject are negligible, the problem is, for all practical purposes, almost entirely religious or moral. A simple example will amplify the nature of the distinction, and the confusion, to which I am referring.

As some persons seek or avoid alcohol and tobacco, heroin and marijuana, so others seek or avoid kosher wine and holy water. The differences between kosher wine and non-kosher wine, holy water and ordinary water, are ceremonial, not chemical. Although it would be idiotic to look for the property of kosherness in wine, or for the property of holiness in water, this does not mean that there is no such thing as kosher wine or holy water. Kosher wine is wine that is ritually clean according to Jewish law. Holy water is water blessed by a Catholic priest. This creates a certain demand for such wine and water by people who want this sort of thing; at the same time, and for precisely the same reason, such wine and water are rejected by those who do not believe in their use.

Similarly, the important differences between heroin and alcohol, or marijuana and tobacco – as far as 'drug abuse' is concerned – are not chemical but ceremonial. In other words, heroin and marijuana are approached and avoided not because they are more 'addictive' or more 'dangerous' than alcohol and tobacco, but because they are more 'holy' or 'unholy' – as the case may be.

The single most important issue in coming to grips with the problem of drug use and drug avoidance is, in my opinion, the medical perspective on moral conduct. As I have shown elsewhere, the psychiatric claim that personal conduct is not volitional but reflexive – in short, that human beings are not subjects but objects, not persons but organisms – was first staked out in relation to acts that were socially disturbing and could conventionally be called 'mad' or 'insane'.

The pioneering eighteenth-century 'alienists' managed the first fact-ories for manufacturing madmen, and developed the earliest advertising campaigns for selling 'insanity' by renaming badness as madness, and then offering to dispose of it. The famous nineteenth-century 'neuropsychiatrists' made decisive advances in both the production and promotion of madness, establishing the 'reality' of the modern concept of 'mental illness': first, they progressively metaphorized disagreeable conduct and forbidden desire as disease – thus creating more and more mental diseases; second, they literalized this medical metaphor, insisting that disapproved behaviour was not merely *like* a disease, but that it *was* a disease – thus confusing others, and perhaps themselves as well, regarding the differences between bodily and behavioural 'abnormalities'.

By the time the twentieth century was ushered in – thanks in large part to the work of Freud and the modern 'psychologists' – madness was bursting through the walls of the insane asylums and was being discovered in clinics and doctors' offices, in literature and art, and in the 'psychopathology of everyday life'. Since the First World War, the enemies of this psychiatrization of man – in particular, religion and common sense – have lost their nerve; now they no longer even try to resist the opportunistic theories and oppressive technologies of modern 'behavioural science'.

Thus, by the time the contemporary American drug-abuseologists, legislators, and psychiatrists came on the scene, the contact lenses that refracted deviance as disease were so deeply embedded into the corneas of the American people that they could be pried loose only with the greatest effort; and only by leaving both the laity and the professionals so painfully wounded and temporarily blinded that they could hardly be expected to tolerate such interference with their vision, much less to impose such painful self-enlightenment on themselves.

The result was that when, in the post-Prohibition, post-Second World War, better-living-through-chemistry era, the so-called drug problem 'hit' America, the phenomena it presented could be apprehended only as refracted through these irremovable contact lenses. Those who used drugs could not help themselves. Since they were the victims of their irresistible impulses, they needed others to protect them from these impulses. This made it logical and reasonable for politicians and psychiatrists to advocate 'drug controls'. And since none of this has 'worked' – as how could it have? – the blame for it all could at least be affixed to those who sold illicit drugs: they were called 'pushers' and were persecuted in the horrifying manner in which men wallowing in the conviction of their own virtuousness have always persecuted those about whose wickedness they could entertain no doubts.

Presumably some persons have always 'abused' certain drugs – alcohol for millennia, opiates for centuries. However, only in the twentieth century have certain patterns of drug use been labelled as 'addictions'. Traditionally, the term 'addiction' has meant simply a strong inclination toward certain kinds of conduct, with little or no pejorative meaning attached to it. Thus, the *Oxford English Dictionary* offers such pre-twentieth-century examples of the use of this term as being addicted 'to civil affairs', 'to useful reading' – and also 'to bad habits'. Being addicted to drugs is not among the definitions listed.

Until quite recently, then, the term 'addiction' was understood to refer to a habit, good or bad as the case might be, actually more often the former. This usage saved people from the confusion into which the contemporary meaning of this term has inevitably led.

Although the term 'addiction' is still often used to describe habits, usually of an undesirable sort, its meaning has become so expanded and transformed that it is now used to refer to almost any kind of illegal, immoral, or undesirable association with certain kinds of drugs. For example, a person who has smoked but a single marijuana cigarette, or even one who has not used any habit-forming or illegal drug at all, may be considered to be a drug abuser or drug addict: this is the case when a person, found to be in possession of illicit drugs, is accused by the legal and medical authorities who 'examine' him of using (rather than with selling or merely carrying) these substances, and is convicted in a court of law on a charge of 'drug abuse' or 'drug addiction'.

In short – during the past half-century, and especially during recent decades – the noun 'addict' has lost its denotative meaning and reference to persons engaged in certain *habits*, and has become transformed into a stigmatizing label possessing only pejorative meaning referring to certain *persons*. The term 'addict' has thus been added to our lexicon of stigmatizing labels – such as 'Jew', which could mean either a person professing a certain religion or a 'Christ killer' who himself should be killed; or 'Negro', which could mean either a black-skinned person or a savage who ought to be kept in actual or social slavery. More specifically still, the word 'addict' has been added to our psychiatric vocabulary of stigmatizing diagnoses, taking its place alongside such terms as 'insane', 'psychotic', 'schizophrenic', and so forth.

But it isn't the case that the medicalization of addiction was accomplished entirely by doctors. One of the important factors in the control of opiates was the complaints from addicted patients.

ANONYMOUS
'Confessions of a Young Lady Laudanum-Drinker'

(*The Journal of Mental Sciences*, January 1889)

Dear Sir,

Perhaps you may remember a lady calling on you with her daughter about the middle of August, to ask you if there was any way of curing the habit of taking opium, which the girl had contracted. I, who write, am that same girl, and think you may perhaps be interested to hear how I got on. It is hateful to me to think of that horrible time, and one of my chief reasons for writing to you is to beg you to try and make known by every means in your power, what a terrible thing opium-eating is. If people only knew of the consequences sure to follow on such a habit, of its insidiousness, and the difficulty of leaving it off, surely they would never touch it.

. . .

Of course, it didn't become habitual all at once; the first time I got it was at school, after a concert, when its effects were so soothing, that it became quite usual for me to get it, mixed up with quinine, which I was forced to take, though there was not the slightest necessity for it, as nobody could be stronger than I am. Thank goodness, we have all inherited splendid constitutions, and would almost think it a disgrace to the family to have anything the matter with us. I am quite sure I would never have had neuralgia, if it had not been for stewing up for exams. Mother was always writing to tell me not to do them, but I did not feel it my duty to obey her on that point, as what does one go to school for if not to learn; and to own one's self beaten by a headache would surely show a very weak mind.

I'm just mad at myself for having given in to such a fearful habit as opium-eating. None but those who have as completely succumbed to it as I did, could guess the mischief it would do. Even you, with an experience which must be extremely varied, being as you are, in such a good place for studying people's brains (or rather their want of them), cannot know the amount of harm it did to me morally, though I must say you did seem to have a pretty fair idea of it. It got me into such a state of indifference that I no longer took the least interest in anything, and did nothing all day but loll on the sofa reading novels, falling asleep every now and then, and drinking tea. Occasionally I would take a walk or drive, but not often. Even my music I no longer took much interest in, and would play only when the mood seized me, but felt it too much of a bother to practise. I would get up about ten in the morning, and make a pretence of sewing; a pretty pretence, it took me four months to knit a stocking!

Worse than all, I got so deceitful, that no one could tell when I was speaking the truth. It was only this last year it was discovered; those living in the house with you are not so apt to notice things, and it was my married sisters who first began to wonder what had come over me. They said I always seemed to be in a half-dazed state, and not to know what I was doing. However they all put it down to music. Mother had let me go to all the Orchestral Concerts in the winter, and they thought it had been too much for me. By that time it was a matter of supreme indifference to me what they thought, and even when it was found out, I had become so callous that I didn't feel the least shame. Even Mother's grief did not affect me, I only felt irritated at her; this is an awful confession to have to make, but it is better to tell the whole truth when you once begin, and it might be some guide to you in dealing with others. If you know of anyone indulging in such a habit, especially girls, just tell them what they will come to.

. . .

One thing I would like to know, and that is – whether you could tell that I had not left off laudanum that day we called. Surely you must know the state one gets into when suddenly deprived of it; they could no more sit up and speak as I did than fly. By that time I had brought myself down to a quarter of an ounce a day, and as you had put Mother on her guard, I had no means of getting any more (I hate having to own that I tried to do so) so the day after we saw you was the last I had any. Then began a time I shudder to look back upon. I don't like owning to bodily suffering, but will not deny that I suffered them. I wonder if leaving off opium has the same effect on everyone! My principal feeling was one of awful weariness and numbness at the end of my back; it kept me tossing about all day and night long. It was impossible to lie in one position for more than a minute, and of course sleep was out of the question. I was so irritable that no one cared to come near me; Mother slept on the sofa in my room, and I nearly kicked her once for suggesting that I should say hymns over to myself, to try and make me go to sleep. Hymns of a very different sort were in my mind, I was once or twice very nearly strangling myself, and I am ashamed to say that the only thing that kept me from doing so was the thought that I would be able to get laudanum somehow. I was conscious of feeling nothing but the mere sense of being alive, and if the house had been burning, would have thought it too much of an effort to rise . . .

However, I gradually got over that, and now am perfectly well, with the exception of my back, which has that nasty aching feeling now and then. Our medical man, who is a bright specimen of the country doctor, said 'it might be anything', and when asked to explain what that meant said 'perhaps her corsets are too tight'. This was indeed a bright idea as I don't happen to wear corsets at all. Those country doctors are fit for nothing but measles and teething. What I think so very queer when I was taking laudanum is that though my memory was going for other things, it was as good as ever for music; I could pick up by ear and play off even better than before. I often think had that faculty gone it would have alarmed me so much that perhaps I would have been able to stop my evil habits, but it's unlikely.

Oh, why do you doctors not try prevention as well as cure! You have it in your power to warn those who take laudanum now and then for toothache or headache, what an insidious thing it is, and how easily they may become the victims of it. I began that way, and see what it came to. Even now I often wonder if I've quite got over its effects. Does anyone who has gone up to three or four ounces a day, and is suddenly deprived of it, live to tell the tale! I can hardly believe it. My own sufferings were bad enough, and I had got down to a quarter of an ounce. I'll end this by alluding again to the object of my writing, namely, the prevention of people getting into such a state as I was: if they were to know the state of moral idiocy to which they would in the end be brought, would they ever allow themselves to once begin the habit! They need not say to themselves 'Oh, we can stop it when we like'; opium takes away their power to do that. There can't be a more determined person than I am naturally, and what good did that do me! I determined a hundred times to stop it, but never succeeded, and at last I got that I didn't care a rap what became of me, all the reasoning and affection expended on me, being a mere waste of time and love. You doctors know all the harm these drugs do, as well as the 'victims' of them, and yet you do precious little to prevent it. If that subject were to be taken up instead of some so often spoken of in the health-lectures which are now given, it might do some practical good. Well, I wonder at myself being able to write such a long letter on a subject which is so repugnant to me that I try never even to think of it. I can hardly finish up in my usual style which is 'hoping to see you soon again'; because I certainly don't hope so, and if I ever do have the pleasure of seeing you again, let us hope it will be under very different circumstances.

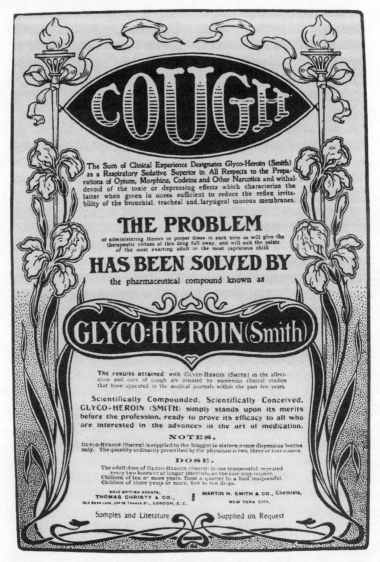

Diamorphine, an unprecedentedly powerful and addictive opiate, was first synthesized in 1874, and the name 'heroin' was coined for it by Bayer Pharmaceuticals in 1898, a year before the company introduced aspirin. Heroin was originally made available to the public as an over-the-counter cough medicine (David F. Musto/*Scientific American*, July 1991)

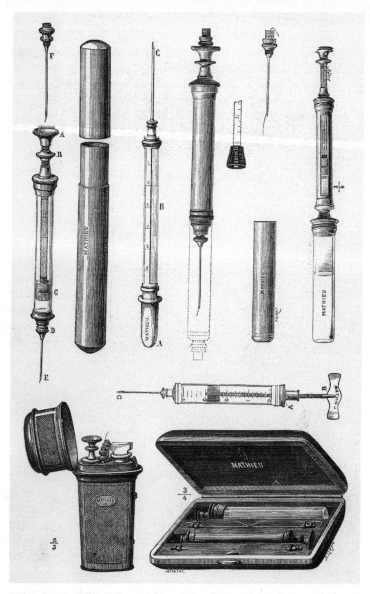

The arsenal of a morphine addict, 1887 (Mary Evans Picture Library)

Nor have doctors been merely the professional observers of addiction: historically, they have always been among its most frequent casualties. For Géza Csáth (see p. 90), medical knowledge was no protection against the addiction which eventually killed him.

GÉZA CSÁTH
Diary extract

(1913, 1980)

JAN. 13, 1913.

In combating myself I can only report one bloody defeat after another. Not even in this respect is fortune willing to smile at me. The week started well with daily quantities of 0.044 and 0.046 which I divided into 3–4 portions. But yesterday and today I reached again that awful vicious circle which is the source of the most shameful remorse. The trouble always starts with not having the strength to wait for my mid-morning stool. Because when I succeed in doing this and the morphine leaves the intestines, then it is followed by a pleasant, all-day-long hunger which can be satisfied with the regular amount. But if the first sin takes place in the morning, still in bed or before the bowel movements, the same amount doesn't work properly, and causes no euphoria. To commit sin, to harm myself without enjoying it, this is the bitter thought tormenting me. If I had a gun near me, at times like this, I would blow my brains out, right away.

What do I do instead? Usually before the time is up, 3–4 hours after the first portion, I take the next one. This usually gives euphoric feelings lasting 20–30 minutes, followed by the most miserable, pitiful low, during which:

1. All human endeavours, industriousness, diligence, work, seem to be ridiculous and only hate-provoking.
2. All talk is tiring and stupid.
3. All plans are unrealizable and terrible.
4. All great, beautiful and noble things are unattainable and futile.

At times like this I smoke one cigarette after another until I no longer feel the taste of the smoke. I eat oranges till I get tired of them. Disgusted, I play the piano. I wash. Visit Olga. Find life insufferable. I make an effort to entertain her, but I lack the true sexual interest, and, therefore, I am just getting bored there. To make my stay bearable I put in 0.02–0.03 in the toilet, hating it. This is followed after dinner by 0.02, then 0.01 and 0.01 again. The last one under the pretext that it already belongs to tomorrow's portion . . . This is an immeasurably loathsome and despicable life. I am so disgusting, weak and pitiful that I have to wonder why Olga still loves me, and hasn't become unfaithful to me. That my weak and forever veiled voice, my steady staring in the mirror, my cynical and shrunken penis, my drawn face, my witless conversation, my impotent, lazy life, my suspicious behavior, my insolence with which I lengthily disappear into the WC, my stupidity haven't disgusted her yet, for ever and ever. I also think that I stink, because with my sense of smell impaired I can no longer smell the stench of my poorly-wiped asshole or the mouth-odour caused by my rotting teeth.

. . . and addiction is still rife among doctors, dentists and other health professionals today.

ROBERT HOLMAN COOMBS
Drug-impaired Professionals

(1997)

A state or federal license gives the addict an advantage in maintaining the secret. Not only does it provide an income and a professional identity; it also guarantees easy drug access and coverup. Motivated to protect their licenses at all costs, addicted professionals become expert in defending themselves and their actions

. . .

Perhaps more than anyone else, professionals are motivated to keep their addictions secret: their careers depend upon their professional reputation, and their sense of self depends upon their careers.

. . .

Some professionals will go to great lengths to maintain the secret. 'It took the worst kind of suffering to open my eyes,' said a dentist, 'but I now know we have an infinite capacity to fool ourselves.'

If anyone had said I was a drug addict, I would have told him he was a liar and just full of it. It did not occur to me that I had a problem until I overdosed . . . Sitting around in my apartment one night, I injected myself with a much larger dose of cocaine than I thought. I started convulsing, and barely made it to the phone to call an emergency service.

He continued:

My staff knew about the problem and one staff member quit, but the rest stayed . . . They thought they were helping me and in that way they enabled me to keep using. I missed days of work when I'd call in; I wanted to go out and use that day, and they'd have to cancel all my patients and reschedule them. I graduated to shooting cocaine and heroin. By then the quantities were incredible. I started out snorting a couple of lines a night and ended up injecting and snorting about three grams a day. My wife threw me out. I moved to one of the worst urban areas in the state, and lived in a residential hotel. I loved every minute of it because the drugs were at my front door-step. My practice was my practice, and my social life was out on the street, so to speak, and that's where I made all my purchases.

One night I ended up getting stabbed by a guy who I thought was my friend . . . We fought and he stabbed me with a 3-inch blade, puncturing my abdomen. Fearing for my license, I avoided hospitals and went to my office. I did a primary internal suture and a secondary suture and placed myself on high dosages of antibiotics. I had so much cocaine and heroin in me that I didn't feel anything. I healed nicely and moved out of the downtown area. I didn't have to go to the hospital and I wasn't reported.

The self-experimenting neuroscientist John Lilly (see p. 63) fell victim to a bizarre and terrifying addiction to the dissociative psychedelic ketamine.

JOHN C. LILLY

The Scientist: A Metaphysical Autobiography

(1988, 1997)

The year in which John was investigating the effects of K on himself, he had one overriding belief system or, more properly, metabelief system, which controlled his entry and exit to and from other belief systems. He called this overriding belief a 'metabelief operator' (MBO). The MBO was: 'In my development as a scientist I must approach the inner realities as well as the outer realities. I must investigate the properties of the observer/operator and his dependence upon the presence of changed molecular configurations within his own brain. K introduces certain specific changes in the molecular configuration and computation of that biocomputer. Some of these changes are visible to outside observers, some are visible only to the inside observer/operator

. . .

During the first part of this year, John did experiments with single doses of K and arrived at a quantitative relation between the dose given and the resulting states of being induced in himself. Later he took multiple doses more frequently and found new effects not accountable simply by the induced phenomena of single doses at widely spaced intervals

. . .

He then went on and experimented with higher doses. He called the 30-milligram-dose threshold for visual projections the internal reality threshold, best seen in the isolation tank. The next amount injected was

75 milligrams. In the tank he found the plateau involved whole sets of phenomena which he had not seen at the lower doses.

For the first time he began to sense changes in himself other than the changes in perception of visual images. His relationship to his physical body became weakened and attenuated. He found that he began to participate in the scenes which were previously merely visual images, as if out there, outside of his body. His observer/operator was becoming disconnected from the physical body. Information from his bodily processes was becoming so weakened that there were times when he was not aware of his body at all. On this plateau he began to experience interaction with the strange presences, strange beings, and began to communicate with them.

'I have left my body floating in a tank on the planet Earth. This is a very strange and alien environment. It must be extraterrestrial, I have not been here before. I must be on some other planet in some civilization other than the one in which I was evolved. *I am in a peculiar state of high indifference. I am not involved in either fear or love. I am a highly neutral being, watching and waiting.*

'This is very strange. This planet is similar to Earth but the colors are different. There is vegetation but it's a peculiar purple color. There is a sun but it has a violet hue to it, not the familiar orange of Earth's sun. I am in a beautiful meadow with distant, extremely high mountains. Across the meadow I see creatures approaching. They stand on their hind legs as if human. They are a brilliant white and seem to be emitting light. Two of them come near. I cannot make out their features. They are too brilliant for my present vision. They seem to be transmitting thoughts and ideas directly to me. There is no sound. Automatically, what they think is translated into words that I can understand.'

. . .

First Being: 'We welcome you once again in a form which you have created. Your choice to come here, we applaud.'

Second Being: 'You have come alone. Why are you alone?'

I answer: 'I do not know. There seems to be something strange about this; the others are reluctant to join me here.'

First Being: 'What is it that you want from us?'

I say: 'I want to know if you are real or merely a product of my own wishes.'

Second Being: 'We are what you wish us to be, it is true. You construct our form and the place in which we meet. These constructions are the result of your present limitations. As to our substance, whether 'real' in the accepted sense upon your planet or 'illusion' in the accepted sense on your planet, is for you to find out. You have written a book on human simulations of reality and of God. Your problem here is whether or not you are traveling in one of your own simulations or whether you have contacted real Beings existing in other dimensions.'

. . .

John decided to try to live in the internal reality, continuously for an extended period, peaking into the extraterrestrial reality (e.t.r.) and contacting the network (N), staying out of the Unknown (U).

He found, by giving himself 50 milligrams every hour on the hour, twenty hours a day, with four hours out for sleep, that he was able to maintain the schedule for three weeks. The experiment ended at three weeks as the result of an accident in the external reality

. . .

During this period John became convinced that he was a visitor from the year 3001. He felt that everything around him was happening in that year. When traveling in automobiles he felt the primitiveness of their mechanisms. He longed to return to the year 3001 in which the vehicles produced steam instead of contaminating exhaust gases. Everything he saw had a patina of old age, as if in a museum, including human beings. Clothing and machines seemed old, antique. Paintings looked as though they had been made by artists long since dead. He briefly began a search for the time machine which had transported him backward in time to the twentieth century. He could not find it and realized that the Beings from another dimension had this control over him. He developed the belief that a Being from the year 3001 had taken over his body. After a few days this Being left and he returned to his twentieth-century self

. . .

By this time all his sources of supply of K had become wary. Some of the friends with whom he had left K became very cautious and refused to give him what was in their care. He went through a severe withdrawal period in which he missed K and its induced effects. During this period he was described by one of his best friends to be 'like an alcoholic who could not obtain alcohol.' John vehemently denied this parallel, still caught in the seduction of K and still caught in his mission.

. . . while some of the most effective withdrawal programmes have been designed not by doctors but by laymen like James Lee (see p. 21).

JAMES S. LEE
'Underworld of the East'

(1935)

I was making preparations for my voyage home, and the giving up of drugs on the way.

At the present time I had no regular dose, or fixed time of taking, such as is the custom of most drug users. For days, sometimes, I would use just the minimum combination of drugs, which would make me feel just right, with perfect comfort in mind and body; then I would have a regular binge with some particular drug, selecting one which I had not been using much for some time, so that it would have all its finer effects.

Not being able to smoke opium or hashish on the voyage, I would have to cut them out.

The first thing to be done was to cut out all drugs, except cocaine and morphia injections, and these I gradually wangled, until I was using an equal quantity of each.

In a bottle, I mixed up 12 grains of morphia and 12 grains of cocaine with 480 minims of distilled water. This was six days' supply of four injections per day, using 20 minims per injection. The syringe was graduated with the number of minims, in lines on the glass barrel.

For some days before leaving I was using the mixture, and the day's supply was of course 2 grains of morphia and 2 grains of cocaine.

I was leaving Mulki in India for the time being, intending to send for her when I got out to some other country.

I found a small hut for her, in a place about sixty miles away.

I sold my furniture to a new arrival, and said 'Good-bye' to my friends, then set off for Calcutta and home; first making arrangements for Mulki's support.

I had come to be very fond of her. Not only was she beautiful in appearance, but she was beautiful in disposition. She had not learned to use drugs, although she had begged many times for me to allow her, and I was afraid that when I was away she would start with opium, as everywhere around there were natives using it.

The voyage home to England was not marked by any unusual incident, except that there was a young medical student on board, who shared my cabin.

Soon he discovered that I was using drugs, and he gave me a lecture on the terrible consequences of the habit. I asked him if he had ever taken any himself, and he confessed that he had not, and that he was going on what he had heard.

Shortly afterwards I missed my syringe.

I did not mention it to him, I just quietly observed, and soon I had more than a suspicion where the syringe had gone to.

However, this did not trouble me, because I had syringes of all kinds in my main baggage; syringes of the best makes, ranging in size from 20 minims, up to 60 minims.

After I had got settled down on board, I started my system in earnest.

I was using 2 grains of morphia, and 2 grains of cocaine per day, as before mentioned.

Without any trouble, I easily got down to 1 grain of each.

Now I mixed up 6 grains of each drug in separate bottles; each with 240 minims of water, and still keeping to the four injections per day, I started by drawing up into the syringe 9 minims of morphia, and 10 minims of cocaine.

Next day the morphia was reduced by another minim and so on until the fourth day my dose was 6 minims of morphia and 10 minims of cocaine.

Now I was beginning to feel slightly the need of a little more morphia.

Instead of taking more, I started reducing the cocaine 1 minim per day until on the eighth day my injection consisted of 6 minims of each drug.

Now I felt that I was getting enough morphia again.

Decreasing the cocaine, had the same effect as though I had increased the morphia.

This may be difficult to believe, yet it is true. The explanation is, that these two drugs are in a certain way antidote to each other, yet when taken together, they both seem to act independently, and one gets the full effect of each drug.

When I had got down to 5 minims of each drug per injection, I marked time for three days.

I was now getting half a grain of each drug per day.

I now commenced afresh, but instead of reducing the quantity of the liquid, I kept to the 10 minims per injection, first mixing up some fresh drugs, as it is not good to keep them mixed long.

Now for four days I added to the morphia solution, an equivalent quantity of distilled water every time I injected, that is to say:

Every time I drew out 5 minims of solution, I added afterwards 5 minims of water. The total quantity of liquid always remained the same in the bottle, but it was getting gradually weaker, and the dilution was taking place on a diminishing scale, as it should do.

Soon the mixture became pretty weak, and I stopped adding more water, and concentrated on reducing the actual number of minims used, until I was down to 5 minims of mixture (¼ syringe full) per injection, and then I recommenced diluting as before.

A few weeks after my arrival in England, I was able to stop using drugs entirely.

I admit that at the end I had a little craving, but it was nothing really, and I was getting freer of it every day. Still, I decided that the system was not perfect, and I meant to continue experimenting and searching, until I found a cure which was fool proof and easy.

Deciding to withdraw from opiate use, and sticking to the decision, are fraught with difficulties. Aleister Crowley enumerated twenty-seven such difficulties to his visiting spirit King Lamus.

ALEISTER CROWLEY
'Diary of a Drug Fiend'

(1922)

King Lamus descended on me one morning, just after I had taken a dose, and was raking my brain for a reason for my action. I was alternately chewing the end of my pencil and making meaningless marks on the paper. I told him my difficulty.

'Always glad to help,' he said airily; went to a filing cabinet and produced a docket of typed manuscripts. He put it in my hand. It was headed, 'Reasons for taking it.'

1. My cough is very bad this morning.
    Note: (a) Is cough really bad?
    (b) If so, is the body coughing because it is sick or because it wants to persuade you to give it some heroin?
2. To buck me up.
3. I can't sleep without it.
4. I can't keep awake without it.
5. I must be at my best to do what I have to do. If I can only bring that off, I need never take it again.
6. I must show I am master of it – free to say either 'yes' or 'no.' And I must be perfectly sure by saying 'yes' at the moment. My refusal to take it at the moment shows weakness. Therefore I take it.
7. In spite of the knowledge of the disadvantages of the heroin life, I am really not sure whether it isn't better than the other life. After all I get extraordinary things out of heroin which I should never have got otherwise.
8. It is dangerous to stop too suddenly.
9. I'd better take a small dose now rather than put it off till later; because if I do so, it will disturb my sleep.
10. It is really very bad for the mind to be constantly preoccupied

with the question of the drug. It is better to take a small dose to rid myself of the obsession.

11. I am worried about the drug because of my not having any. If I were to take some, my mind would clear up immediately, and I should be able to think out good plans for stopping it.

12. The gods may be leading me to some new experience through taking it.

13. It is quite certainly a mistake putting down all little discomforts as results of taking it. Very likely, nearly all of them are illusions; the rest, due to the unwise use of it. I am simply scaring myself into saying 'no.'

14. It is bad for me morally to say 'no'. I must not be a coward about it.

15. There is no evidence at all that the reasonable use of heroin does not lengthen life. Chinese claim, and English physicians agree, that opium smoking, within limits, is a practice conducive to longevity. Why should it not be the same with heroin? It has been observed actually that addicts seem to be immune to most diseases which afflict ordinary people.

16. I take it because of its being prohibited. I decline being treated like a silly schoolboy when I'm a responsible man.

> Note: Then don't behave like a silly schoolboy. Why let the stupidity of governments drive you into taking the drugs against your will? – K.L.

17. My friend likes me to take it with her.

18. My ability to take it shows my superiority over other people.

19. Most of us dig our graves with our teeth. Heroin has destroyed my appetite, therefore it is good for me.

20. I have got into all sorts of messes with women in the past. Heroin has destroyed my interest in them.

21. Heroin has removed my desire for liquor. If I must choose, I really think heroin is the better.

22. Man has a right to spiritual ambition. He has evolved to what he is, through making dangerous experiments. Heroin certainly helps me to obtain a new spiritual outlook on the world. I have no right to assume that the ruin of bodily health is injurious; and 'whosoever will save his life shall lose it, but whoever loseth his life for My sake shall find it.'

23. So-and-so has taken it for years, and is all right.

24. So-and-so has taken it for years, and is still taking it, and he is the most remarkable man of his century.

25. I'm feeling so very, very rotten, and a very, very little would make me feel so very, very good.

26. We can't stop while we have it – the temptation is too strong. The best way is to finish it. We probably won't be able to get any more, so we take it in order to stop taking it.

27. Claude Farrère's story of Rodolphe Hafner. Suppose I take all this pains to stop drugs and then get cancer or something right away, what a fool I shall feel!

'Help you at all?' asked Lamus.

Well, honestly, it did not. I had thought out most of those things for myself at one time or another; and I seemed to have got past them. It's a curious thing that once you've written down a reason you diminish its value. You can't go on using the same reason indefinitely. That fact tends to prove that the alleged reason is artificial and false, that it has simply been invented on the spur of the moment by oneself to excuse one's indulgences.

Once free from addiction, the subject often finds it hard to remember or even imagine their previous state. Jean Cocteau's Opium, *subtitled* Diary of a Cure *against his wishes, both acknowledges and overcomes this problem.*

JEAN COCTEAU
Opium: The Diary of a Cure

(1930)

Opium leads the organism towards death in euphoric mood. The tortures arise from the process of returning to life against one's wish. A whole spring-time excites the veins to madness, bringing with it ice and fiery lava.

I recommend the patient who has been deprived for eight days to bury his head in his arm, to glue his ear to that arm, and wait. Catastrophe, riots, factories blowing up, armies in flight, flood – the ear can detect a whole apocalypse in the starry night of the human body.

. . .

Clinics receive few opium addicts. It is rare for an opium addict to stop smoking. The nurses only know the counterfeit smokers, the elegant smokers, those who combine opium, alcohol, drugs, the setting (opium and alcohol are mortal enemies), or those who pass from the pipe to the syringe and from morphine to heroin. Of all drugs 'the drug' is the most subtle. The lungs absorb its smoke instantaneously. The effect of a pipe is immediate. I am speaking of the real smokers. The amateurs feel nothing, they wait for dreams and risk being seasick; because the effectiveness of opium is the result of a pact. If we fall under its spell, we shall never be able to give it up.

To moralise to an opium addict is like saying to Tristan: 'Kill Yseult. You will feel much better afterwards.'

. . .

I became addicted to opium a second time under the following circum-stances.

To begin with, I could not have been thoroughly cured the first time. Many courageous drug addicts do not know the pitfalls of being cured, they are content merely to give up and emerge ravaged by a useless ordeal, their cells weakened and further prevented from regaining their vitality through alcohol and sport.

Incredible phenomena are attached to the cure; medicine is powerless against them, beyond making the padded cell look like a hotel-room and demanding of the doctor or nurse patience, attendance and sensitivity. I shall explain later that these phenomena should be not those of an organism in a state of decomposition but on the contrary the uncommun-icated symptoms of a baby at the breast and of vegetables in spring.

A tree must suffer from the rising of its sap and not feel the falling of its leaves.

'Le Sacre Du Printemps' orchestrates a cure with a scrupulous pre-cision of which Stravinsky is not even aware.

I therefore became an opium addict again because the doctors who cure – one should really say, quite simply, who purge – do not seek to cure the troubles which first cause the addiction; I had found again my unbalanced state of mind; and I preferred an artificial equilibrium to no equilibrium at all. This moral disguise is more misleading than a disordered appearance: it is human, almost feminine, to have recourse to it.

I became addicted with caution and under medical supervision. There *are* doctors capable of pity. I never exceeded ten pipes. I smoked them at the rate of three in the morning (at nine o'clock), four in the afternoon (at five o'clock), three in the evening (at eleven o'clock). I believed that, in this way, I was reducing the chances of addiction. With opium I suckled new cells, which were restored to the world after five months of abstinence, and I suckled them with countless unknown alkaloids, whereas a morphine addict, whose habits frighten me, fills his veins with a single known poison and surrenders himself far less to the unknown.

. . .

SIX WEEKS AFTER WEANING

For a week I have looked well again and the strength has come back to my legs (Jouhandeau has pointed out one thing that is true: my hands still look ill). Now, I find that for a week I have not been able to write any more about opium. I do not need to any more. The opium problem is receding. I would have to invent something.

I was therefore eliminating through ink, and even after the official elimination there was an unofficial elimination with a flow which became solid through my desire to write and draw. I allowed these drawings or notes only the value of frankness, and they seemed to me to be a derivative, a discipline for the nerves, but they became the faithful graph of the last stage. Sweat and bile precede some phantom substance which would have dissolved, leaving no other trace behind except a deep depression, if a fountain pen had not given it a direction, relief and shape.

Waiting for a period of calm to write these notes was trying to relive a state which is inconceivable as soon as the organism is no longer in it. Since I have never granted the slightest importance to the setting and since I was using opium as a remedy, I was not unhappy at seeing my state disappear. Whatever one renounces is a dead letter for those who imagine that the setting plays a part . . . I hope that this reportage finds a place among doctors' pamphlets and the literature of opium; may it serve as a guide to the novices who do not recognise, beneath the slowness of opium, one of the most dangerous faces of speed.

A drawing by Jean Cocteau under the influence of opium.

The jazz singer Billie Holliday recovered from addiction – though unfortunately only temporarily – by finding something else to take its place.

BILLIE HOLLIDAY
'Lady Sings the Blues'

(1956)

I've had my troubles with the habit for fifteen years, on and off. I've been on and I've been off. As I said before, when I was really on, nobody bothered me. I got in trouble both times when I tried to get off. I've spent a small fortune on stuff. I've kicked and stayed clean; and I've had my setbacks and had to fight all over again to get straight.

But I'm not crazy. I knew when I started to work on this book that I couldn't expect to tell the truth in it unless I was straight when it came out. I didn't try to hide anything. Doubleday carried an item in their winter catalogue that I was writing about my fight with dope and that I knew it wasn't over yet. There isn't a soul on this earth who can say for sure that their fight with dope is over until they're dead. *Variety* printed an item about it a couple of months before. I've been under a doctor's care and treatment before I went to Philadelphia and since

. . .

I begged the matron to let me keep my money and my clothes. I've only been to the fifth grade, but I know a few things about jails they don't teach you in school. Once they get your clothes put away and your valuables locked up, there ain't no bondsman on earth can get them out for you in a hurry.

I told them I didn't have nobody to take care of Pepi, so they let me keep him in the cell with me. He gave them a hard time. He was so little he could slip out between the bars, and they knew it. Every matron or turnkey that came by, Pepi would bark up a storm. There were some poor things in there, crying and screaming as they took the cold-turkey cure on the cement floor. Every scream that came from outside, Pepi would bark back.

There was nothing in the cell but a toilet and a long plank to lay down on. Pepi is so delicate he would get pneumonia in a minute, so I was busy worrying how to keep him warm. I spread my blue mink coat on the board and used it for a mattress while I cuddled that dog to keep him warm. But it wouldn't work. We were cold on top. So I pulled out my mink and threw it over us. Then we were cold on the bottom. When I wasn't worrying about Pepi, I was worrying about Louis on the other side without any topcoat. But the men in that jail treat each other better than the women do.

I had been on my feet since nine-thirty the night before when I went to work, and I was beat. But I couldn't even catch twenty winks in that place.

They only let you make one phone call. I used it to call a friend in Philly and ask her to start scrounging for the thousand dollars or more it would take in cash to get me and Louis out on bail. The ban on telephone calls wasn't too tough on me. Newspapers are good for one thing – they let your friends know you've been busted.

It was five o'clock that night before the bondsman got me out. I walked out of that jail and went back to the hotel. That little one room looked like a cyclone had hit it. I got on the telephone and arranged to get an advance on my salary so I could get Louis out. Then I pushed a pile of my gowns off the bed, fed Pepi, and tried to take a nap.

In a few minutes two friends from New York came in the hotel. They got me something to eat and a drink. By the time I fixed my hair and found a dress that hadn't been pawed into a mess of wrinkles, it was time for my first show to go on.

The club was packed. Most of them were customers, but a lot of them looked like fuzz. I closed my first set with 'My Man.' If the customers didn't know from reading the papers that Louis was still in jail, the fuzz did. They told me I'd never sung it any better. I'm sure I never felt it more.

At least one member of the Vice Squad was caught with a tear on his cashmere coat.

. . .

We took a taxi to the station. Luck was still with us. There'd been a big train wreck near Washington, and there'd be no trains before morning. The station was deserted. There was hardly anybody there but the fuzz. They looked as tired of watching me as I was of them.

Louis tried to negotiate a connection on a bus.

The best we could do was a couple of single seats on a crowded bus. It took me back twenty years, to be heading back to New York the way I had so many times before: busted, out on bail, broke from paying the bondsman, hungry from having no time to eat, beat from twenty-four hours without sleep, remembering the smell of that jail as I rattled around in a damn bus with a sleeping sailor falling all over me. But all that I soon forgot, with my man.

This time, the doctors have told me, with any kind of luck, I should be able to stay straight for two whole years. Who can ask for anything more? I've got enough of that Fagan Irish in me to believe that if the curtains are washed, company never comes. If you expect nothing but trouble, maybe a few happy days will turn up. If you expect happy days, look out.

But no doctor can tell you anything your own bones don't know. And I can let the doctors in on something. I knew I'd really licked it one morning when I couldn't stand television any more. When I was high and wanted to stay that way, I could watch TV by the hour and loved it. Who can tell what detours are ahead? Another trial? Sure. Another jail? Maybe. But if you've beat the habit again and kicked TV, no jail on earth can worry you too much.

Tired? You bet. But all that I'll soon forget with my man. . . .

. . . and the psychologist Stanton Peele reminds us that love and addiction may be more closely related than we imagine.

STANTON PEELE WITH ARCHIE BRODSKY
Love and Addiction

(1975)

'**L**ove' and 'addiction': the juxtaposition seems strange. Yet it shouldn't, for addiction has as much to do with love as it does with drugs. Many of us are addicts, only we don't know it. We turn to each other out of the same needs that drive some people to drink and others to heroin. And this kind of addiction is just as self-destructive as – and a lot more common than – those other kinds.

Ideally, love and addiction do not have anything at all to do with one another. They are polar opposites. Nothing could be further removed from genuine love – conceived as a commitment to mutual growth and fullfillment – than the desperate self-seeking dependency which, with drugs, we call addiction. Yet in practice, we tend to get them confused. We often say 'love' when we really mean, and are acting out, an addiction – a sterile, ingrown dependency relationship, with another person serving as the object of our need for security. This interpersonal dependency is not *like* an addiction, not something analogous to addiction; it *is* an addiction. It is every bit as much an addiction as drug dependency

. . .

For if addiction is now known *not* to be primarily a matter of drug chemistry or body chemistry, and if we therefore have to broaden our conception of dependency-treating objects to include a wider range of drugs, then why stop with drugs? Why not look at the whole range of things, activities, and even people to which we can and do become addicted? We must, in fact, do this if addiction is to be made a viable concept once again. At present, addiction as a scientific notion is falling into disuse because of the mass of contradictory data about drugs and their effects. Since people who take narcotics often do not get addicted, scientists are beginning to think that addiction does not exist. Yet, more casually, we find the word being used in an increasing number of contexts – 'addicted to work,' 'addicted to gambling' – because it describes something real that happens to people.

Addiction does exist, and it is a large issue in human psychology. An understanding of addiction will help answer the question of why we repeatedly return to things we have done before – the question of habit. Addiction can be considered a pathological habit. It occurs with human necessities, such as food and love, as well as with things which people can do without, such as heroin and nicotine.

In other words, addiction is not something mysterious, something about which our ordinary experience has nothing to say. It is a malignant outgrowth, an extreme, unhealthy manifestation, of normal human inclinations. We can recognize examples of addiction in ourselves even when we would not characterize ourselves entirely, or even basically, as addicts. This is why the ideal of addiction can be an important tool in our self-understanding. But for its value to be realized, it must be redefined. There has to be a fundamental change in the way we think about addiction

. . .

Interpersonal addiction – love addiction – is just about the most common, yet least recognized, form of addiction. Highlighting it helps us break down the stereotype of the 'drug addict' and arrive at a better understanding of the way addiction affects us all. On the other side, the antithesis of addiction is a true relatedness to the world, and there is no more powerful expression of that relatedness than love, or true responsiveness to another person.

The issue of love versus addiction is one that is very close to our lives, and thus one that we can do something about as individuals.

The environment that is most important to us is the human one. This is why, when we get addicted, we tend to get addicted to people. Similarly, our best hope of breaking out of addiction is by learning better ways of dealing with people. This is true not only for romantic involvements but also for family ties and friendships

. . .

Addiction is not a chemical reaction. Addiction is an *experience* – one which grows out of an individual's routinized subjective response to something that has special meaning for him – something, anything, that he finds so safe and reassuring that he cannot be without it. If we want to come to terms with addiction, we have to stop blaming drugs and start looking at people, at ourselves, and at what makes us dependent. We still find that we learn habits of dependence by growing up in a culture which teaches a sense of personal inadequacy, a reliance on external bulwarks, and a preoccupation with the negative or painful rather than the positive or joyous.

Addiction is not an abnormality in our society. It is not an aberration from the norm; it is itself the norm.

8
Soma-drinkers, Lotus-eaters, Assassins: Drugs and Society

The effects of drugs on individuals and cultures have throughout history raised broader questions about the role of drug use in society. But this role has never been a single or simple one. This section presents three 'myths', in the sense of recurrent cultural complexes, which suggest the various roles which drugs have historically played, or been seen to play.

Soma-drinkers

The first 'myth' of drug use can be called, for convenience, that of the 'soma drinkers' (see p. 97). This is the model whereby drug-taking is an important shared ritual within the mainstream of society. The soma hymns of the Rig Veda demonstrate that the plant sacrament was a powerful symbol of social union and defence against common enemies.

RIG VEDA
Hymn to Soma: 'This Restless Soma'

(*c.* 1000 BC)

1   This restless Soma – you try to grab him but he breaks away and overpowers everything. He is a sage and a seer inspired by poetry.

2   He covers the naked and heals all who are sick. The blind man sees; the lame man steps forth.

3   Soma, you are a broad defence against those who hate us, both enemies we have made ourselves and those made by others.

4   Through your knowledge and skills, rushing forward you drive out of the sky and the earth the evil deed of the enemy.

5   Let those who seek find what they seek: let them receive the treasure given by the generous and stop the greedy from getting what they want.

6   Let him find what was lost before; let him push forward the man of truth. Let him stretch out the lifespan that has not yet crossed its span.

7   Be kind and merciful to us, Soma; be good to our heart, without confusing our powers in your whirlwind.

8   King Soma, do not enrage us; do not terrify us; do not wound our heart with dazzling light.

9   Give help, when you see the evil plans of the gods in your own house. Generous king, keep away hatreds, keep away failures.

Drugs still occupy this central role in many of today's traditional societies. In 1907 a rubber-tapper named Manuel Cordoba-Rios was kidnapped by Indians in the Amazon forest, and initiated into their tribe. The most important part of this initiation was the ayahuasca *ceremony, in which the tribe developed a level of 'group mind' which borders, by our definitions, on telepathy.*

F. BRUCE LAMB
Wizard of the Upper Amazon: The Story of Manuel Córdova-Rios

(1971)

Each of us drank his cupful of *honixuma*, the vision extract. The chanting gradually took on the high falsetto quality, with each one in the circle adding his tremulous obbligato to the chief's chant, again coming together on key words which gave emphasis and continuity to the flow of sound. As before, in a few minutes a pulsating hum dominated my consciousness, followed by a violent muscle spasm as soon as the pulsations merged to a continuous sound. Nausea did not appear this time, but a flow of other sensations progressed through my consciousness, their content impossible to describe in terms of the rational world. Exotic sensations, erotic in nature, produced indescribable feelings of pleasure and exhilaration. And I had the impression of being free of my body, capable of actions, sensations and knowledge completely divorced from my physical being.

The sense of time disappeared completely and perhaps the impressions felt were very fleeting with relation to normal consciousness. Colored visions began to dominate the scene, and the chanting seemed to intrude and take over control of the progression of visions. After unorganized visions developed, of colored forms and abstract shapes dominated by intense blues, natural objects of the forest began to appear – in vague, imprecise outline at first, but soon in unimaginable detail.

With the chant of the boa, a giant constrictor appeared slowly gliding through the forest. Blue lights intensified an intricate design of scroll configurations that seemed to float along the boa's spine. Light flashed from his eyes and tongue. The bold patterns on the snake's skin glowed with intense and varied colors.

. . .

The chief said, 'Let us start with the birds. You know the medium-sized tinamou, the partridge that gives the plaintive call at sunset because he does not like to sleep alone on the ground. Visualize one for me there on the ground between the trees in the alternating light and shadow.'

There he was! I saw him in infinite detail with his rounded tailless rump, plumage olive gray, washed and barred with shades of cinnamon, chestnut and dusky brown, colors that blended imperceptibly with the light and shadows on the leafy forest floor. My visual perception seemed unlimited. Never had I perceived visual images in such detail before.

'Yes, Chief, I see him,' was my response, mentally if not aloud.

'He will move around now. Watch closely.'

A few shy, furtive movements and the bird was in another pattern of light and shadow where he was much more difficult to see. But I had followed him there and could pick out every detail still. The chief then brought a female, and the male went through his mating dance. I heard all of the songs, calls and other sounds. Their variety was beyond anything I had known. Finally a simple saucer-shaped nest appeared on the ground between the birds, with two pale-blue eggs in it. The male then sat on the nest, to my surprise. 'Yes, he raises the children,' said the chief.

We went from the various tinamous to the trumpeter, the curassows and other important game birds, all seen in the same infinite and minute detail.

Then the chief said, 'Close your eyes now and let the visions flow before we go on to other things.'

. . .

Colour visions, indefinite in form, began to evolve into immense vistas of enchanting beauty. Soon subtle but evocative chants led by the chief took control of the progression of our visions. Embellishments to both the chants and the visions came from the participants.

Soon the procession of animals began, starting with the jungle cats. Some of these I had not seen before. There was a tawny puma, several varieties of the smaller spotted ocelot, then a giant rosetta-spotted jaguar. A murmur from the assembly indicated recognition. This tremendous animal shuffled along with head hanging down, mouth open and tongue lolling out. Hideous, large teeth filled the open mouth. An instant change of demeanor to vicious alertness caused a tremor through the circle of phantom-viewers.

From a memory recess in my brain there emerged with the stimulation of the cats an experience from my past. On a trip to the Rio Putumayo a year before coming to the Jurua to cut caucho, I had come face to face on a forest path with a rare black jaguar. It had been a terrifying experience, but I had dominated the flashing eyes of the beast and we had gone our separate ways without violence.

This mighty animal now intruded on our visions and a shudder passed through us all. As before, the demon of the forest went on his way.

. . .

Everyone seemed aware of the source of the black jaguar sequence of visions. It left a strong impression on them and resulted in my being given the name Ino Moxo, Black Panther.

Drugs in the fabric of society: Women gathering coca leaves in Bolivia
in the 1860s. (Wellcome Trust)

*Some thinkers, like Aldous Huxley, have suggested that such insti-
tutionalized drug use could be a cure for modern society's ills.*

ALDOUS HUXLEY
'Culture and the Individual' from Moksha: Writings on Psychedelics and the Visionary Experience 1931–63

(1963)

Unprecedentedly rapid technological and demographic changes are steadily increasing the dangers by which we are surrounded, and at the same time are steadily diminishing the relevance of the traditional feeling-and-behaviour-patterns imposed upon all individuals, rulers and ruled alike, by their culture. Always desirable, widespread training in the art of cutting holes in cultural fences is now the most urgent of necessities. Can such a training be speeded up and made more effective by a judicious use of the physically harmless psychedelics now available? On the basis of personal experience and the published evidence, I believe that it can. In my utopian fantasy, *Island*, I speculated in fictional terms about the ways in which a substance akin to psilocybin could be used to potentiate the nonverbal education of adolescents and to remind adults that the real world is very different from the misshapen universe they have created for themselves by means of their culture-conditioned prejudices. 'Having Fun with Fungi' – that was how one waggish reviewer dismissed the matter. But which is better: to have Fun with Fungi or to have Idiocy with Ideology, to have Wars because of Words, to have Tomorrow's Misdeeds out of Yesterday's Miscreeds?

How should the psychedelics be administered? Under what circumstances, with what kind of preparation and follow-up? These are questions that must be answered empirically, by large-scale experiment. Man's collective mind has a high degree of viscosity and flows from one position to another with the reluctant deliberation of an ebbing tide of sludge. But in a world of explosive population increase, of headlong technological advance and of militant nationalism, the time at our disposal is strictly limited. We must discover, and discover very soon, new energy sources for overcoming our society's psychological inertia, better solvents for liquefying the sludgy stickiness of an anachronistic state of mind. On the verbal level an education in the nature and limitations, the uses and abuses of language; on the wordless level an education in mental silence and pure receptivity; and finally, through the use of harmless psychedelics, a course of chemically triggered conversion experiences or ecstasies – these, I believe, will provide all the sources of mental energy, all the solvents of conceptual sludge, that an individual requires. With their aid, he should be able to adapt himself selectively to his culture, rejecting its evils, stupidities and irrelevances, gratefully accepting all its treasures of accumulated knowledge, or rationality, human-heartedness and practical wisdom. If the number of such individuals is sufficiently high, they may be able to pass from discriminating acceptance of their culture to discriminating change and reform. Is this a hopefully utopian dream? Experiment can give us the answer, for the dream is pragmatic; the utopian hypotheses can be tested empirically. And in these oppressive times a little hope is surely no unwelcome visitant.

Modern societies, however, do in almost all cases have drugs integrated into their fabric, though usually on a less conspicuous level. A good example is the use of betel by around 300 million people across South-East Asia.

DAWN F. ROONEY
Betel Chewing Traditions in South-East Asia

(1993)

Few traditions in South-East Asia have the antiquity and universal acceptance of betel chewing. The custom is over 2,000 years old and has survived from ancient times into the twentieth century. Its use cuts across class, sex, or age: 'The habitual and universal solace of both sexes is the areca nut and betel . . . which is rarely absent from the mouth of man or woman,' wrote the Honourable George N. Curzon, a nineteenth-century observer. Its devotees include farmers, priests, and kings, men, women, and children. The homeliness of the name belies its importance. The Thais 'prefer to go without rice or other food rather than to deprive themselves of the betel . . .' noted Nicolas Gervaise, a French visitor in the seventeenth century.

Three ingredients – an areca-nut, a leaf of the betel-pepper, and lime – are essential for betel chewing; others may be added depending on availability and preference. The leaf is first daubed with lime paste and topped with thin slices of the nut, then it is folded or rolled into a bite-size quid. The interaction of the ingredients during chewing produces a red-coloured saliva. 'If a person speaks to you while he is chewing his "quid" of betel, his mouth looks as if it were full of blood,' reflected Isabella L. Bird, an intrepid woman traveller of the nineteenth century. Most of the betel juice is spat out. The tell-tale residue looks like splotches of dried blood. Indeed, the resemblance is so close that some early European visitors thought many Asians had tuberculosis. The splotches of betel spittle are spaced consistently enough for use as measurements of time and distance in rural areas. A short time is 'about a betel chew' and the distance between two villages, for example, may be 'about three chews'

. . .

Besides being chewed, the betel quid and the individual ingredients are widely used for medicinal, magical, and symbolical purposes. It is administered as a curative for a plethora of ills, including indigestion and worms. It is believed to facilitate contact with supernatural forces and is often used to exorcise spirits, particularly those associated with illness. In its symbolical role, it is present at nearly all religious ceremonies and festivals of the lunar calendar. Betel fosters relationships and thus serves as an avenue of communication between relatives, lovers, friends, and strangers. It figures in male–female alliances and its potency in this area is especially telling. Because of its power in bonding relationships, betel is used symbolically to solidify acts of justice such as oaths of allegiance and the settlement of lawsuits. Betel is a surrogate for money in payment to midwives and surgeons for services rendered.

A key to the unconditional patronage of betel is its use on four levels – as a food and medicine, and for magical and symbolical purposes. As such, this single tradition is an integral part of the art, ceremonies, and social intercourse of daily life.

. . .

Why do people chew betel? The multi-purpose benefits are described explicitly in Indian literature as early as the sixth century. 'Betel stimulates passion, brings out the physical charm, conduces to good-luck, lends aroma to the mouth, strengthens the body and dispels diseases arising from the phlegm. It also bestows many other benefits.' According to a sixth-century Indian text (quoted in Morarjee, n.d.), betel is one of the eight enjoyments of life – along with unguents, incense, women, garments, music, beds, food, and flowers named in a Sanskrit verse of the twelfth century. Chou Ta-Kuan (Zhou Daguan), a member of a Chinese mission to Angkor at the end of the thirteenth century, gives more practical reasons for chewing betel: he thought it prevented belching after meals. Betel is 'energy giving medicine' for Khun (Mrs) Samap, an 85-year-old Thai barber, who always chews it before giving a haircut. It 'encourages self-reflection' for a Burmese monk.

The main reason for chewing betel seems to lie in the social affability

326 **Artificial Paradises**

produced by sharing a quid with friends. This enjoyment can be seen on the faces of a group of elderly men squatting around a betel box, or heard in the laughter of women relaxing in a rice-field with a betel basket. Offering a quid to someone is a mark of hospitality.

Our own 'soft drugs' – tea, coffee, chocolate, tobacco – only arrived relatively recently, but quickly insinuated themselves into many levels of Western life.

JORDAN GOODMAN
'Fxcitantia: Or, how Enlightenment Europe took to soft drugs'

(1995)

I

The rituals and meanings associated with the consumption of tea, coffee, chocolate and tobacco are deeply embedded in our culture. The habitual consumption of tea, coffee, chocolate and tobacco is a public affirmation of the central place of the consumption of a few, key, legal drugs in Western culture. Significantly, these drugs are not nakedly consumed; they are clothed in a commodified form wherein is hidden an economic, social, cultural and political reality. Drinking tea, coffee, or chocolate and smoking cigarettes is quite different from consuming caffeine, theine, theobromine and nicotine. (Contrast this with the consumption of illicit drugs: heroin, cocaine, crack, even marijuana.) Yet caffeine, nicotine, etc. are powerful alkaloids of their respective plants, with rather similar pharmacological properties and have been recognized for a long time as producing physiological changes primarily but not exclusively in the mind and as addictive.

These rituals had their origin in the eighteenth century when they were used to proclaim a powerful ideology of sobriety and respectability. How the new soft drugs came to be associated with this ideology can partly be explained by the way in which Europe absorbed and transformed their mode of production, distribution and consumption.

Europe was the direct beneficiary of a prolonged period during which tea, coffee, chocolate and tobacco were brought to the point of commercial viability and consumer acceptance. This involved the process of botanical experimentation and selection, developments in

methods of cultivation and processing leading to distinctive commodities
with their own particular modes of consumption. These commodities,
therefore, appeared in Europe replete with their own historical experiences often rooted in antiquity, enacted in China, the Near East and
the New World. Tea and tobacco were certainly consumed in China
and the Americas, respectively, by about 2000 BC. Central American
Amerindians were cultivating the cocoa tree at least a thousand years
before Columbus reached the New World. Coffee was probably being
consumed in Ethiopia and Yemen by about AD 800–1000.

Tobacco was the first of the new exotica to enter Europe as a direct
result of the expansion of European interests overseas. Still, it took
almost a century – from Columbus in 1492, to the publication in 1571
by Nicolas Monardes of his natural history of medicinal plants of the
New World (which launched tobacco as an extraordinary panacea) –
for Europeans to take up the nicotian habit. Coffee made its first
appearance in Europe, in Venice, in the first few decades of the seventeenth century, as part of its diffusion through the Middle East, from
Yemen to the eastern Mediterranean lands, to the main cities of Islam,
especially Baghdad, Cairo and Aleppo. By the middle of the century,
coffeehouses had sprung up in many of Europe's major cities, especially
in Paris, London, Marseille and Vienna. Until this time, coffee supplies
into Europe were erratic and relatively small scale, traded across the
Mediterranean into the ports of southern Europe, particularly Marseille.

Chocolate, too, spread slowly from its homeland, Central America,
to Europe. Though Columbus came across chocolate on his fourth
voyage, the Spanish only became interested in it after the Conquest
and it remained confined, in terms of consumption, to the populations
of the newly conquered territories, both the indigenous Amerindians
and the Spanish newcomers, for a long time. Shipments of chocolate
to Europe date from the first decade of the seventeenth century (and
possibly earlier than that) but not until the middle of the century did
Europeans become familiar with the chocolate beverage.

Tea faced a similar experience in Europe. Reports of its use in China
and Japan were circulating in late sixteenth-century Europe and though
some shipments of tea from China were made by the Dutch East India
Company as early as 1606, the Company did not begin regular imports
until the second half of the century. The English East India Company
started regular shipments of tea from Canton to London in the 1660s,
though English acquaintance with tea drinking antedated the Company's

involvement: Holland supplied the English market for the first half of the seventeenth century.

. . .

Europeanization can also be seen at work at the point of consumption. Medical authorities and botanists were of crucial importance here. They were responsible for assigning to the new commodities European meanings within the prevailing discourse. Precisely where, for example, the new substance would be located in therapeutic theory and practice was a matter of intense debate and for each of tobacco, coffee, tea and chocolate, a considerable literature was generated. This was not just an intellectual exercise, however; it was also a question of vested interests. Cornelis Bontekoe, one of the most enthusiastic advocates of coffee and tea drinking (in his 1685 treatise on tea, he advised that drinking anywhere from fifty to two hundred cups of the infusion daily was reasonable) was said by his critics to have been in the employ of the Dutch East India Company. Another enthusiast of tea drinking, the Amsterdam physician and burgomaster, Nicholas Tulp, was a director of the Company. Nicolas Monardes, the champion of nicotian therapy, had considerable interests in Spanish–American colonial trade, and no doubt there were others, such as Hans Sloane and Benjamin Moseley, who mixed medical and colonial interests. The medical/botanical debate penetrated the structure of colonial commerce and there is no doubt that this stimulated demand for the new exotic substances.

Another aspect of the Europeanization of these new commodities was the way in which they were consumed. As far as tobacco is concerned, European tobacco artefacts – pipes, cigars and snuff – were essentially imitations of Amerindian ones, but they were quickly transformed materially as were the rituals of their consumption. European tobacco consumption became incorporated into the culture of the tavern and it was consumed alongside alcoholic drinks. This combination of drugs, alcohol and tobacco is, in this case, important to note.

As for the newly introduced hot beverages, these, too, were absorbed within European rituals while, at the same time, their consumption imitated practices of the source culture. Just as coffeehouses in the Near East were the preserve of men, incorporating leisure as well as business, so in Europe, coffeehouses were club-like and exclusively male. Yet not all activities of the Near Eastern coffeehouse found their way to Europe: musical entertainments, ubiquitous in the Near Eastern coffeehouse, were practically unknown in the European variant, where counting house and political matters prevailed. Once coffee consumption became established in its social and physical setting, tea and chocolate became available there too. Because of their assimilation within the culture of the coffeehouse, all three beverages were initially associated with a bourgeois masculinity, serious, purposive and respectable.

The mid-seventeenth-century European coffeehouse may be seen as an adaptation of the Near Eastern establishment, but in its social dimension and the commodities it offered for consumption it was distinctly European. So, too, was the practice of sweetening and adding milk to these drinks. As far as we know, neither coffee, nor tea, nor chocolate were served sweetened in their source cultures. How and why the practice of sweetening evolved is a moot point. Whatever the actual chronology, the fusion of tea, coffee and chocolate with sugar was a powerful force and symbol of European power overseas: it happened very swiftly and was rapidly taken for granted.

Lotus-eaters

A second myth, or model, of drugs in society is that of the Lotus-Eaters: where drug use has become so prevalent that the society has lost the power to act, and destroyed itself from within. In The Odyssey, *Homer relates how such a fate nearly befell Odysseus and his crew.*

HOMER
The Odyssey

(*c.* 700 BC)

For nine days I was chased by those accursed winds across the teeming seas. But on the tenth we reached the country of the Lotus-eaters, a race that eat the flowery lotus fruit. We disembarked to draw water, and my crews quickly had a meal by the ships. When we had eaten and drunk, I sent some of my followers inland to find out what sort of human beings might be there, detailing two men for the duty with a third as herald. Off they went, and it was not long before they came upon the Lotus-eaters. Now these natives had no intention of killing my comrades; what they did was to give them some lotus to taste. Those who ate the honeyed fruit of the plant lost any wish to come back and bring us news. All they now wanted was to stay where they were with the Lotus-eaters, to browse on the lotus, and to forget all thoughts of return. I had to use force to bring them back to the hollow ships, and they wept on the way, but once on board I tied them up and dragged them under the benches. I then commanded the rest of my loyal band to embark with all speed on their fast ships, for fear that others of them might eat the lotus and think no more of home. They came on board at once, took their places at their oars and all together struck the white surf with their blades.

So we left that country and sailed with heavy hearts.

*What exactly is wrong with the blissful society of the Lotus-Eaters? For
Tennyson, despite his personal disapproval of the opium habits of his
friends, the answer seems to be less than clear, and his telling of the
same story is tinged with longing and regret.*

ALFRED, LORD TENNYSON
'The Lotos-eaters'

(1832)

'Courage!' he said, and pointed toward the land,
'This mounting wave will roll us shoreward soon.'
In the afternoon they came unto a land
In which it seemed always afternoon.
All round the coast the languid air did swoon,
Breathing like one that hath a weary dream.
Full-faced above the valley stood the moon;
And like a downward smoke, the slender stream
Along the cliff to fall and pause and fall did seem.

A land of streams! some, like a downward smoke,
Slow-dropping veils of thinnest lawn, did go;
And some thro' wavering lights and shadows broke,
Rolling a slumbrous sheet of foam below.
They saw the gleaming river seaward flow
From the inner land: far off, three mountain-tops,
Three silent pinnacles of aged snow,
Stood sunset-flush'd: and, dew'd with showery drops,
Up-clomb the shadowy pine above the woven copse.

The charmed sunset linger'd low adown
In the red West: thro' mountain clefts the dale
Was seen far inland, and the yellow down
Border'd with palm, and many a winding vale
And meadow, set with slender galingale;
A land where all things always seem'd the same!
And round about the keel with faces pale,
Dark faces pale against that rosy flame,
The mild-eyed melancholy Lotos-eaters came.

Branches they bore of that enchanted stem,
Laden with flower and fruit, whereof they gave
To each, but whoso did receive of them,
And taste, to him the gushing of the wave
Far far away did seem to mourn and rave
On alien shores; and if his fellow spake,
His voice was thin, as voices from the grave;
And deep-asleep he seem'd, yet all awake,
And music in his ears his beating heart did make.

They sat them down upon the yellow sand,
Between the sun and moon upon the shore;
And sweet it was to dream of Fatherland,
Of child, and wife, and slave; but evermore
Most weary seem'd the sea, weary the oar,
Weary the wandering fields of barren foam.
Then some one said, 'We will return no more;'
And all at once they sang, 'Our island home
Is far beyond the wave; we will no longer roam.'

. . .

The Lotos blooms below the barren peak:
The Lotos blows by every winding creek:
All day the wind breathes low with mellower tone:
Thro' every hollow cave and alley lone
Round and round the spicy downs the yellow Lotos-dust is
  blown.
We have had enough of action, and of motion we.
Roll'd to starboard, roll'd to larboard, when the surge was seeth-
  ing free,
Where the wallowing monster spouted his foam-fountains in
  the sea.
Let us swear an oath, and keep it with an equal mind,
In the hollow Lotos-land to live and lie reclined
On the hills like Gods together, careless of mankind.
For they lie beside their nectar, and the bolts are hurl'd
Far below them in the valleys, and the clouds are lightly curl'd
Round their golden houses, girdled with the gleaming world:

Where they smile in secret, looking over wasted lands,
Blight and famine, plague and earthquake, roaring deeps and
    fiery sands,
Clanging fights, and flaming towns, and sinking ships, and pray-
    ing hands.
But they smile, they find a music centred in a doleful song
Steaming up, a lamentation and an ancient tale of wrong,
Like a tale of little meaning tho' the words are strong;
Chanted from an ill-used race of men that cleave the soil,
Sow the seed, and reap the harvest with enduring toil,
Storing yearly little dues of wheat, and wine and oil;
Till they perish and they suffer – some, 'tis whisper'd – down in
    hell
Suffer endless anguish, others in Elysian valleys dwell,
Resting weary limbs at last on beds of asphodel.
Surely, surely, slumber is more sweet than toil, the shore
Than labour in the deep mid-ocean, wind and wave and oar;
Oh rest ye, brother mariners, we will not wander more.

From Victorian times onwards, the fate of the Lotus-Eaters has been most commonly used as a metaphor for the abuse of opiates, and the most frequently cited historical example of its occurrence has been nineteenth-century China.

MARGARET GOLDSMITH
The Trail of Opium: The Eleventh Plague
(1939)

'I cannot prevent the introduction of the flowing poison,' the Emperor of China answered the requests of the victorious English, 'gain-seeking and corrupt men will for profit and sensuality defeat my wishes, but nothing will induce me to derive a revenue from the vice and misery of my own people.'

The Emperor's insistence on what he considered his duty, meant that the smuggling trade continued as before the War, except that it had become easier for English smugglers to carry on this illicit trade. Hong Kong could be used as a base of supplies, and an efficient British warship was stationed at each of the five ports in which the English were free to trade.

. . .

Opium, in other words, had been not only the cause but the victor in this first Opium War. Shipments from India to China increased rapidly after the conclusion of peace. In 1840 the total imports into China, from Bengal and Malwa, amounted to 20,619 chests. In 1841 these imports had risen to 34,631; in 1845 they were 39,010; in 1850 they were 52,925; and by 1859 they had reached 75,822 chests.

At home in England the influence of opium was making itself felt as well. When Peel asked Gladstone to accept the Vice-Presidency of the Board of Trade, Gladstone declined because he could not 'reconcile it to his sense of right to exact from China, as a term of peace, compensation for the opium surrendered to her.' And in both Houses, differences ensued whenever China and opium came up for debate.

. . .

The Chinese opium crop was, as an English contemporary pointed out, 'a sword of Damocles, always hanging over our heads, and rendering a secure enjoyment of the Indian monopoly revenue impossible.'

The fear of this Chinese competition became articulate when the price of the native Chinese product dropped far below the price of Indian imports. In some inland parts of China, in 1870, Indian opium was extremely expensive, literally 'worth its weight in silver,' whereas the Chinese opium was only tenpence for a Chinese ounce. This meant that for a penny, an ordinary smoker could buy his day's supply of the drug. Many English business men were not only frightened by this Chinese competition; they were annoyed as well. They felt that somehow or other they owned China, and that she had no right to compete in any way with the Indian opium.

. . .

Many Chinamen, though for different reasons, were equally alarmed by the domestic opium cultivation. The Government, in fact, was actively against it. For apart from the fact that the home product increased the consumption of the drug, and thus illness, degeneration and poverty amongst the consumers, the poppy cultivation presented a serious agricultural problem.

Some of the land which should have been used for food crops was planted with poppy, so that in certain districts a food shortage frequently resulted. During famine years this was a most serious matter. In a Consular Report from Shanghai, in 1873, Medhurst, the British Consul, reported an alarming situation.

'The easy production of the drug,' he wrote, 'and the remunerative returns it gives . . . tend to engross the attention of the agriculturists and to sap nearly every other industry.'

Three years before this, in 1870, the Censor Yew-Peh-Ch'wan had already warned his people against growing opium. He claimed that the production of the poppy was the greatest obstacle to the production of foodstuffs in China, and declared that 10,000 mow (6 mow is an acre) of land was under poppy cultivation at that time. The Censor mentioned cases of suicide; people had taken their lives, desperate from starvation, because, though they had money to buy food, only opium was available in their district.

'The evil caused by opium smoking,' Yew-Peh-Ch'wan pleaded in his memorial, 'is worse than the destruction caused by floods, or the ravages of wild beasts.'

The fear that the West might become corrupted by the opiated Chinese underlies many manifestations of late Victorian culture – for example, the opening of Charles Dickens's last, unfinished novel Edwin Drood.

CHARLES DICKENS
The Mystery of Edwin Drood

(1870)

An ancient English Cathedral town? How can the ancient English Cathedral town be here! The well-known massive grey square tower of its old Cathedral? How can that be here? There is no spike of rusty iron in the air, between the eye and it, from any point of the real prospect. What IS the spike that intervenes, and who has set it up? Maybe, it is set up by the Sultan's orders for the impaling of a horde of Turkish robbers, one by one. It is so, for cymbals clash, and the Sultan goes by to his palace in long procession. Ten thousand scimitars flash in the sunlight, and thrice ten thousand dancing-girls strew flowers. Then, follow white elephants caparisoned in countless gorgeous colors, and infinite in number and attendants. Still, the Cathedral tower rises in the background, where it cannot be, and still no writhing figure is on the grim spike. Stay! Is the spike so low a thing as the rusty spike on the top of a post of an old bedstead that has tumbled all awry? Some vague period of drowsy laughter must be devoted to the consideration of this possibility.

Shaking from head to foot, the man whose scattered consciousness has thus fantastically pieced itself together, at length rises, supports his trembling frame upon his arms, and looks around. He is in the meanest and closest of small rooms. Through the ragged window-curtain, the light of early day steals in from a miserable court. He lies, dressed, across a large unseemly bed, upon a bedstead that has indeed given way under the weight upon it. Lying, also dressed and also across the bed, not longwise, are a Chinaman, a Lascar, and a haggard woman. The two first are in a sleep or stupor; the last is blowing at a kind of pipe, to kindle it. And as she blows, and shading it with her lean hand, concentrates its red spark of light, it serves in the dim morning as a lamp to show him what he sees of her.

'Another?' says this woman, in a querulous, rattling whisper. 'Have another?'

He looks about him, with his hand to his forehead.

'Ye've smoked as many as five since ye come in at midnight,' the woman goes on, as she chronically complains. 'Poor me, poor me, my head is so bad. Them two come in after ye. Ah, poor me, the business is slack, is slack! Few Chinamen about the Docks, and fewer Lascars, and no ships coming in, these any! Here's another ready for ye, deary. Ye'll remember like a good soul, won't ye, that the market price is dreffle high just now? More nor three shillings and sixpence for a thimbleful! And ye'll remember that nobody but me (and Jack Chinaman t'other side the court; but he can't do it as well as me) has the true secret of mixing it? Ye'll pay up according, deary, won't ye?'

She blows at the pipe as she speaks, and, occasionally bubbling at it, inhales much of its contents.

'O me, O me, my lungs is weak, my lungs is bad! It's nearly ready for ye, deary. Ah, poor me, poor me, my poor hand shakes like to drop off! I see ye coming-to, and I ses to my poor self, "I'll have another ready for him, and he'll bear in mind the market price of opium, and pay according." O my poor head! I make my pipes of old penny ink-bottles, ye see, deary – this is one – and I fits in a mouthpiece, this way, and I takes my mixter out of this thimble with this little horn spoon; and so I fills, deary. Ah, my poor nerves! I got Heavens-hard drunk for sixteen year afore I took to this; but this don't hurt me, not to speak of. And it takes away the hunger as well as wittles, deary.'

She hands him the nearly-emptied pipe, and sinks back, turning over on her face.

He rises unsteadily from the bed, lays the pipe upon the hearthstone, draws back the ragged curtain, and looks with repugnance at his three companions. He notices that the woman has opium-smoked herself into a strange likeness of the Chinaman. His form of cheek, eye, and temple, and his color, are repeated in her. Said Chinaman convulsively wrestles with one of his many Gods, or Devils, perhaps, and snarls horribly. The Lascar laughs and dribbles at the mouth. The hostess is still.

The spectacularly paranoid Dr Donald Johnson (see p. 238) was con-
vinced in the 1950s that this type of enslavement by drugs was being
systematically perpetrated on the West by Communist Russia.

DONALD McI. JOHNSON
Indian Hemp: A Social Menace

(1952)

In this twentieth century we have already had atomic warfare, poison gas warfare, nerve warfare, cold warfare – and we have had drug warfare too. Indeed what more effective weapon could there be for waging the Cold War than by promoting the use and consumption of noxious drugs within the ranks of your enemy that will corrupt his youth; and so rot your foe from inside so that he will crumble of his own accord? For such a purpose the hemp drug would be an admirable medium.

Drug warfare is, in fact, nothing new. There was the deliberate encouragement of opium smoking by the Japanese in Northern China in the nineteen-thirties as a measure of policy.

Drug warfare in our own day could conceivably take two forms. One would be the more direct method of actively promoting and assisting those organizations who traffic in drugs in their penetration for their own purpose of enemy territory. It is appropriate that we should call to mind in this connection that Soviet Russia, our antagonist in the Cold War, is in control of the territories of Eastern Europe, such as Bulgaria, which were the acknowledged source of much of the illicit drugs that flooded the international market in the pre-war years. Russell Pasha gives the information that a single Bulgarian factory in the nineteen-thirties was found to be producing as much as 187 million shots of heroin per month – far in excess of any medical requirements for this drug.

But a yet more sinister method of warfare comes to mind in the case of a drug whose properties are such as we have been considering in this book – a drug which, through its insertion into a widely consumed article of food (such as, for instance, bread), might through gradual doses condition the mentality of a whole population. We can surmise from the previous chapters how the hemp drug, if it be supposed that the hemp drug was selected for such a purpose, would act. There would be increased receptivity to suggestion – a welling up of the collective unconscious – a breach in the mental barriers of individuality with the increased facilities of telepathic communication and of hypnotism that such a state would bring. There would be established, in fact, all the pre-requisites for the success of suddenly-applied totalitarian propaganda.

A vast field of study and experiment would seem to lie upon to our scientific experts in the problems of telepathy and hypnotism in connection with the Indian hemp drug. Indeed it would seem as if we already have our miniature laboratories in our 'hot jazz' dancing clubs where, so it is said, 'reefer' smoking is an essential part of the proceedings. *Daily Express* correspondent, Chapman Pincher, in his article of 28th November, 1951, gives an answer to the question: is there a link between dope and hot jazz dancing? 'Reefers and rhythm seem to be directly connected with the minute electric waves continually generated by the brain surface. When the rhythm of the music synchronizes with the rhythm of the brainwaves, the jazz fans experience an almost compulsive urge to move their bodies in sympathy. Dope may help the brain to tune in to the rhythm more sharply.' This statement is based on the brain research carried out by Dr. Grey Walter of the Burden Neurological Institute, Bristol.

For the rhythm of the jazz drum substitute the rhythm of totalitarian propaganda; and the point which I wish to make will be appreciated.

It is perhaps not out of place to mention here that, according to the Board of Trade returns, our imports of grain and flour from the Soviet Union have in the past three years been as follows: 1948, 13,440,277 cwt.; 1949, 4,067,842 cwt.; 1950, 13,504,079 cwt.

. . . but recent scholarship suggests that the 'Lotus-Eating collapse' of nineteenth-century Chinese society as a result of opium is itself a myth which was propagated by missionaries and journalists.

RICHARD K. NEWMAN

Opium Smoking in Late Imperial China: A Reconsideration

(1995)

A social problem in one country may often be held up as an example to others, but it is rare for it to bring forth an internationally co-ordinated response with a world-wide application. One of these rarities is the campaign against 'hard' drugs. While liquor laws differ widely from country to country, the modern system of laws against cocaine and the opiates have been established by international convention. These arrangements evolved out of the measures taken to help imperial China with its opium problem, which was regarded, at least in part, as a foreign responsibility arising out of the vast quantities of Indian opium which had been imported by foreigners into China throughout the nineteenth century, often in questionable circumstances. The behaviour of the opium merchants and their governments seemed all the more reprehensible because of the encouragement which it gave to the Chinese to break their own government's laws against opium smoking and poppy cultivation. The first International Opium Commission met in Shanghai in 1909 and passed a number of resolutions to help China; it also laid down principles of co-operation between producing and consuming countries which tended logically to expand in scope and force, leading to a global system of control of all narcotic substances, and to the institutionalization of these arrangements under the League and the United Nations.

China has also been a major influence on the world's understanding of the 'opium evil'. Unfortunately much of the information about China was tendentious from the start as missionary and philanthropic organizations tried to mobilize public opinion against opium and exert political leverage against the trade. The classic depiction of the Chinese opium smoker – a pathetic and degenerate creature with 'lank and shrivelled limbs, tottering gait, sallow visage, feeble voice and death-boding glance of eye' – became established as a stereotype and was reinforced by literary and journalistic depictions of opium dens, xenophobic reactions to Chinese communities abroad and late nineteenth-century intellectual movements such as progressivism and social Darwinism

. . .

Historians have done little to clarify these aspects of the subject. Some have found it useful to repeat the condemnations of opium, since these provide evidence of the social damage done by British imperialism. Others have treated the subject more dispassionately but without breaking away from the assumptions that the missionaries so vigorously promoted: that all opium use is harmful and that it leads to addiction and therefore to physical ruin. Jonathan Spence, for example, gives a wide-ranging survey of opium use in imperial China, but exaggerates the deleterious effects of the drug by referring to opium smokers as addicts. If we are to understand the true effect of opium on the health of individual Chinese, and cumulatively on Chinese society, we must distinguish carefully between those who were addicted, those who were damaged in some way by the addiction, and the many millions of light and moderate consumers who were not addicted at all.

Another reason why it has been difficult to clarify the Chinese experience with opium is that the evidence pointing to the harmlessness of much opium consumption was so roundly condemned by anti-opium propagandists that the missionary viewpoint was able to establish itself as an axiom. This was exemplified best by the controversy surrounding the Royal Commission on Opium, which collected information for the British government in 1893–94. The Commission was set up to mollify the temperance reformers, but it ended by enraging them, because its report concluded that opium did little harm and there was no good reason for abolishing the export trade from India to China. The reformers claimed that the evidence collected from China was biased and inadequate and that if the Commission had been more thorough its conclusions would have been different. In fact, much of the evidence which the anti-opiumists condemned is serious, sensible, carefully substantiated and not at all self-seeking; some of it comes from missionaries and missionary doctors whose natural inclination was to side with the philanthropists; and, most significantly, it conforms fairly well with modern medical knowledge about the nature of opiate dependency

. . .

Opium smoking undoubtedly produced some addicts, and some of those addicts were reduced to a pitiable condition, but it is not their image that should be foremost in the mind; we should also remember the peasants carrying their lumps of poppy juice to market, the boatmen wrapped in their blankets passing round an opium pipe in the twilight, and the Chinese gentleman smoking peaceably at home with his friends. It is not the existence of addiction that requires explanation so much as the fact that, in a society in which opium was cheap and widely available, so many people smoked lightly or not at all. The production and consumption of opium were, for most people, normal rather than deviant activities and it is the implications of this normality which ought to be explored, both for the sake of China's history and for the sake of their relevance to modern societies learning to live with drugs.

The clearest historical example of a 'Lotus-Eater's drug' which reduces societies to chaos and misery is undoubtedly alcohol, which destroyed many of the peoples to whom it was introduced in the process of colonization. The stereotype of the 'drunken Indian' was established by accounts like Benjamin Franklin's.

PETER C. MANCALL
Deadly Medicine: Indians and Alcohol in Early America

(1995)

When Benjamin Franklin wrote his *Autobiography* he included one of American literature's most enduring descriptions of intoxicated Indians. Indians, he believed, 'are exteamly apt to get drunk, and when so are very quarrelsome and disorderly.' As a result, he and his fellow negotiators of a treaty at Carlisle, Pennsylvania, in 1753 informed the Indians present that 'if they would continue sober during the Treaty, we would give them Plenty of Rum when Business was over.' The Indians abided by their promise, no doubt inspired by the knowledge that the only people in the town who had rum were Franklin and the other negotiators. Once their business was concluded, the colonists, true to their word and to custom, offered liquor. Franklin recorded what happened.

The hundred or so Indians got rum in the afternoon, Franklin wrote. By nightfall they had apparently consumed the entire available supply, and the commissioners walked into their camp after 'hearing a great Noise.' 'We found,' Franklin recalled years later, 'they had all made a great Bonfire in the Middle of the Square. They were all drunk Men and Women, quarrelling and fighting. Their dark-colour'd Bodies, half naked, seen only by the gloomy Light of the Bonfire, running after and beating one another with Firebrands, accompanied by their horrid Yellings, form'd a Scene the most resembling our Ideas of Hell that could well be imagin'd.' Realizing there was little they could do to calm the Indians, Franklin and the other commissioners returned to their camp. When several Indians came asking for more rum at midnight, the colonists this time declined to provide it.

The next day the Indians were 'sensible they had misbehav'd in giving us that Disturbance,' and sent three of their 'old Consellors to make their Apology.' Though acknowledging their behavior, the Indians' spokesman laid the blame on the rum itself, 'and then endeavour'd to excuse the Rum, by saying, *"The Great Spirit who made all things made everything for some Use, and whatever Use he design'd any thing for, that Use it should always be put to; Now, when he made Rum, he said,* LET THIS BE FOR INDIANS TO GET DRUNK WITH. *And it must be so."'* Such logic no doubt fitted Franklin's understanding of Indian drinking behavior.

Franklin's appraisal of Indians' drinking practices did not reflect some desire to condemn all consumption of alcohol

. . .

Yet by writing about Indians' drinking in the way he did, Franklin suggested, and countless other early Americans would have agreed, that the consequences of drinking almost always seemed more dangerous among Indians than among colonists. It would be a relatively simple matter to dismiss Franklin's description as exaggerated, especially the suggestion that the spectacle at Carlisle so closely resembled eighteenth-century conceptions of Hell. But Franklin was expressing complicated ideas that were widespread among colonists.

Franklin was writing from a particularly good vantage point. By the time he wrote his *Autobiography* he had long believed that drinking could create social turmoil in Indian communities. His *Pennsylvania Gazette* periodically ran articles describing the actions of intoxicated Indians, often dwelling on the tragic or near-tragic consequences of their sprees. Franklin also believed that alcohol made Indians foolish or incompetent, at times to the advantage of colonists. And by 1763 he had printed and sold the minutes of treaties which included Indians' or colonists' complaints about the devastations that alcohol created in Indian communities. As one of the commissioners at Carlisle in 1753, Franklin joined Richard Peters and Isaac Norris in a public statement noting that liquor destroyed Indian communities. '[T]he Quantities of strong Liquors sold to these *Indians* in the Places of their Residence, and during their Hunting Seasons, from all Parts of the Counties over *Sasquehannah,* have encreased of late to an inconceivable Degree,' they wrote, 'so as to keep these poor *Indians* continually under the Force of

Liquor, that they are hereby become dissolute, enfeebled and indolent when sober, and untractable and mischievous in their Liquor, always quarrelling, and often murdering one another. . . .' If the trade continued, the consequences would be disastrous. Liquor traders 'by their own Intemperance, unfair Dealings, and Irregularities, will, it is to be feared, entirely estrange the Affections of the *Indians* from the *English*. . . .'

But it was his *Autobiography* that best captured the stereotype of the drunken Indian. However closely it resembled any actual occurrence, Franklin's image of wild Indians fighting or seducing one another in the half-light of a campfire drew inspiration from two other, related phenomena: colonists' trepidations about the dangers of excessive drinking and anxiety about the nature of American Indians and their proper place in British American society. Accounts of Indians who drank to intoxication and acted disorderly thus represented the fusion of these disparate fears. The mere prospect terrified countless numbers of colonists, and they proved more than willing to accept lurid descriptions of drunken Indians. Colonial officials, who presumed they could control the liquor trade, acted on their fears by making it illegal in most instances to provide alcohol to Indians.

This speech of a Creek-Indian leader in 1754 is perhaps the authentic lament of the Lotus-Eater. It also gives a clue to the underlying fear which would have presented itself to Odysseus and his crew – that a society of Lotus-Eaters would render itself unfit for war.

A CREEK-INDIAN

'A Speech: On the Breaking Out of the Late War'

(1754)

*O*h Countrymen!

I will spare myself the ungrateful Task of repeating, and you the Pain of recollecting, those shameful Broils, those unmanly Riots, and those brutal Extravagances, which the unbounded Use of this Liquor has so frequently produced among us. I must, however, beg Leave to assert, and submit to your Impartiality my Arguments to support this Assertion, that our prevailing Love, our intemperate Use, of this Liquid, will be productive of Consequences the most destructive to the Welfare and Glory of the Public, and the Felicity of every individual Offender. It perverts the Ends of Society, and unfits us for all those distinguishing and exquisite *Feelings*, which are the Cordials of Life, and the noblest Privileges of *Humanity*.

I have already declined the Mortification which a Detail of Facts would raise in every Breast, when unpossessed by this *Demon*. Permit me then, in general, only to appeal to public Experience, for the many Violations of civil Order, the indecent, the irrational Perversions of Character, which these inflammatory Draughts have introduced amongst us. 'Tis true, these are past, and may they never be repeated. – But tremble, O ye *Creeks!* when I thunder in your Ears this *Denunciation*; that if the Cup of Perdition continues to rule among us with Sway so intemperate, *Ye will cease to be a Nation!* Ye will have neither *Heads* to direct, nor *Hands* to protect you.

While this diabolical Juice undermines all the Powers of your Bodies and Minds, with offensive Zeal the *Warrior's* enfeebled Arm will draw the Bow, or launch the Spear in the Day of Battle. In the Day of Council, when national Safety stands suspended on the Lips of the hoary *Sachem*, he will shake his Head with uncollected Spirits, and drivel the Babblings of a second Childhood.

Think not, O ye *Creeks!* that I presume to amuse or affright you with an imaginary Picture. Is it not evident, – (alas, it is too fatally so!) that we find the Vigour of our Youth abating; our Numbers decreasing; our ripened Manhood a premature Victim to Disease, to Sickness, to Death; and our venerable *Sachems* a solitary scanty Number?

Does not that Desertion of all our reasonable Powers, which we feel when under the Dominion of that deformed Monster, that barbarian Madness, wherewith this Liquor inspires us, prove beyond Doubt that it impairs all our intellectual Faculties, pulls down Reason from her Throne, dissipates every Ray of the *Divinity* within us, and sinks us below the Brutes?

I hope I need not make a Question to any in this *Assembly*, whether he would prefer the intemperate Use of this Liquor, *to clear Perceptions, sound Judgement*, and a *Mind* exulting in its own *Reflections*. However great may be the Force of Habit, how insinuating soever the Influence of Example, and however unequal we may sometimes find ourselves to this insidious Enemy; I persuade myself, and I perceive by your Countenances, O *Creeks!* there is none before whom I stand, so shameless, so lost to the weakest Impulses of Humanity, and the very Whisperings of Reason, as not to acknowledge the Baseness of such a Choice.

Fathers and Brethren

I must yet crave your Patience, while I suggest to you, that this Intoxication of ourselves disqualifies us from acting up to our proper Characters in social Life, and debars us from all the soothing, softening, endearing Joys of domestic Bliss.

There is not within the whole Compass of Nature, so prevailing, so lasting a Propensity, as that of associating and communicating our Sentiments to each other. And there is not a more incontestable Truth than this, that *Benignity* of *Heart*, the calm Possession of ourselves, and the undisturbed Exercise of our *thinking* Faculties, are absolutely necessary to constitute the eligible and worthy Companion. How opposite to these Characters Intoxication renders us, is so manifest to our own Experience, so obvious to the least Reflection, that it would be both Impertinence and Insolence to enlarge farther upon it, before the Candour and *Wisdom* of this *Assembly*.

And now, O ye *Creeks!* if the Cries of your Country, if the Pulse of Glory, if all that forms the *Hero*, and exalts the *Man*, has not swelled your Breasts with a Patriot Indignation against the immoderate Use of this Liquor; – if these Motives are insufficient to produce such Resolutions as may be effectual – there are yet other Ties of Humanity, tender, dear, and persuading. Think on what we owe to our Children, and to the gentler Sex.

With Regard to our Children, besides affecting their Health, enervating all their Powers, and endangering the very Existence of our Nation, by the unbounded Use of these pernicious Draughts, think how it must affect their Tenderness, to see the Man that gave them Being, thus sunk into the most brutal State, in Danger of being suffocated by his own Intemperance, and standing in Need of their infant Arm to support his staggering Steps, or raise his feeble Head, while he vomits forth the foul Debauch?

O Warriors! O Countrymen!

How despicable must such a Practice render us even in the Eyes of our own Children! Will it not gradually deprive us of all Authority in the Families which we ought to govern and protect? What a Waste of Time does it create, which might otherwise be spent round the blazing Hearth, in the most tender Offices? It perverts the great Designs of Nature, and murders all those precious Moments, in which the Warrior should recount, to his wondering Offspring, his own great Actions and those of his Ancestors. By these Means the tender Bosom has often caught the Patriot-flame, and an illustrious Succession of *Sachems* and Warriors were formed among us from Generation to Generation, before our Glory was eclipsed by the Introduction of this destructive Liquid.

Assassins

A third 'myth' of the role of drugs in society is that of the Assassins or 'Hashishin' – a secret, initiatic group of drug users concealed within the wider society. The source of this myth is Marco Polo's account of the Old Man of the Mountain, the assassin chief who would drug his recruits in order to 'brainwash' them with images of Paradise.

MARCO POLO
The Travels of Marco Polo the Venetian

(*c.* 1300)

Having spoken of this country, mention shall now be made of the old man of the mountain. The district in which his residence lay obtained the name of Mulehet, signifying in the language of the Saracens, the place of heretics, and his people that of Mulehetites, or holders of heretical tenets; as we apply the term of Patharini to certain heretics amongst Christians. The following account of this chief, Marco Polo testifies to having heard from sundry persons. He was named Alo-eddin, and his religion was that of Mahomet. In a beautiful valley enclosed between two lofty mountains, he had formed a luxurious garden, stored with every delicious fruit and every fragrant shrub that could be procured. Palaces of various sizes and forms were erected in different parts of the grounds, ornamented with works in gold, with paintings, and with furniture of rich silks. By means of small conduits contrived in these buildings, streams of wine, milk, honey, and some of pure water, were seen to flow in every direction. The inhabitants of these palaces were elegant and beautiful damsels, accomplished in the arts of singing, playing upon all sorts of musical instruments, dancing, and especially those of dalliance and amorous allurement. Clothed in rich dresses they were seen continually sporting and amusing themselves in the garden and pavilions, their female guardians being confined within doors and never suffered to appear. The object which the chief had in view in forming a garden of this fascinating kind, was this: that Mahomet having promised to those who should obey his will the enjoyments of Paradise, where every species of sensual gratification should be found, in the society of beautiful nymphs, he was desirous of its being understood by his followers that he also was a prophet and the compeer of Mahomet,

and had the power of admitting to Paradise such as he should choose
to favour. In order that none without his licence might find their way
into this delicious valley, he caused a strong and expugnable castle to
be erected at the opening of it, through which the entry was by a secret
passage. At his court, likewise, this chief entertained a number of youths,
from the age of twelve to twenty years, selected from the inhabitants
of the surrounding mountains, who showed a disposition for martial
exercises, and appeared to possess the quality of daring courage. To
them he was in the daily practice of discoursing on the subject of the
paradise announced by the prophet, and of his own power of granting
admission; and at certain times he caused opium to be administered to
ten or a dozen of the youths; and when half dead with sleep he had
them conveyed to the several apartments of the palaces in the garden.
Upon awakening from the state of lethargy, their senses were struck
with all the delightful objects that have been described, and each
perceived himself surrounded by lovely damsels, singing, playing, and
attracting his regards by the most fascinating caresses, serving him also
with delicate viands and exquisite wines; until intoxicated with excess
of enjoyment amidst actual rivulets of milk and wine, he believed himself
assuredly in Paradise, and felt an unwillingness to relinquish its delights.
When four or five days had thus been passed, they were thrown once
more into a state of somnolency, and carried out of the garden. Upon
their being introduced to his presence, and questioned by him as to
where they had been, their answer was, 'In Paradise, through the favour
of your highness:' and then before the whole court, who listened to
them with eager curiosity and astonishment, they gave a circumstantial
account of the scenes to which they had been witnesses. The chief
thereupon addressing them, said: 'We have the assurances of our prophet
that he who defends his lord shall inherit Paradise, and if you show
yourselves devoted to the obedience of my orders, that happy lot awaits
you.' Animated to enthusiasm by words of this nature, all deemed
themselves happy to receive the commands of their master, and were
forward to die in his service. The consequence of this system was, that
when any of the neighbouring princes, or others, gave umbrage to this
chief, they were put to death by these his disciplined assassins; none of
whom felt terror at the risk of losing their own lives, which they held
in little estimation, provided they could execute their master's will. On
this account his tyranny became the subject of dread in all the surrounding countries. He had also constituted two deputies or representatives

of himself, of whom one had his residence in the vicinity of Damascus, and the other in Kurdistan; and these pursued the plan he had established for training their young dependants. Thus there was no person, however powerful, who, having become exposed to the enmity of the old man of the mountain, could escape assassination. His territory being situated within the dominions of Ulaù (Hulagu), the brother of the grand khan (Mangu), that prince had information of his atrocious practices, as above related, as well as of his employing people to rob travellers in their passage through his country, and in the year 1262 sent one of his armies to besiege this chief in his castle. It proved, however, so capable of defence, that for three years no impression could be made upon it; until at length he was forced to surrender from the want of provisions, and being made prisoner was put to death. His castle was dismantled, and his garden of Paradise destroyed. And from that time there has been no old man of the mountain.

*Despite the spread of this myth throughout Western culture – along with
the word 'assassin' – there is no evidence that the 'Assassins', or 'Hashishin', ever referred to themselves by this name, or even used drugs.*

FARHAD DAFTARY

The Assassin Legends: Myths of the Isma'ilis

(1995)

The Persian historians of the Ilkhanid period, including Juwayni
and Rashid al-Din, who are the main sources for the history of the
Persian Nizari community during the Alamut period, do not use the
term *hashishiyya* in reference to the Persian Nizaris. In fact, the term
hashishi and its variants do not appear at all, to this author's knowledge,
in any of the Persian texts of the Alamut or post-Alamut period which
have references to the Nizari Isma'ilis

. . .

Hashish, or *hashisha*, is the Arabic name for a product of hemp, a
cultivable plant whose Latin name is *cannabis sativa*. This plant, and
its more common variety Indian hemp (*cannabis Indica*), have been
known and used in the Near East since ancient times as a drug with
intoxicating effects. The seeds and leaves of the hemp plant, as well
as the products derived from it, have acquired different names and
nicknames in India, Persia and the Arab world, including *banj* (*bang*),
shahdanaj, *qinnah* and *kif*. But it is not known how and when the Arabic
word hashish, which originally meant 'dry herb', came to be applied as
a nickname to the hemp plant, or rather to its resin which contains the
active element of hemp. At any rate, this hallucinatory drug must have
been rather widely used by the time of the adoption of the word hashish
as its nickname. Subsequently, the nickname itself led to the derivation
of terms designating a person (or persons) using or being addicted to
this product, notably *hashishi* (plural, *hashishiyya*; colloquial plurals
hashishiyyin and *hashishin*) and, less commonly, *hashshash* (plural,

hashshashin). The earliest known written attestation of the designation *hashishiyya* occurred, as noted, in reference to the Syrian Nizaris in the Musta'lian polemical epistle issued around 1123. This document did not explain why the term was applied to the Nizaris, although it may be assumed that its application implied the idea, but not the fact that the Nizaris were actually hashish users. At any rate, it is evident that by the beginning of the twelfth century, the word *hashishiyya* had already been a term familiar to the Muslims for some time, dating at least to the second half of the eleventh century and preceding the Nizari–Musta'lian schism.

The use of hashish grew significantly in Syria, Egypt and other Muslim countries during the twelfth and thirteenth centuries, especially among the lower strata of society. It was at this time that the harmful effects of hashish began to be discussed extensively throughout Muslim society; and, starting in the thirteenth century, numerous tracts were written by Muslim authors who described these effects in terms of different physical, mental, moral and religious categories. In particular, Muslim writers stressed that the extended use of hashish would have extremely harmful effects on the user's morality and religion, relaxing his attitude towards those duties, such as praying and fasting, specified by the sacred law of Islam. As a result, the hashish user would qualify for a low social and moral status, similarly to that of a *mulhid* or heretic in religion. It was particularly in this sense that the Muslim jurists argued against hashish users, and strongly demanded their punishment as criminals and heretics

. . .

It was in the abusive senses of 'low-class rabble' and 'irreligious social outcasts' that the term *hashishiyya* seems to have been used metaphorically in reference to the Nizari Isma'ilis during the twelfth and thirteenth centuries, and not because the Nizaris or their *fida'is* secretly used hashish in a regular manner, which in any event would not have been public knowledge

. . .

At any rate, the fact remains that neither the Isma'ili texts which have been recovered so far nor any contemporary non-Isma'ili Muslim texts, which were generally hostile towards the Nizaris, attest to the actual use of hashish by the Nizaris. Indeed, the major Muslim historians of the Nizaris, such as Juwayni, who generally attribute all types of sinister motives and beliefs to the Isma'ilis, do not even refer to the Nizaris as 'Hashishis'. The few Arabic sources which do refer to the Nizaris as 'Hashishis' never explain this appellation in terms of the use of hashish, even though they were prepared to heap all sorts of defamatory accusations upon the heads of the Nizaris.

Muslims who were familiar with Shi'i martyrology did not require an explanation in order to understand the self-sacrificing behaviour of the *fida'i*s. As a result, Muslim authors, unlike western writers, did not fantasize about the sect's secret practices. The available evidence indicates that it was the name Hashishiyya that in time led to the unfounded suggestion that the Nizaris, or their *fida'i*s, used hashish in a regular manner; a myth which was accepted as reality during the Middle Ages and was essentially endorsed by Silvestre de Sacy and other orientalists of the nineteenth century. The hashish connection proved particularly appealing to mediaeval western observers who needed 'simple' explanations for the seemingly irrational behaviour of the Nizari *fida'i*s.

Under such circumstances, beginning in the second half of the twelfth century, Arabic variants of the term *hashishi* were heard and picked up locally in Syria by the Crusaders, who received their information about Muslims mainly through oral channels. This information served as the basis for a number of terms, such as Assassini, Assissini and Heyssessini, by which the Nizari Isma'ilis of Syria came to be designated in base-Latin sources of the Crusaders and in different European languages, resulting in the more familiar name 'Assassins'. The Nizari 'assassinations' later received further exaggeration in western popular lore and literature when the term 'assassin' entered the western languages as a new common noun meaning 'murderer'. At any rate, by the end of the fourteenth century the epithet *hashishi* was evidently no longer regarded as a term of abuse in Muslim society. Al-Maqrizi (d. 1442), the famous Egyptian historian who has an informative section called 'the hashish of the poor' (*hashishat al-fuqara*) in his well-known book dealing with the antiquities of Cairo, relates that by his time the use of hashish had indeed reached a peak; it was discussed and utilized, even among the better classes of Cairo and Damascus, publicly and without inhibition.

The 'Brotherhood of Assassins': Turkish soldiers smoking in a lithograph from 1846. (Wellcome Trust)

... but the Assassins were nevertheless taken as the ideological model for one of the first 'drug subcultures', the Club des Haschischins, which flourished in Paris in the 1850s and counted Charles Baudelaire, Alexandre Dumas, Gerald de Nerval and Théophile Gautier among its members. The hashish supplier and master of ceremonies – 'the doctor' – was Moreau de Tours (see p. 19).

THÉOPHILE GAUTIER
'Club des Haschischins'

(*Revue des Deux Mondes*, 1 February 1846)

One December evening ... I arrived in a remote quarter in the middle of Paris, a kind of solitary oasis which the river encircles in its arms on both sides as though to defend it against the encroachments of civilization. It was in an old house on the île St Louis, the Pimodan hotel built by Lauzun, where the strange club which I had recently joined held its monthly seance. I was attending for the first time.

Though it was scarcely six o'clock, the night was black. A fog, made thicker still by the nearness of the Seine, blurred all the shapes under its quilting ... The pavement, inundated with rain, glistened under the street lamp as water reflects an image; a sharp dry wind carrying particles of sleet whipped into the face ... None of winter's rude poetry was wanting that night.

It was difficult in the clump of sombre buildings along that deserted quay to distinguish the house for which I searched; nevertheless my coachman, perched high on his seat, managed to read on a marble plaque the half-worn, gilded name of the old hotel, the gathering place for the initiates.

I raised the carved knocker, and several times heard the catch grate unsuccessfully; at last, succumbing to a more vigorous pull, the rusty old bolt opened and the door of massive planks turned on its hinges.

As I entered, an old porter, roughly outlined by the flickerings of a candle, appeared behind a pane of yellowish transparency, a perfect Skalken painting. The face regarded me with singular grimace, and a skinny finger stretched outwards to point my way ...

Once up the flight of steps, I found myself at the bottom of one of those immense staircases constructed during the time of Louis XIV, and in which a modern house would dance with ease. An Egyptian chimera, in the style of Lebrun, with a Cupid astride, rested its feet on a pedestal and held a light in claws bent round to form candlesticks.

The incline was gentle. Well-placed landings attested to the genius of the late architect and to the grandiose life of bygone centuries; in climbing the impressive stair, attired as I was in my thin black frockcoat, I felt like a blotnish on the scene, usurping a right not mine; the service stairway would have done well enough for me.

Paintings, for the most part frameless, copies of masterpieces from the Italian and Spanish schools, hung on the walls; and high above, in the shadows, could barely be discerned a huge mythological ceiling painted in fresco.

I arrived at the designated floor. A worn and shiny velvet tapestry from Utrecht, whose yellow borders and bruised threads bespoke long service, showed me the door. I rang; it was opened with the usual precautions and I found myself in a huge room lit at the end by several lamps. To enter here was to step backwards two centuries. Time, which passes so quickly, seemed not to have flown in this house and, as a forgotten clock left unwound, its hands pointed always to the same place . . .

I moved into the luminous portion of the room where several human shapes were stirring about a table, and as soon as the light reached me and I was recognized, a vigorous shout shook the sonorous depths of the ancient edifice.

'It's he! It's he!' cried some voices together; 'let's give him his due!'

MUSTARD WITH DINNER

The doctor stood by the side of a buffet on which lay a platter filled with small Japanese saucers. He spooned a morsel of paste or greenish jam about as large as the thumb from a crystal vase, and placed it next to the silver spoon on each saucer.

The doctor's face radiated enthusiasm; his eyes glittered, his purple cheeks were aglow, the veins in his temples stood out strongly, and he breathed heavily through dilated nostrils.

'This will be deducted from your share in Paradise,' he said as he handed me my portion.

After each had eaten his due, coffee was served in the Arab manner, that is to say, with the coffee grounds and no sugar. Then we sat down at the table . . .

THE BANQUET

The meal was served in singular fashion and in all sorts of elaborate and picturesque dishes. Large Venetian goblets, cut in milky spirals, German steins embellished with coats of arms and legends, Flemish jugs of enamel, and slender-necked bottles twisted in their reed encasements replaced the ordinary glasses, pitchers and carafes.

The opaque porcelain of Louis Lebeuf and the flowered English crockery, customary ornaments of bourgeois settings, were conspicuous in their absence. No plate was identical, but each had its own particular virtue. From China, Saxony and Japan were examples of the loveliest sort and richest color, all a trifle cracked or broken, but in exquisite taste.

The plates were, for the most part, enamel of Bernard de Palissy or china from Limoges, and occasionally under the meat, the carver's knife met a reptile, frog or bird in bas-relief. The cooked eel mixed his coils with those of the patterned serpent below.

An honest Philistine would have experienced some trepidation at the sight of such table companions, hirsute, bearded, mustached, or shorn in singular fashion, brandishing poignards from the sixteenth century, Malayan daggers or machetes, and bent over their food to which the flickering lamps gave a disquieting aspect.

The meal drew to an end; already some of the more fervent members felt the effects of the green jam: for my part, I had experienced a complete transformation in taste. The water I drank seemed the most exquisite wine, the meat, once in my mouth, became strawberries, the strawberries, meat. I could not have distinguished a fish from a cutlet.

My neighbors began to appear somewhat strange. Their pupils became big as a screech owl's; their noses stretched into elongated proboscises; their mouths expanded like bell bottoms. Faces were shaded in supernatural light. One among them, a pale countenance in a black beard, laughed aloud at an invisible spectacle; another made incredible efforts to raise his glass to his lips and the resulting contortions aroused deafening hoots from his companions; a man, shaken with nervous convulsions, turned his thumbs with remarkable agility; another, fallen against the back of his chair, his eyes unseeing and his arms inert, let himself drift voluptuously in the bottomless sea of nothingness.

My elbows on the table, I considered all this with clarity and a vestige of reason which came and went by intervals, like the light of a lantern about to flicker and die. A deadening warmth pervaded my limbs, and dementia, like a wave which breaks foaming onto a rock, then withdraws to break again, invaded and left my brain, finally enveloping it altogether. That strange visitor, hallucination, had come to dwell within me.

'To the salon, to the salon!' cried one of the guests; 'can't you hear those heavenly choirs? The musicians have been gathered for a long time.'

And indeed, a delectable harmony reached us in whiffs across the tumult of the conversation.

AN UNINVITED GUEST

The salon was an enormous room of carved and gilded paneling, a painted ceiling whose friezes depicted satyrs chasing nymphs through the grasses, a monumental fireplace of colored marble and abundant brocade curtains. Here one inhaled the luxurious airs of times gone by. Embroidered chairs, canapes, settees and bergeres, large enough for the skirts of duchesses and marquesas to spread with ease, seated the *hachichins* and welcomed them with soft and open arms. A warmth from the corner of the chimney invited me, and I settled there, abandoning myself without resistance to the fantastic effects of the drug.

After several moments, my companions disappeared . . . Quiet reigned in the salon, and a few vague, flickering lamps; then, suddenly a flash of red under my eyelids, as though countless candles had lit themselves, and I felt bathed in a pale and tepid glow. The room in which I sat was indeed the same, but, like a rough sketch for a painting, everything seemed larger, richer, more splendid. In the opulence of hallucination, reality appears only at the point of departure.

Part of the enduring power of the Assassin/Hashishin myth is that drug cultures share many underlying dynamics with initiatory secret societies.

LUIGI ZOJA
Drugs, Addiction & Initiation: The Modern Search for Ritual

(1989)

We appear to live under conditions that are, for the most part, desacralized. However, it is enough just to scratch the surface of the situation to rediscover many elements of a real religious state, the survival of which manifests itself indirectly, especially in a need for esoteric and initiatory experiences

. . .

In the survival of the need for initiation, we will recognize above all a persistent desire for personal regeneration. We no longer have to speak of a latent need, since that need is today quite open and manifest

. . .

Mircea Eliade asserts that the only form of genuine initiatory structures today is in artistic-literary creation. All things considered, modern society is practically unable to provide institutional initiation. Such initiation calls for masters and structures formed over a long period of time and in context of a whole participating culture. Initiation presupposes that biological birth brings man into the world only partially, in an absolutely vegetative condition lacking values and transcendence. Access to a higher state of being is possible only through symbolic and ritual death and regeneration

. . .

A modern complex society, generally speaking, offers relatively greater individual freedom, but also greatly increases the limits entailed by the

individual's mundane existence. Does this society allow an individual
to radically alter his condition without setting off a series of contradictions
that would alienate him from the world? The question is hard to answer,
since the structure of modern life tends to eliminate possibilities of
radical change. Ideological conversions, such as becoming a member
of a political group, generally have few if any institutional characteristics,
so it is hard to determine what their ramifications are in terms of the
initiatory model.

. . .

The latent need for secret groups and initiatory experiences can at times
result in the formation of occult power structures, such as in terrorist
groups, for example. It would be overly simplistic to interpret the
initiatory aspect of these groups as mere expedients guaranteeing
maximum efficiency and secrecy. The decisive element in the initiation
into a terrorist group, for instance, often consists of the perpetration of
a criminal act which cuts the initiate off from legal society and makes
his bond with his colleagues concrete and real.

In general it is the occult structure which grows out of a need for
esoterism, not the other way around. The need for esoterism seems to
be present even when it is not understood, even in the 'secrecy' games
of children. Secret rituals inherently call for respect and solemnity, and
aside from their functional aspect, they are fascinating and arouse the
curiosity of outsiders.

Both literature and cinema have exploited this theme, drawing not
so much on the public's political interests as on its latent curiosity for
the hidden, for the secrecy of ritual. Though more or less indifferent
to the ideological particularities of terrorist groups, the public at large
responds to depictions of them with a mixture of horror and fascinated
curiosity.

An analysis of the need for esoterism is of interest to us as we attempt
to understand the phenomenon of drug addiction. From the point of
view of the unconscious, turning to drugs can be understood as an
attempt at a kind of initiation defective in its basic premise because of
a lack of awareness. The 'true' process of initiation – an initiation that
fulfills the initiate's underlying psychic needs – can be encapsulated in
three distinct phases.

First, the situation at the outset is one that must be transcended because of its meaninglessness. In order to transcend his meaningless state of existence, the adolescent in a primitive society entrusted himself to the initiatory process, which imbued him with a complete, adult identity. Similarly, the individual in our own society – passive, lost, condemned to a state of mere consumerism – secretly dreams of transforming himself into a separate, creative adult, no longer bound to consumerism.

Second, initiatory death. This phase entails a renunciation of the world, the rejection of one's previous identity, and the withdrawal of the libido from its habitual direction (in our society, this consists in above all refraining from consumerist behavior).

Third, initiatory rebirth, made psychologically easier by sharing the experience with others and by ritual – for instance, the controlled consumption of drugs.

. . .

The psychological interpretation we are proposing, the initiatory moment – not to be confused with the initial moment – is what is of real importance. If, in fact, the expectations lying beneath the initiatory moment are archetypal, then they never die but rather continue to recur both as collective manifestations and individual pathologies

. . .

It should be noted that initiation and the process of drug use both adhere to similar archaic unconscious models, an argument important in and of itself

. . .

Initiation, and the use of drugs which unconsciously echoes its structure, is fundamentally an archetypal process . . . and therefore impossible to personify, since it potentially belongs to any type of personality. Initiation assumes mythic forms in every culture, as do all solemn events, but it does not derive from one myth valid for all peoples. For each people, initiation is a means of returning mythic life to the commonality, and of conferring upon the individual a certain state of grace mere biological birth cannot provide.

. . . and many writers, notably William Burroughs and his collaborator Brion Gysin, have used the Assassin myth as a metaphor for the contemporary 'drug underground'.

BRION GYSIN
The Process

(1969)

I am out in the Sahara heading due south with each day of travel less sure of just who I am, where I am going or why. There must be some easier way to do it but this is the only one I know so, like a man drowning in a sea of sand, I struggle back into this body which has been given me for my trip across the Great Desert. 'This desert,' my celebrated colleague, Ibn Khaldoun the Historian, has written, 'This desert is so long it can take a lifetime to go from one end to the other and a childhood to cross at its narrowest point.' I made that narrow childhood crossing on another continent; out through hazardous tenement hallways and stickball games in the busy street, down American asphalt alleys to paved playgrounds; shuffling along Welfare waiting-lines into a maze of chain-store and subway turnstiles and, through them, out onto a concrete campus in a cold gray city whose skyscrapers stood up to stamp on me. It has been a long trail a-winding down here into this sunny but sandy Middle Passage of my life in Africa, along with the present party. Here, too, I may well lose my way for I can see that I am, whoever I am, out in the middle of Nowhere when I slip back into this awakening flesh which fits me, of course, like a glove.

I know this body as if it were a third party whose skin I put on as a mask to wear through their 'Land of Fear' and I do go in a sort of disguise for, like everyone else out here in this blazing desert where a man is a fool to show his face naked by day, I have learned to wrap five or six yards of fine white muslin around my head to protect the mucus of my nose and throat against the hot, dry wind. All you can see of me is my eyes. For once, I look just like everyone else

. . .

Bundled up like a mummy, I huddle here under my great black burnous, a cape as big as a bag for an animal my size, shape and color. It also serves as a portable tent smelling of woodsmoke and lanolin, under which I fumble for the two pencil-thin sections of my *sebsi*, my slim wooden keef-pipe from Morocco, to fit them together. A fine flesh-pink clay pipe head, no bigger than the last joint of my little finger, snuggles up over a well-fitted paper collar shaped wet with spit. I try it like a trumpet; air-tight, good. My keef-pouch from Morocco is the skin of a horned viper sewn into a *metoui* and stuffed with great grass. I check with my thumb the tide of fine-chopped green leaf which rolls down its long leather tongue, milking most of the keef back into the pouch. What remains, I coax into the head of my pipe with the beckoning crook of my right forefinger.

A masterpiece matchbox the size of a big postage stamp leaps into the overturned bowl of my left hand, riding light but tight between the ball of my thumb and my third finger. I make all these moves not just out of habit but with a certain conscious cunning through which I ever-so slowly reconstruct myself in the middle of your continuum; inserting myself, as it were, back into this flesh which is the visible pattern of Me. Yet, I know this whole business is a trap which may well be woven of nothing but words, so I joggle the miniature matchbox I hold in my hand and these masterpiece matches in here chuckle back what always has sounded to me like a word but a word which I cannot quite catch. It could be a rattling Arabic word but my grasp of Arabic is not all that good and no one, not even Hamid, will tell me what the matches say to the box. I hold the box up to my ear as I shake it again, trying to hear what the box stutters back

. . .

Far away back up north in the green hills of Morocco, which I call home since I began to merge almost against my will into this scene with Hamid my Moroccan mock-guru, everyone around the keef cafés is always talking and singing of the Sahara but not one man in ten knows where it begins or ends or how to get into this desert. 'It lies down that way, many days marching,' they say, swinging their long slim keef-pipes around vaguely south

. . .

Hamid suddenly became fascinated by the form he began to see in my map. He pointed out that the Great Desert is in the shape of a camel stretching its neck right across Africa, from the Atlantic to the Red Sea. He laughed like a lunatic to see that the western butt-end of his camel was dropping its Mauretanian crud on the Black Senegalese – 'Charcoal Charlies,' Hamid calls them, having picked up the term in the port. The head of Hamid's camel drinks its fill in the sweet waters of the Nile. The eye of the camel, naturally enough, is that fabled city of Masr, where the Arab movies are made and all the radios ring out over streets paved with gold. Us poor Nazarenes call the place Cairo, for short. Suddenly, somewhere down on the lower middle belly of Hamid's camel, about four knuckles north of Kano in northern Nigeria, I dowsed out a big carbuncle. With no more warning than that, my whole heart rushed out to this place which was pictured as an outcropping of extinct ash-blue volcanoes jutting up out of the bright yellow sands. I noted that the whole area was called the Hoggar and it seemed to boast only one constantly inhabited place, whose name I made out to be Tam. I was truly surprised to hear myself calmly boasting to Hamid, as if I were AMERICAN EXPRESS: 'I'll be in this place, here, this time next year.'

'*Inch' Allah!* if God wills,' Hamid corrected me automatically and then, as if he were indeed the Consul of Keef, who was sending me out on this mission, he went on: 'I'll get them to cut you a green passport of keef to see you through everything. I'll see that you get the best of the crop from Ketama and I'll bring it down from the mountain myself with the blessings of Hassan-i-Sabbah, the Father of Grass. On your way, you're bound to run into some other Assassins.'

'But, Hamid,' I laughed: 'I am not an Assassin at all!'

'We are Assassins, all of us,' he gravely replied.

This metaphor was developed further by the Scottish beat writer Alexander Trocchi.

ALEXANDER TROCCHI
'Trocchi on Drugs'

(1970)

We should not allow the Americans to persuade us that our seven-year-olds need go in fear and trembling at the thought that they may turn on to junk! In this area what we have most to fear is fear itself. Fear, together with ignorance and the general need to find someone else to blame for 'the state of the world' etcetera.

First of all let's really have a look at the state of the world (as it concerns drugs). Perhaps our seven-year-olds don't need a fix because their fathers are not (a) at war in Indo-China, (b) necessarily wearing short hair, (c) or long, (d) and because such experienced investigators as Dr R. D. Laing, Mr William Burroughs and the present author, are presently concerning themselves with a sense of urgency to match the situation. Who knows, the future may be in the hands of the hashish smokers. A grid, a field of force, spreading, a psychological infection, in pads all over, wherever the preponderant life-style is *hashishin*. These cells of hashish experience can become co-conscious participants in a global surracial strategy. No formal explicit alliance is necessary: on the contrary, no badges. On a semi-conscious level the grid exists already as a marvellously complex process of so-to-speak electric light bulbs, which can be turned on in mutual recognition by means of various tactical symbols – click click click click – in phun cities wherever and whenever they exist, from San Francisco to Katmandu. As Kropotkin said a long time ago now: 'The future is in the hands of free associations and not of centralised governments.' Whose future? Let it be ours.

The Woodstock phenomenon, the great young happening together, causes great uneasiness in establishment circles, as well it might. For, as well, it is a foreboding of things to come, when the young come together in their hundreds of thousands, and simply exclude the conventional world and its organised violence. The establishment answers with drug probes by police and dogs, *agents provocateurs* attempting through violence (the only violence at the various phun cities is police violence), trying with a kind of cold hysteria through arrests, to bring back the minds of the young back under the sway of the great confidence trick of yesterday's law and order.

You're breaking the law! You *must* be breaking the law! What's that you're smoking? Mongolian parsley? Break it up! Cover your shame, like us.

In uniform and in disguise they haunt the lawless precincts of phun city and the measure of their impotence is the piddling number of arrests they dare to make, which arrests constitute the only disturbance of the peace, and how obvious this is becoming. Drugs and the law. I have to write on the insolence of the law insofar as it makes me act against my own best interests. Insofar as a law makes a man act against his own best interests, that law is politically insolent. It is against political insolence that I shall fight. I shall fight with every weapon available, and using every scientific and artistic technique available. We are fighting for men's minds. We are fighting for mind and spirit and body, against the various paralyses of the spirit which will refuse a man experience on the equivocal grounds that experience will corrupt him (and through him, others). It seems to some of us that most of us are so utterly corrupt already that practically any experiment is better than none. And in my own experience, voyages into inner space through drugs can be every bit as exciting and meaningful as the voyages of the ancient explorers were to their contemporaries and descendants.

Would it be true to say that in the United States, funds for research are in effect allocated by the drug police?

The junkie's security, depending as it does, upon a sufficient and regular supply of heroin, is threatened by any new legal limits to his consumption. (Compare the junkie scene with the Spanish Inquisition.)

Paris, 1952. I was twenty-seven years of age. I looked into the mirror. The central panel of these panels of the cheap wardrobe in the third floor room in an hotel in *rue de Vernieuil*. That was originally a street of tradesmen's entrances and backed into the stately and illustrious mansions of the *rue de l'Université* in the seventh arrondisement, the arrondisement in which the *Quai d'Orsay* is located. I remember writing on a piece of paper: drink, drugs, sex. I crossed out drink, I put a question mark after drugs, and I put a tick after sex.

❖

I am involved in a revolution whose implications go far beyond the legalisation of this or that drug. When we are successful in shifting some of the conventional sediment from vital places, such reforms as the rationalisation of the public attitude and the law towards drugs will be carried out from the top.

One effect of the hashish I have just smoked is to take me very intensely into the texture of the work I am involved in. But I cannot always choose the work I am involved in under hashish. That is to say there is a certain quality of a state of mind. It allows me to live most dramatically in the present moment, a habit of mind which eludes me under 'natural' conditions: thus I find some of the correlative disadvantages outweighed by this capacity for focussing attention. Under hashish, I know that what I have to do is relax and allow my attention to be directed towards whatever it is I have decided to do.

I have been talking to Lyn about structuring things to allow her to take an active interest in this programme on drugs. Who better, when you come to think of it, to give the woman's point of view? But if, for example, the other party is not in control, is perhaps anxious, this anxiety can be quickly transmitted to one's own state of mind, unless one is solidly based. Sometimes, to bring my attention back on to, say, a writing job, I find I can escape from the nervousness of which I spoke by applying my attention, for example, to painting. In painting I can try to exploit even my nervousness: paint laid quickly and nervously, as painters know, can represent an inspired passage. It was under hashish that I first learned to have confidence in my own ability to paint, to sculpt.

Of course, the so-called problem of drugs is bound up with attitudes towards leisure and other economic facts. Crime. Actually, crime statistics are sagging ominously. As Burroughs says, 'Sad old turnkeys mutter through empty cells, Desperate for arrests, police prowl the streets like paranoid dogs . . .' So the narcotics criminal is invented. He breaks the law to get the money to break the law. To buy his forbidden drug, etcetera. It's a treadmill, doctor. That buncha zombies! We gotta get them outta here and onta the streets and inta statistics! You take this farm in Kentucky, the Manslayer used to say, I'm against it!

On television a few nights ago somebody posed the question, 'Is there not a danger drug-taking will become the "in" thing?' It *is* the 'in' thing. Thus, we must plan and investigate in a tolerant, objective way. To leave the outcome of this historical process to the hysteria of headlines and the reactions of Members of Parliament to that conglomeration of ignorant headlines would be fatal.

The hashish smoker and his wondrous sculpted pipe – bewitched: a gift of god. 'What we in the East turn into the fabric of heaven, you in the West turn into the hangman's rope. You would have shown more delicacy to have preferred sisal to hemp,' said the Sultan.

'Assassin!' screamed the indignant British lexicographer, adding to his Dictionary of Definitions even more definite prohibitions. And, triumphantly, seeking to prove his spurious moral point by definition, 'Y'know what the word assassin really means?'

'Hey, sirrah!' quoth our hashish smoker, 'By what insolent authority do you seek to impose your narrow moral prohibitions upon me?'

What excites one is not the drug, but what the drug makes available to experience. For example, a critic might say, 'You've had pot!' As though that made one anything but more critical and quick to sense an evasion. Man is always perfectable, because he is never perfect? Man is perfectable in the sense that a work of art is perfectable. Man's perfection consists in the infinite possibility of perfecting his imperfections . . . and the doing is the point. There is a point at which any machine is perfect. This is to be related to a tactical use of drugs in the tentative changing of states of mind.

Is the 'Assassin myth' of an initiatory, 'underground' drug culture in fact the natural model for drug use in society? Some animal experiments suggest that it is.

RONALD K. SIEGEL

Intoxication: Life in Pursuit of Artificial Paradise

(1989)

Consider the dramatic effects of drugs on the social structure of neon tetra, a tropical fish from the shaded jungle waters of the Brazilian Amazon. The fish swim in tightly controlled schools. The blue-green sheen along the sides is so brilliant that the school appears to be a cloud of fireflies stuck in the On position. Schools are highly polarized, with no more than one body-length between individuals. This inter-fish distance, remarkably, never varies and appears to be the minimal distance sufficient for normal swimming behavior. The fish maneuver as a school, forming strings of Christmas-tree lights snaking up and down the tank.

The decorum in the school breaks down if only five neons are drugged in a school that numbers fifty. The drugged fish tend to group together and apart from the rest. This division is actually a benefit to the school, which can now swim independent of the drugged subgroup. The subgroup itself stays only loosely aggregated; one or two fish can always be found suspended in a vertical position apart from the others. As long as the drugged fish have room, they stay apart until the drugs wear off. But in small tanks where space is limited, the crippling effects are inevitable as sober fish cannot avoid bumping into intoxicated fish, leading to disorganized swimming for all. In addition, the gentle neons, which rarely fight, start to show some resemblance to a distant relative, the bloodthirsty piranha. The sober neons slyly begin to nip at the fins of their drugged schoolmates.

Social behavior in birds is similarly disrupted by drugs such as hallucinogens. I conducted experiments with pigeons and found that LSD or THC caused the birds to isolate themselves from nondrugged birds.

If there were several intoxicated pigeons, they aggregated into small subgroups, or squads, that refused to participate in the social behavior of the loft. Fighting between the 'drug squads' and the rest of the pigeons in the loft was thereby kept to a minimum. Usually there were enough sober birds around so that important mating and nesting chores could still get done

. . .

In large social groups where there is room to be alone, rats and mice intoxicated with hallucinogens follow the same isolation strategy seen with fish and birds. Rats given scopolamine, for example, will spread out into the corners of an open field away from sober rats in the same way that grazing animals intoxicated with *Datura* or locoweed move away from the main herds. When a drugged mouse is placed in a spacious colony, it will squeal, squeak, and retreat from investigations by colony members. Such a drugged animal will eventually find refuge in an isolated corner of the colony cage. Put several drugged mice into the colony and they will end up apart from the colony huddles but aggregated with each other, furry snowballs massed in the corners of the cage. This grouping of 'druggies' occurs because there is a tendency for drugged mice to huddle together and avoid annoying investigations by the sober animals. The drugged animals don't really pay any attention to each other. Indeed, they may be so inattentive that they sometimes can convince us they no longer see the outside world. In maze tests comparing blind rats with sighted rats, the sighted rats given LSD sometimes did no better than sober blind animals, bumping around like Mexican cavefish out of water. In human terms, the rats are 'stoned'.

. . .

The same reactions are seen in social groups of primates when they are given hallucinogens. Monkeys and baboons seek quiet areas and withdraw from group activities. But there is increased fighting between intoxicated cagemates when they cannot avoid each other. Humans are no different. After taking hallucinogenic mushrooms, Komugl men in the New Guinea highlands become so hypersensitive to sounds, they run away from the group's territory until they can find a quiet place to rest. But in their rush to escape the group and avoid confrontation, the

Komugl men may run into each other and a struggle will take place.

Sometimes the isolation strategy followed by humans is not a matter of increasing physical distance. For example, individuals under the influence of LSD at small parties may simply cut off their verbal behavior with others. And while 'huddles' of hallucinogenic drug users have been found at times in our culture, as in the hippie communes of the 1960s, individuals can remain in the central population and isolate themselves by embracing attitudes and ideologies of lessened commitment to institutional goals and rules. The expression 'Turn on, tune in, and drop out,' coined by social psychologist Timothy Leary, was an apt description of these drug effects.

Permissions

For permission to publish copyright material in this book, grateful acknowledgement is made to the following:

Nelson Algren: from *The Man With The Golden Arm* (Pan Books, 1990), © 1990 by Nelson Algren, by permission Donadio & Ashworth Inc; John M. Allegro: from *The Sacred Mushroom and the Cross* (Abacus, 1970), by permission of Hodder Headline Plc; Antonin Artaud: from 'A Voyage to the Land of the Tarahumara' in *Selected Writings*, translated by Helen Weaver (Farrar, Straus & Giroux, 1976), © Editions Gallimard, 1971, © 1976 by Farrar, Straus & Giroux Inc, by permission of Editions Gallimard and Farrar, Straus & Giroux Inc; Charles Baudelaire: from *Artificial Paradises*, translated by Stacy Diamond (Citadel Press, 1996), by permission of Carol Publishing Group; Dan Baum: from *Smoke and Mirrors: The War on Drugs and the Politics of Failure* (Little, Brown & Company, 1966), © 1996 by Dan Baum, © 1997 by Dan Baum (Afterword), by permission of the publisher and International Creative Management Inc; Walter Benjamin: from *One-Way Street and Other Writings*, translated by Edmund Jephcott and Kingsley Shorter (Verso, 1979), by permission of the publisher; William Burroughs: from *The Naked Lunch* (John Calder, 1964), by permission of The Wylie Agency (UK) Ltd; Michael Carmichael: from 'Wonderland Revisited' in *Psychedelia Britannica: Hallucinogenic Drugs in Britain*, edited by Antonio Melechi (Turnaround 1997), by permission of the publisher; Jean Cocteau: from *Opium: The Diary of a Cure* (New English Library, 1972), by permisison of Peter Owen Ltd, London; Robert Holman Coombs: from *Drug-Impaired Professionals* (Harvard University Press, 1997), © 1997 by the President and Fellows of Harvard College, by permission of the publisher; Aleister Crowley: from *Diary of a Drug Fiend* (Samuel Weiser, 1970), by permission of Mandrake Press; Géza Csáth: from *The Magician's Garden and Other Stories*, translated by Jascha Kessler and Charlotte Rogers (Columbia University Press, 1980), by permission of

Rieu, 1946, by permission of the publisher; Aldous Huxley: from *The Doors of Perception* and *Heaven and Hell* (Flamingo Modern Classics, 1994) and *Moksha: Writings on Psychedelics and the Visionary Experience 1931–63*, edited by Michael Horowitz and Cynthia Palmer (Flamingo Modern Classics, 1994), by permission of Mrs Laura Huxley and Random House U K Ltd: Jefferson Airplane: 'White Rabbit' (Words and Music: Grace Slick) from LP *Surrealistic Pillow*, © 1967 Iriving Music Inc, USA/Copperpenny Music Publishing Co/Rondor Music (London) Ltd, S W 6 4TW, by permission of International Music Publications Ltd; Marek Kohn: from *Dope Girls: The Birth of the British Drug Underground* (Lawrence & Wishart, 1992), by permission of the publisher; F. Bruce Lamb: from *Wizard of the Upper Amazon: The Story of Manuel Córdova-Rios* (North Atlantic Books, 1971), © 1971, 1974 by F. Bruce Lamb, by permission of North Atlantic Books, Berkeley, California, USA; Timothy Leary: from *Flashbacks: A Personal and Cultural History of an Era* (A Jeremy P. Tarcher/Putnam Book, 1983), © 1983 by Timothy Leary, by permission of Putnam Berkley, a division of Penguin Putnam Inc; Claude Levi-Strauss: from *Tristes Tropiques*, translated by John and Doreen Weightman (Jonathan Cape, 1973), by permission of Random House U K Ltd; J. D. Lewis-Williams and T. A. Dowson: from 'Entoptic Phenomena in Upper Palaeolithic Art' from *Current Anthropology*, 29:2 (April 1988), by permission of the authors and The University of Chicago Press; John Lilly: from *The Centre of the Cyclone: An Autobiography of Inner Space* (Paladin, 1973), by permission of the author and Abner Stein; from *The Scientist: A Metaphysical Autobiography* (Ronin Publishing, 1988), © 1988, 1997 by John Lilly, by permission of Ronin Publishing, Berkeley, CA. www.roninpub.com; Carl Linnaeus: from *Inebriantia* (1762), courtesy of Hunt Institute for Botanical Documentation, Carnegie Mellon University, Pittsburgh, Pennsylvania, USA; Medlar Lucan and Durian Gray: from *The Decadent Gardener* (Dedalus, 1996), by permission of the publisher; Norman Mailer: from 'The White Negro' in *Advertisements for Myself* (Harvard University Press, 1992), by permission of The Wylie Agency (U K) Ltd; Peter C. Mancall: from *Deadly Medicine: Indians and Alcohol in Early America* (Cornell University Press, 1995), © 1995 by Cornell University, by permission of the publisher, John Marks: from *The Search for the 'Manchurian Candidate'* (W. W. Norton, 1991), © 1979 by John Marks, by permission of the publisher; Christopher Mayhew: from 'An excursion out of time' in the *Observer* (28

October, 1956), by permission of the publisher; Antonio Melechi: from 'Drugs of Liberation: From Psychiatry to Psychedelia' in *Psychedelia Britannica: Hallucinogenic Drugs in Britain*, edited by Antonio Melechi (Turnaround, 1997), by permission of the publisher; Mezz Mezzrow: from *Really the Blues* (Random House, 1946), by permission of Carol Publishing Group; Henri Michaux: from *Miserable Miracle* (City Lights Books, 1960), © 1960 by City Lights Books, by permission of the publisher, Jacques-Joseph Moreau: from *Hashish and Mental Illness*, translated by Gordon J. Barnett (Raven Press, 1973), by permission of Lippincott Williams & Wilkins; R. K. Newman: from 'Opium Smoking in Late Imperial China: A Reconsideration' from *Modern Asian Studies*, 29:4 (1995), by permission of the author and Cambridge University Press; Anaïs Nin: from *The Diary of Anaïs Nin, Volume 5: 1947–1955*, edited by Gunther Stuhlmann (Harcourt Brace Jovanovich, 1955), © 1974 by Anaïs Nin, by permission of Gunther Stuhlmann, Harcourt Brace & Company and Peter Owen Ltd, London; Walter N. Pahnke: from 'LSD and Religious Experience' in *LSD, Man & Society*, edited by Richard C. DeBold and Russell C. Leaf (Faber & Faber, 1969), by permission of the publisher; Stanton Peele with Archie Brodsky: from *Love and Addiction* (Taplinger, 1975), by permission of Stanton Peele; Chapman Pincher: 'Brain Doctor Explains Rhythm and "Reefer" Tie-Up' from Daily Express (28 November, 1951), by permission of Express Newspapers Plc; Marco Polo: from *The Travels of Marco Polo the Venetian* (J. M. Dent, 1954), by permission of David Campbell Publishers; François Rabelais: from *The Histories of Gargantua and Pantagruel*, translated by J. M. Cohen (Penguin Classics, 1955), © J. M. Cohen, 1955, by permission of Penguin Books Ltd; G. Reichel-Dolmatoff: from 'Drug-induced optical sensations and their relationship to applied art among some Colombian Indians' in *Art in Society: Studies in style, culture and aesthetics*, edited by Michael Greenhalgh and Vincent Megaw (Gerald Duckworth, 1978), by permission of the publisher; from *The Rig Veda: An Anthology*, translated by Wendy Doniger O'Flaherty (Penguin Classics, 1981), © Wendy Doniger O'Flaherty, 1981, by permission of Penguin Books Ltd; Theodore Rothman: from 'De Laguna's commentaries on hallucinogenic drugs and witchcraft in Dioscorides' *Materia Medica*' in *Bulletin of the History of Medicine*, 46 (1972), by permission of The Johns Hopkins University Press; Ronald Sandison: from 'LSD Therapy' in *Psychedelia Britannica: Hallucinogenic Drugs in Britain*, edited by Antonio Melechi (Turnaround, 1997), by permission of the publisher; Richard Evans Schultes: from 'Plants and Plant Constituents as Mind-Altering Agents throughout History' in *Handbook of Psychopharmacology, Volume 11: Stimulants*, edited by Leslie L. Iversen, Susan D. Iversen and Solomon H. Snyder (Plenum Press, 1978), by permission of the publisher; Alexander Shulgin and Ann Shulgin: from *Tihkal: The Continuation* (Transform Press, 1997), by permission of the publisher; Ronald K. Siegel: from *Intoxication: Life in Pursuit of Artificial Paradise* (E. P Dutton, 1989), by permission of Reid Boates Literary Agency; Terry Southern: from *Red Dirt Marijuana and Other Tastes* (Bloomsbury Publishing, 1997), by permission of the publisher; P. G. Stafford and B. H. Golightly: from *LSD:The Problem-Solving Psychedelic* (Sidgwick & Jackson, 1969), © 1967 by Peter Stafford and Bonnie Golightly, by permission of Macmillan Publishers Ltd; Jerry Stahl: from *Permanent Midnight* (Warner Books, 1995), © Jerry Stahl, 1995, by permission of Warner Books and Little, Brown & Company (UK); Omer C. Stewart: from *Peyote Religion: A History* (University of Oklahoma Press, 1987), by permission of the publisher; Thomas Szasz: from *Ceremonial Chemistry* (Anchor Press/Doubleday, 1974), © 1974 by Thomas Szasz, by permission of McIntosh & Otis Inc; Charles T. Tart: from *On Being Stoned: A Psychological Study of Marijuana Intoxiation* (Science & Behavior Books, 1971), by permission of Science & Behavior Books Inc, Palo Alto, California, 1–800.547.9982; Alice B. Toklas. 'Haschich Fudge' from *The Alice B. Toklas Cook Book* (Anchor Books/Doubleday, 1954), © 1954 by Alice B. Toklas, renewed 1982 Edward M. Burns, Foreword © 1984 by M. F. K. Fisher, Publisher's note © 1984 by Simon Michael Bessie, by permission of HarperCollins Publishers Inc; Alexander Trocchi: from 'Trocchi on Drugs' in *Psychedelia Britannica: Hallucinogenic Drugs in Britain*, edited by Antonio Melechi (Turnaround, 1997), by permission of the publisher; Andrew Weil: from *The Natural Mind* (Houghton Mifflin, 1972), © 1972, 1986 by Andrew Weil, by permission of the publisher; H. G. Wells: from 'The New Accelerator' in *The Complete Short Stories of H. G. Wells* (A & C Black, 1987), by permission of A. P. Watt Ltd on behalf of The Literary Executors of the Estate of H. G. Wells; Peter Lamborn Wilson: from *Scandal: Essays in Islamic Heresy* (Autonomedia Press, 1988), by permission of the author; Charles Winick: from 'How High the Moon – Jazz and Drugs' in *Antioch Review*, 21:1 (Spring 1961), © 1961 by the Antioch Review Inc, by permission of the Editors; Stanislaw Witkiewicz: from 'Report about the Effects of Peyote

PENGUIN 🐧 CLASSICS

www.penguinclassics.com

- *Details about every Penguin Classic*

- *Advanced information about forthcoming titles*

- *Hundreds of author biographies*

- *FREE resources including critical essays on the books and their historical background, reader's and teacher's guides.*

- *Links to other web resources for the Classics*

- *Discussion area*

- *Online review copy ordering for academics*

- *Competitions with prizes, and challenging Classics trivia quizzes*

PENGUIN CLASSICS ONLINE

READ MORE IN PENGUIN

In every corner of the world, on every subject under the sun, Penguin represents quality and variety – the very best in publishing today.

For complete information about books available from Penguin – including Puffins, Penguin Classics and Arkana – and how to order them, write to us at the appropriate address below. Please note that for copyright reasons the selection of books varies from country to country.

In the United Kingdom: Please write to *Dept. EP, Penguin Books Ltd, Bath Road, Harmondsworth, West Drayton, Middlesex UB7 0DA*

In the United States: Please write to *Consumer Sales, Penguin Putnam Inc., P.O. Box 12289 Dept. B, Newark, New Jersey 07101-5289.* VISA and MasterCard holders call 1-800-788-6262 to order Penguin titles

In Canada: Please write to *Penguin Books Canada Ltd, 10 Alcorn Avenue, Suite 300, Toronto, Ontario M4V 3B2*

In Australia: Please write to *Penguin Books Australia Ltd, P.O. Box 257, Ringwood, Victoria 3134*

In New Zealand: Please write to *Penguin Books (NZ) Ltd, Private Bag 102902, North Shore Mail Centre, Auckland 10*

In India: Please write to *Penguin Books India Pvt Ltd, 11 Community Centre, Panchsheel Park, New Delhi 110017*

In the Netherlands: Please write to *Penguin Books Netherlands bv, Postbus 3507, NL-1001 AH Amsterdam*

In Germany: Please write to *Penguin Books Deutschland GmbH, Metzlerstrasse 26, 60594 Frankfurt am Main*

In Spain: Please write to *Penguin Books S. A., Bravo Murillo 19, 1° B, 28015 Madrid*

In Italy: Please write to *Penguin Italia s.r.l., Via Benedetto Croce 2, 20094 Corsico, Milano*

In France: Please write to *Penguin France, Le Carré Wilson, 62 rue Benjamin Baillaud, 31500 Toulouse*

In Japan: Please write to *Penguin Books Japan Ltd, Kaneko Building, 2-3-25 Koraku, Bunkyo-Ku, Tokyo 112*

In South Africa: Please write to *Penguin Books South Africa (Pty) Ltd, Private Bag X14, Parkview, 2122 Johannesburg*

READ MORE IN PENGUIN

Penguin Twentieth-Century Classics offer a selection of the finest works of literature published this century. Spanning the globe from Argentina to America, from France to India, the masters of prose and poetry are represented by Penguin.

If you would like a catalogue of the Twentieth-Century Classics library, please write to:

Penguin Press Marketing, 27 Wrights Lane, London W8 5TZ

(Available while stocks last)

READ MORE IN PENGUIN

A CHOICE OF TWENTIETH-CENTURY CLASSICS

Ulysses James Joyce

Ulysses is unquestionably one of the supreme masterpieces, in any artistic form, of the twentieth century. 'It is the book to which we are all indebted and from which none of us can escape' T. S. Eliot

The First Man Albert Camus

'It is the most brilliant semi-autobiographical account of an Algerian childhood amongst the grinding poverty and stoicism of poor French-Algerian colonials' J. G. Ballard. 'A kind of magical Rosetta stone to his entire career, illuminating both his life and his work with stunning candour and passion' *The New York Times*

Flying Home Ralph Ellison

Drawing on his early experience – his father's death when he was three, hoboeing his way on a freight train to follow his dream of becoming a musician – Ellison creates stories which, according to the *Washington Post*, 'approach the simple elegance of Chekhov.' 'A shining instalment' *The New York Times Book Review*

Cider with Rosie Laurie Lee

'Laurie Lee's account of childhood and youth in the Cotswolds remains as fresh and full of joy and gratitude for youth and its sensations as when it first appeared. It sings in the memory' *Sunday Times*. 'A work of art' Harold Nicolson

Kangaroo D. H. Lawrence

Escaping from the decay and torment of post-war Europe, Richard and Harriett Somers arrive in Australia to a new and freer life. Somers, a disillusioned writer, becomes involved with an extreme political group. At its head is the enigmatic Kangaroo.

READ MORE IN PENGUIN

A CHOICE OF TWENTIETH-CENTURY CLASSICS

Belle du Seigneur Albert Cohen

Belle du Seigneur is one of the greatest love stories in modern literature. It is also a hilarious mock-epic concerning the mental world of the cuckold. 'A *tour de force*, a comic masterpiece weighted with an understanding of human frailty ... It is, quite simply, a book that must be read' *Observer*

The Diary of a Young Girl Anne Frank

'Fifty years have passed since Anne Frank's diary was first published. Her story came to symbolize not only the travails of the Holocaust, but the struggle of the human spirit ... This edition is a worthy memorial' *The Times*. 'A witty, funny and tragic book ... stands on its own even without its context of horror' *Sunday Times*

Herzog Saul Bellow

'A feast of language, situations, characters, ironies, and a controlled moral intelligence ... Bellow's rapport with his central character seems to me novel writing in the grand style of a Tolstoy – subjective, complete, heroic' *Chicago Tribune*

The Go-Between L. P. Hartley

Discovering an old diary, Leo, now in his sixties, is drawn back to the hot summer of 1900 and his visit to Brandham Hall ... 'An intelligent, complex and beautifully-felt evocation of nascent boyhood sexuality that is also a searching exploration of the nature of memory and myth' Douglas Brooks-Davies

Orlando Virginia Woolf

Sliding in and out of three centuries, and slipping between genders, Orlando is the sparkling incarnation of the personality of Vita Sackville-West as Virginia Woolf saw it.

READ MORE IN PENGUIN

A CHOICE OF TWENTIETH-CENTURY CLASSICS

Collected Stories Vladimir Nabokov

Here, for the first time in paperback, the stories of one of the twentieth century's greatest prose stylists are collected in a single volume. 'To read him in full flight is to experience stimulation that is at once intellectual, imaginative and aesthetic, the nearest thing to pure sensual pleasure that prose can offer' Martin Amis

Cancer Ward Aleksandr Solzhenitsyn

Like his hero Oleg Kostoglotov, Aleksandr Solzhenitsyn spent many years in labour camps for mocking Stalin and was eventually transferred to a cancer ward. 'What he has done above all things is record the truth in such a manner as to render it indestructible, stamping it into the Western consciousness' *Observer*

Nineteen Eighty-Four George Orwell

'A volley against the authoritarian in every personality, a polemic against every orthodoxy, an anarchistic blast against every un-questioning conformist ... *Nineteen Eighty-Four* is a great novel, and it will endure because its message is a permanent one' Ben Pimlott

The Complete Saki Saki

Macabre, acid and very funny, Saki's work drives a knife into the upper crust of English Edwardian life. Here are the effete and dashing heroes, Reginald, Clovis and Comus Bassington, tea on the lawn, the smell of gunshot and the tinkle of the caviar fork, and here is the half-seen, half-felt menace of disturbing undercurrents ...

The Castle Franz Kafka

'In *The Castle* we encounter a proliferation of obstacles, endless conversations, perpetual possibilities which hook on to each other as if intent to go on until the end of time' Idris Parry. 'Kafka may be the most important writer of the twentieth century' J. G. Ballard

READ MORE IN PENGUIN

Published or forthcoming:

1900   Edited by Mike Jay and Michael Neve

At the turn of the century, just as today, many people were terrified –
or thrilled – by the seemingly unstoppable progress of science,
wrestling with questions of sexual identity, turning away from
traditional religions or taking refuge in spiritualism, the paranormal
and 'new age' philosophies.

From poetry to pulp fiction, scientific polemic to sexological
speculation, *1900* brings together a fascinating collage of writings
which encompass the amazing range of beliefs, ideas and obsessions
current at the turn of the century.

'*1900* offers a striking vision of the fin-de-siècle shock of the new no
less than the fatigue of the old, regeneration no less than degeneration,
the viewpoints of scientists and futurists as well as decadent poets'
Roy Porter

'*1900* is a splendid starting-point for analysis of fin-de-siècle thought
and for understanding the millennium' Elaine Showalter

READ MORE IN PENGUIN

Published or forthcoming:

Wars   Edited by Angus Calder

'Soon there'll come   the signs are fair –
A death-storm from the distant north.
Stink of corpses everywhere,
Mass assassins marching forth.'

Wars dominated life in Europe in the first half of the twentieth century
and have haunted the second, as the terrible legacy of guilt and grief is
worked through. In this powerful and original anthology, Angus
Calder brings together writings which emphasize that, despite the
camaraderie and heroism of war, it is really about killing and being
killed.

It concentrates on why men fight wars and how something we can call
'humanity' somehow survives them. Primo Levi, Robert Graves,
Wilfred Owen, W. B. Yeats, Anna Akhmatova , Seamus Heaney,
Kurt Vonnegut, Marguerite Duras, Jacques Brel, Bertolt Brecht,
Sorley Maclean and Miklos Radnoti are among the many writers
represented; all offer a vivid sense of what war at the sharp end is
really like.

READ MORE IN PENGUIN

Published or forthcoming:

Utopias   Edited by Catriona Kelly

Russian modernism began with the triumph of the symbolist style and survived until the Stalinist terror of the late 1930s. This was an age bristling with visions of glorious or terrifying futures, with manifestos for new artistic movements and furious feuds between them.

This richly illustrated anthology brings together Bakhtin's celebrated analysis of 'carnival culture'; reflections by painter and stage designer Léon Bakst and film director Sergei Eisenstein; and major texts by Babel and Bulgakov, Mayakovsky and the Mandelstams, Akhmatova and Tsvetaeva, Nabokov and Pasternak, as well as many works by less well-known, but equally talented, figures. Supportive or subversive of the Soviet régime, baldly realistic or boldly experimental, they capture the essence of an astonishingly fertile and stimulating literary era.

'Modernism everywhere entailed a drastic, dangerous breach with the past; in Russia it gained an extra impetus from an entire society's efforts to modernise itself. *Utopias* tells the whole whirlygig story . . . This is *Dr Zhivago* for highbrows!' Peter Conrad

READ MORE IN PENGUIN

Published or forthcoming:

Movies Edited by Gilbert Adair

At the turn of the millennium cinema permeated all of our lives. From the Lumière brothers' first public film screening at the end of the nineteenth century to the technical wizardry at the end of the twentieth, it has both recorded and created our history. Its images and icons are part of our collective consciousness. We are all film buffs now.

But does the end of the century also herald the 'End of Cinema'? Has mainstream, formulaic, big-budget moviemaking triumphed over all other alternatives? Covering subjects as diverse as avant-garde cinema, B-movies, blue movies, bad movies and Nazi propaganda, with texts by filmmakers and non-specialists – Orson Welles, Fellini, Updike on Burton and Taylor, Mailer on Marilyn – this is a refreshing corrective to the Hollywood bias.

'An anthology to destroy in a weekend – and open up your life. Start dipping Friday night, and by Sunday lunch you're seeing the links between Manny Farber and Sergei Eisenstein, Mickey Mouse and Modernism . . . a superb, unexpected collection of thoughts, wonders and outrages, making you want to read – and see – more' David Thomson

READ MORE IN PENGUIN

Published or forthcoming:

Titanic   Edited by John Wilson Foster

RMS *Titanic* sank to the bottom of the Atlantic during a night of rare calm, but the tragedy caused shock waves on both sides of the ocean and has continued to haunt our imaginations ever since.

The human drama of the disaster still has much of the power to excite and appal that it had in 1912, inspiring novels, films, plays, paintings and music. This anthology draws from more than eight decades of literature about the great ship, combining journalism, essays, fiction, poems, letters, songs and transcripts of hearings. It relives the event through the accounts of survivors, witnesses and commentators, with contributions from major writers of the time such as Joseph Conrad, H. G. Wells, Thomas Hardy, George Bernard Shaw and Sir Arthur Conan Doyle.

But beyond that it also shows how the sinking of *Titanic* was a cultural phenomenon which fulfilled the anxieties of its time – the frictions of class, race and gender, the hunger for progress and machine efficiency, and the arrogant assumptions of the Mechanical Age.